JESUIT POSTMODERN

JESUIT POSTMODERN

Scholarship, Vocation, and Identity in the 21st Century

Edited by
Francis X. Clooney, S.J.

LEXINGTON BOOKS
A Division of
ROWMAN & LITTLEFIELD PUBLISHERS, INC.
Lanham • Boulder • New York • Toronto • Oxford

LEXINGTON BOOKS

A division of Rowman & Littlefield Publishers, Inc.
A wholly owned subsidiary of The Rowman & Littlefield Publishing Group, Inc.
4501 Forbes Boulevard, Suite 200
Lanham, MD 20706

PO Box 317
Oxford
OX2 9RU, UK

British Library Cataloguing in Publication Information Available

Library of Congress Cataloging-in-Publication Data

Jesuit postmodern : scholarship, vocation, and identity in the 21st century / edited by
Francis X. Clooney.
    p. cm.
  Includes bibliographical references.
  ISBN-13: 978-0-7391-1400-1 (cloth : alk. paper)
  ISBN-10: 0-7391-1400-X (cloth : alk. paper)
  ISBN-13: 978-0-7391-1401-8 (pbk. : alk. paper)
  ISBN-10: 0-7391-1401-8 (pbk. : alk. paper)
    1. Jesuits—United States. 2. Intellectuals—United States. 3. Learning and scholarship—
United States—History—20th century. 4. United States—Intellectual life—20th century.
I. Clooney, Francis Xavier, 1950– . II. Title.
BX3708.J39 2006
271'.53—dc22   2005029532

Printed in the United States of America

∞™ The paper used in this publication meets the minimum requirements of American
National Standard for Information Sciences—Permanence of Paper for Printed Library
Materials, ANSI/NISO Z39.48-1992.

Contents

1

Introducing Ourselves

Francis X. Clooney, S.J.

I. Introduction

IN *JESUIT POSTMODERN* EIGHT AMERICAN JESUIT SCHOLARS teaching in institutions of higher education in the United States—three universities, a college, and two schools of theology, all of which we shall hereafter refer to under an abbreviated title, "universities"—reflect on our scholarly work, why we engage in it, and how the work we do coheres with our self-understanding as Jesuits. Most of us work at Jesuit institutions, and even the two of us now teaching elsewhere (Francis Clooney and Roger Haight) spent most of their careers at Jesuit institutions. A ninth Jesuit scholar, also at a Jesuit university, offers a rejoinder that enriches the conversation, but to some extent also makes us think twice about what we have written. (We offer a little more information on ourselves on the Contributors page at the end of the book.)

At this writing, we range in age from our forties to our sixties. We entered the Society as long ago as 1954 and as recently as 1985. All but one of us were born in the United States. We do not pretend to speak for Jesuits in other countries, but we hope that our reflections will be of interest internationally, in a Society of Jesus and Church having to face questions analogous to those we raise. Many of us are philosophers (the Aristotelian tradition in its sources and today, French deconstruction and the encounter with the Holocaust, reflection on the meeting points of medicine and ethics, science and technology studies, and ethical-political theory) and theologians (Christology and ecclesiology, liturgical theology, comparative theology and the encounter with other religions), and we also include the historian and philosopher of science

and the scholar of contemporary literature and literary theory. In our essays
we trace and sort out several particular strands making up who we are:

- We live in the early twenty-first century, at a time marked by cultural and
  religious fragmentation, retrenchment and expansion, the breakdown of
  coherent traditions and yet also their revitalization in new combinations
  with elements from other cultures.
- We are Roman Catholic Christians and all but one of us are ordained
  priests, formed largely in the post–Vatican II Church; we need to attend
  to the specific nature of Catholic identity today and how our time and
  place have affected how we understand and express our faith.
- We are Jesuits—companions of Jesus—in a Society that had its ways of
  living and thinking transformed in the 1960s and 1970s, by events in the
  Church and world and by Jesuit events such as the 31st and 32nd General
  Congregations, and by a whole series of subsequent changes as this "new
  Society"—shifting from its immediate past, seeking original roots—was
  further contested and reshaped in the decades thereafter.
- We are scholars, academics, and all but two of us work in institutions of
  Catholic and Jesuit higher education; this environment gives us opportu-
  nities to enhance our scholarly identities, but the safe and secure boundaries of academe—whether the tower is ivory or not—can also soften and
  banalize the powers and passions of true inquiry.
- We explore questions arising in different disciplines, related to theological, philosophical, ethical, scientific, historical, and literary matters. No
  Jesuit scholar has exactly the same questions, or resources for answers, as
  another, nor will he investigate these questions entirely for the same reasons as another Jesuit.

These five threads (themselves woven of more slender and subtle threads)
are best traced as woven together in the fabric of our work as Jesuit scholars,
in the texture of our particular writing. Were the threads of culture, religion,
scholarly discipline, personal journey merely gathered—as if the (re)integra-
tion of Jesuit life, scholarship, and ministry were simply the sum of disparate
elements in one's life—they would not constitute the fabric of a solution.
Hence our decision in *Jesuit Postmodern* to write personal accounts of our
scholarship, to place our works in contexts described in ways that seemed apt
to us individually and as a group, guided by our individual intuitions as to
how best this might be described. None of our essays is simply autobiographical, but they all include autobiographical elements; none is an impar-
tial history, but they are all mindful of our past and all evoke the Jesuit tradition of research and writing; each of us has thought about our particular

instances of current Jesuit scholarship, as located within a 450-year tradition, and we tried to uncover how we as individuals imagine ourselves part of that tradition.

Common concerns and questions notwithstanding, each essay retains its own characteristic tone, because we found ourselves stubbornly committed to differing styles and intensities of autobiographical specification, writing styles, levels of formality and informality, all leading to differing degrees of specificity in conclusion; and we are often talking about different modes of scholarship engaged from different starting points in the first place. Although we all engage the same range of thematic issues, the results are different, eight times over, as we pursue our own themes: theology as an intellectual pursuit today; Aristotle; medical ethics; the Holocaust; the history and location of physics; liturgy as practice and scholarship; gay identity as lived, written, and taught; the encounter with other religions. Our respondent multiplies the differences yet again as he poses to us questions about the limits of what we have said and not said.

We believe that even the largest and most important issues are best addressed on the local level, and our accounts aim to suggest fresh starting points for reflection on the Jesuit scholarly life, that is, the Jesuit intellectual life as lived and practiced today in its particularly intense and professionalized forms. *Jesuit Postmodern* proceeds on the premise that it is wiser to begin with accounts of what Jesuit scholars actually do and think, moving from those accounts toward theories about the Jesuit intellectual life, rather than using personal narratives merely to illustrate already established and essential principles about the religious and intellectual life of Jesuits. As will be emphasized below, however, we very much hope that our singular conversation will become part of much larger new and renewed conversations.

In agreeing to work together on this book, we agreed that we do have much in common among ourselves and with other Jesuits, and that we share areas of common concern. But we also agreed that these do not presume or reduce to a timeless essence flowing beneath the surface of Jesuit or Catholic intellectual life. While there are many standard and conventional phrases and formulae that describe what Jesuit education is all about, these do not succeed in capturing our Jesuit way of acting and thinking. What we have in common is more the act of writing, this composition of essays and a book, in resistance to both separation (individual Jesuit scholars on their own, doing their own thing) and overgeneralization (a confidence that deep down we all agree and our scholarship converges, whatever it might happen to be). To highlight the problematic facing us, we have allowed difference to reign in our essays, discussed in their draft and nearly final forms. We did not aim for a uniformity that would homogenize our nine different voices.

Of course, we hope that the volume still reads coherently, perhaps as a kind of symphony or intelligently contrapuntal endeavor, to an overall good effect that is more than the sum of the disjointed parts. It may even be the case that in the future Jesuits might weave back together a common rhetoric about Jesuit intellectual identity. William Rehg, our respondent, suggests that we should indeed still hope for more—right now—since there is still an effective charism and common discourse—recorded in the books and documents mentioned earlier, lived in the lives of individual Jesuits—that remains the authoritative Jesuit tradition in which we live, pray, and work. We do not disagree in any definitive fashion, but we think that right now there is no agreed upon set of words that succeeds in expressing our Jesuit way of acting and thinking, nor any singular, shared memory nor set of images that might translate the Jesuit scholarly enterprise or our particular essays into a discourse that would serenely float above the particulars.

II. Our Discontent

Jesuit Postmodern grows out of a conversation among Jesuits in the Boston area in the late 1980s and 1990s, and its basic strength lies particularly in those years in which we talked together on a regular basis. But we must first clarify our project's motivation by putting it in perspective.

Our essays are rooted in scholarly work that has been done on the campuses of our universities, amidst the usual array of teaching, campus activities, and pastoral ministries. We have managed to write as well as teach, in part because Jesuit institutions have been and are good to us, and we are grateful. Nevertheless, in the 1980s and 1990s we also found our work to be increasingly marginal to the expected, conventional forms of Jesuit presence on campus and even to the life of our Jesuit communities. Jesuit presence and Jesuit ministries still matter, but there has been no clear opening on campus for a corresponding recognition of new directions in scholarship—as intellectually, practically, and religiously important. Our universities, while expanding wonderfully, have not taken into account how the ways we think of ourselves culturally, philosophically, and religiously have also been changing. As a result, and despite a growing professionalization of the faculty and higher profile of our universities as research institutions, it was no longer clear how what scholars actually think and write might matter in contemporary, pragmatically defined educational institutions, Jesuit universities included. Although we have remained enthused by our scholarship—we hope this is evident in our essays—over the past years we have found it hard to discover where we could talk about our work, even with other Jesuits. As we have been doing scholarly work that problematizes any expectation of a simple, neat conversation about who Jesuits are, at the same moment university administrators have been finding it necessary to distill Jesuit identity down to a few key themes and even public relations slogans, buttressed with quotations from our founder, Saint Ignatius Loyola, and later Jesuit saints, poets, and scholars. Indeed, we have often been puzzled at the stories our institutions insist on telling about the Jesuit scholarly and intellectual tradition—and so too about us. We have wondered who is listening to whom.

Jesuit intellectual tradition has always combined a theoretically open-ended "quest to find God in all things" with a more pragmatic utilization of scholarship as an instrument of evangelization. There are in our history stellar examples of great Jesuit scholars, but many more examples of intelligent and well-educated Jesuits choosing not to be scholars and write books, and rather to put their gifts to work in building and influencing institutions. Various features of modern Jesuit educational institutions have accentuated the tension between these two dynamics: never before have we had so many readily available resources—money, time, opportunity, tenure, and professionalization—that make scholarly practice more easily available to Jesuits and more likely to bear fruit, and yet too more noticeably sidelined in relation to the actual management of the universities as Jesuit institutions of learning. The original Jesuit intellectual tradition had its own possibilities and problems, but these provide only a general frame for our essays. As postmodern scholars—exploring the irreducible diversity of our experiences and critical of the modern Jesuit heritage of the late twentieth century—we hoped to problematize the nearer and dominant modern synthesis that shaped Jesuit institutions of higher education from the 1960s to the 1990s; as will be noted in a separate section below, this is a key version of the "modern" to which this volume opposes itself as "postmodern."

Throughout, we have had to ask ourselves how the Jesuit scholar can best resist the commodification of Jesuit identity as a selling point in a university's self-promotion, and how to make clear that the content of scholarship matters as well as the formalities of degree, publication, and tenure—while yet also acknowledging the Jesuit tradition of learning that makes our own scholarship possible. We do not wish to say that the realities of Catholic tradition and Christian faith no longer pertain, nor that the grand verities of Jesuit tradition are untrue, nor that the synthesis given to us in our generations in the Jesuit universities of the United States has been unproductive. But still, we have found, our modern institutions and conversations about what counts in Jesuit life have marginalized and muffled the scholars among us—precisely when there are more Jesuit scholars than ever before, with more new ideas promising more change and more growth.

Although this volume is not the place for the necessarily related analysis of Jesuit communities and their intellectual profile, we agree too that within our communities' generally friendly and supportive fraternal environment we found a similar benign neglect of the substance of the work we do and the questions raised; our communities have been dedicated to the work of the university as institution, and happy to lend the name "Jesuit" to many aspects of university life, without entertaining the tougher intellectual questions that arise out of the work of scholars. Perhaps no one is to blame; perhaps we all are simply at a loss as to how to carry on such conversations today.

In the late 1980s a number of us at Boston College were discontented with our feeling of marginalization; we felt that others were speaking authoritatively for the "Jesuit tradition" not only without consulting us, but also without taking the voice of the Jesuit scholar into account. At times it felt as though being a scholar rather than "a man about campus" diminished the likelihood of being listened to. But we decided that absence, silence, and marginalization are best remedied by honest conversation attending directly to what particular Jesuit scholars actually think and write. *Jesuit Postmodern* and the conversations preceding it could take shape rather easily, even naturally, because most of us were in the Boston area during at least part of the 1980s and 1990s, and so could share our concerns. We therefore decided to talk about our work as Jesuits and scholars in a way that would give visibility to Jesuit ways of scholarship, while yet preserving the actual dynamic of the actual scholarship of particular scholars. We were hoping that such a conversation could become the locale for an honest critique of the standard rhetoric about Jesuit intellectual tradition, as well as a forum in which we could actually talk about the research we were doing. So we convened and shared a series of conversations among a wide range of Jesuit scholars. Individual sessions—more than thirty between 1989 and 1999—most often consisted of a Sunday afternoon discussion followed by dinner; they took place in and around Boston College, participants coming and going from meeting to meeting, visitors always welcome.

III. Our Institutions, Our History

In taking up the challenge of the conversation and this volume following from it, we have been well aware that there is no dearth of good and worthy books about Jesuits and the Jesuit scholarly tradition, including works that tell the story of the Society as an intellectual Order. Members of the Society of Jesus itself, along with numerous other scholars and more popular writers, have been describing, defending, or criticizing Jesuits almost from the beginning of the Order. Professionals and amateurs have studied us, quietly or sensationally, lamenting or celebrating continuities and shifts in Jesuit life and ministry. Official sources have offered measured pronouncements on what the Jesuit contribution to the intellectual life ought to be, most recently with Decree 16 of the 1995 Thirty-fourth General Congregation, "The Intellectual Dimension of Jesuit Ministries." Standard histories examine the Society of Jesus as an intellectual, cultural, and religious force, histories for the most part composed by scholars inside Society, including J. de Guibert, S.J., *The Jesuits: Their Spiritual Doctrine and Practice* (1964); William V. Bangert, S.J., *A History of the Society of Jesus* (1986); John W. O'Malley, S.J., *The First Jesuits* (1993), and with several co-editors, *The Jesuits: Cultures, Sciences, and the Arts, 1540–1773* (1999). Regarding more recent developments we find studies such as Joseph M. Becker, S.J., *The Re-formed Jesuits* (1992); and Peter McDonough, *Men Astutely Trained* (1992). Among the books focused on Jesuit higher education in the United States, we have John W. Donohue, S. J., *Jesuit Education: An Essay on the Foundations of Its Idea* (1963); Paul A. FitzGerald, S. J., *The Governance of Jesuit Colleges in the United States, 1920–1970* (1984); and William P. Leahy, S. J., *Adapting to America: Catholics, Jesuits, and Higher Education in the Twentieth Century* (1991). The tradition of writing about Jesuits continues, as a glance at recent arrivals shows us: Peter McDonough and Eugene C. Bianchi, *Passionate Uncertainty: Inside the American Jesuits* (2002); Michael Bunker, *Swarms of Locusts: The Jesuit Attack on the Faith* (2002); Jonathan Wright, *God's Soldiers: Adventure, Politics, Intrigue, and Power—A History of the Jesuits* (2004). There are also important essays to be considered, such as John Coleman, S.J.'s "A Company of Critics: Jesuits and the Intellectual Life" (*Studies in the Spirituality of Jesuits*, 1990), and Peter McDonough's "Clenched Fist or Open Palm? Five Jesuit Perspectives on Pluralism" (*Studies in the Spirituality of Jesuits*, 2005), which also reconsider and retell aspects of the great story of how Jesuits have learned and taught over the centuries.

We acknowledge and respect this impressive body of writing. Certainly, no one should turn to *Jesuit Postmodern* in order to learn the basics about the Jesuits or the standard Jesuit view of the intellectual life, and we do not venture an overview of that tradition. Readers of this volume will profit from exploring some of the above-mentioned works in conjunction with ours, since *Jesuit Postmodern* seeks to complement and in a way contest this rich body of writings by and about Jesuits. While admiring the work of our many predecessors, we have not found in those writings insights and modes of expression such as would help us in exploring the particular energies that make our scholarship possible, urgent, exciting. By our conversations and then this book, we hope to have probed those energies more deeply. We have spoken stubbornly from within our actual scholarship, rather than about it, and given priority to first-person accounts of what it means to be a Jesuit scholar, as we have lived and

understood the particular trajectories of our work. Accordingly, we have resisted the accustomed concepts and words with which "Jesuit intellectual tradition and ministry" are usually described. Rather, by accounts that weave together our scholarly lives and personal stories, we explore what some Jesuit
scholars do, and ask what it means when we say that Jesuits conceive of scholarship as genuinely Christian and Jesuit. *Jesuit Postmodern* is an answer, our
current answers.

IV. Contesting "Jesuit Modern"

We are very conscious of the postmodern world in which we all live and write
as scholars today; in a sense, we are all postmoderns. But in a rather modest
and more pointed sense we also ambition a postmodern persona for this
book, in what we say and how we say it. In part, we aim to interrogate and
problematize the great modern synthesis of the Society of Jesus as an educational religious order in the United States, entertaining the notion that what
we know and what we do no longer fit together into an administrator's dream
of the perfect harmony of a Catholic, Jesuit, scholarly, educational, spiritual
whole that also succeeds as a very modern university. We therefore presuppose
a sense of "Jesuit Modern"—as we shall call it—as a complex of principles, attitudes, and practices still held by many if not most American Jesuits involved
in higher education today. Three basic principles in particular stand out: the
unity of all truth, the sanctity of creation and human intellectual activity, and
the universal reach of divine grace. These are wonderful and unexceptionable,
but their dynamic becomes more problematic when we reflect on Jesuit education in the modern era. And for this, we must also say a few things about the
classical Jesuit understandings of education and intellectual life to which Jesuit Modern was a reaction. For the latter is by no means identical with the
classical Jesuit understanding of education or education or intellectual life.

    The classical Jesuit program of education had its glories; they were many,
and we have benefited greatly. It is open to question whether the classical Jesuit program was actually responsible for all these glories, but the glories were
many. Nonetheless, it also suffered from three major deficiencies that became
increasingly obvious as the twentieth century wore on. First, taking its inspiration from Saint Ignatius's First Principle and Foundation—everything we
are and do is from God, for God, in God—the classical Jesuit view of education was strongly teleological. It valued intellectual activities and educational
institutions to the extent, and only to the extent, that they help people to save
their souls. (John Donohue's classic *Jesuit Education* is good on this point.)
Second, this teleological or instrumental view of learning applied, at least in

theory, both to the programs of study in Jesuit colleges and universities and to the formation and activities of the Jesuit professors themselves. Learning was instrumental, and individual Jesuits could be assigned this or that academic discipline; thus, Jesuits used to be assigned to higher studies in fields in which they took no deep personal interest. Third, taking its impulse from the Constitutions of the Society of Jesus, the classical view provided for Jesuit religious superiors to exercise a high degree of control and supervision over educational institutions. Thus, fifty or sixty years ago, a provincial might attempt to standardize the textbooks in the colleges of his province, so that faculty could be more easily transferred from one college to another.

By the 1960s and 1970s the principles of Jesuit Modern had all the power of ideas whose time had come. Although the colleges and universities founded by the Society of Jesus were legally incorporated as institutions independent of the Society, nonetheless they quickly reincarnated as "the Jesuit colleges" and "the Jesuit universities," institutions bearing a remarkable (and not yet well studied) influence on the attitudes and practices of the Society of Jesus.

Without attempting to give a full description of all the attitudes and practices currently prevalent in Jesuit higher education, we suggest that the following are characteristic attitudes of Jesuit Modern:

- *A strong sense of the autonomy and worth of the individual scholarly disciplines, and a dedication to work in the disciplines.* This has led Jesuits to unprecedented levels of achievement and recognition in their scholarly disciplines.
- *A strong focus on Jesuit administration as the core of the university, defining the university's identity and mission, along with readiness to accept a strongly centralized model of governance.* It may be asked how this focus on Jesuit administration coheres with a strong sense of the autonomy and worth of the disciplines. The most common response would be something like "we do our job, and the president runs the university." The focus on Jesuit administration can involve impatience with, for example, faculty demands for a larger share in governance. And we have even run into Jesuits who seem to feel that it is unfair of boards of trustees to exercise power over Jesuit presidents.
- *A close visceral identification of Jesuits with the university, enthusiasm for its mission, and a strong sense of the continuing Jesuitness of the university.* There is certainly much to be enthusiastic about in the contemporary Jesuit university. And yet we sometimes wonder if this close identification with the university is in part a response to signs of decline in the Society and to problems in the institutional church. It is only human to identify oneself with a success.

- *A high degree of sensitivity to criticism of the contemporary Jesuit university, along with a tendency to interpret criticism as stemming from one or more forms of negative mindset (antiquated, authoritarian, Jansenist, Manichaean, extrinsicist, fideist, anti-intellectual, right-wing, etc.).*

While it would be a mistake to distinguish attitudes and practices too sharply, we can also mention some of the practices typical of Jesuit Modern:

- *Progressive assimilation to the dominant American academic culture.* In the longstanding and ongoing debate within American Catholicism on the pros and cons of assimilation to American ways of life, Jesuit Modern stands on the assimilationist side, as opposed to any movement towards Catholic separatism or (as Jesuit Moderns might put it) sectarianism or ghettoization.
- *Resolute insistence on institutional autonomy.* The autonomy of Jesuit colleges and universities was secured in the first instance by the separate incorporation of the local Jesuit communities in the 1960s and 1970s. More recent evidence of this insistence on autonomy may be found in the responses to the document *Ex corde ecclesiae,* to the requirement of canon 812 that theology faculty seek a *mandatum* from their local bishop, and to the assertion that the property of Catholic colleges and universities is ecclesiastical property within the meaning of canon law. In all these cases the consistent practice of Jesuit Modern has been to insist on institutional autonomy.
- *A large measure of presidential independence from Jesuit supervision.* A major part of the post 1960s settlement has been that Jesuit presidents are accountable to their boards of trustees, not to their Jesuit superiors (provincials, local rectors) for the governance of their college or university. Further, while the old rector-presidents generally served for six years or less, the tendency of Jesuit Modern, like other academic sites, favors a longer-term presidency. This gives Jesuit presidents an additional protection against interference from religious superiors: they generally outlast those superiors.
- *Representation of the Society by the president rather than by the community rector or by the community functioning as a group.* We are not sure whether this practice goes to the core of Jesuit Modern, or whether it is simply a historical contingency. When the offices of president and rector were separated, nothing guaranteed that the presidents would be the spokesmen for the Society while the rectors focused on issues internal to the Jesuit community; but that is how things have worked out.
- *Public identification of the university with the Society.* This identification with the university includes not only the local Jesuit community but also

the wider Society. Thus the Jesuit provincial superior may ceremonially entrust the president with his mission. And the Jesuit Superior General makes occasional well-publicized visits to Jesuit universities, delivering statements of Jesuit educational principles, and suggesting that the universities are still in some sense directed by the Society.

- *Assertion of continuity with classical Jesuit humanism.* Here we are thinking of attempts to explain what Jesuit higher education is about by going back to Renaissance humanism, the first college for lay students at the Jesuit college in Messina, and the like. We are also thinking of attempts to suggest that contemporary Jesuit education is (or should be) marked by a specifically Jesuit pedagogy—a pedagogy that draws not so much on the classical *Ratio Studiorum* or on the historical Jesuit tradition as on Ignatius's *Spiritual Exercises.*
- *Narratives of progress.* While insisting on its continuity with Jesuit tradition, the Jesuit Modern university also asserts the superiority of current arrangements to those prevailing thirty, forty, or fifty years ago, and thus presents its history as a narrative of progress. Whig history is a standard institutional practice and a standard public relations practice. It is particularly understandable as a response to occasional fulminations from those disposed to insist that the older system was better than what replaced it.
- *Regular legitimation by reference to basic principles.* The three principles of Jesuit Modern—the unity of all truth, the sanctity of creation and human intellectual activity, and the universal reach of divine grace—are the common denominator of Jesuit higher education rhetoric today. When on occasion Jesuits have had to defend their educational institutions against criticism, their counterattacks regularly appeal to one or more of these basic principles, which critics are said to misunderstand or overlook.

Jesuit Modern was and is a powerful synthesis and in many ways an admirable synthesis. We owe it much. It has allowed us to cultivate the study of Greek and philosophy without worrying too much about their relevance to the salvation of souls or the liberation of the poor. It has encouraged us to immerse ourselves in the works of non-Christians with the attitude that we were likely to learn things that were worth learning, even if their traditions are rarely allowed to teach us something truly new or truly unsettling. It has enabled us to pursue philosophy without having our methods or conclusions set for us by religious authorities. Why, then, do we take critical distance from Jesuit Modern, when we admit its rationale and coherence and gratefully acknowledge its benefits? Are we not biting the hand that has so generously fed us?

To answer this question, let us consider some signs of tension within Jesuit Modern. First, we suggest that as the Society of Jesus tried to adapt to American modernity and to win for its educational institutions the acceptance of the American educational community, it became increasingly clear that the classical Jesuit view was constrained in its teleology, instrumental in its love of learning, and overly managed in its execution of actual education. Jesuits such as Paul FitzGerald and William Leahy have chronicled the waning of the classical Jesuit view (for diverse reasons, including those to which we point, but also others) and the changes that transformed Jesuit colleges and universities in the 1960s and 1970s. We do not propose to go over all that ground again. We would like to suggest, however, that this transformation was largely motivated and justified by a set of philosophical and theological principles, principles that quickly took on institutional embodiment and gave rise to the practices and attitudes that strongly characterize Jesuit higher education today. It is this complex of principles, practices, and attitudes that we term for short Jesuit Modern.

Or to put it another way: one of the most important positive contributions of Jesuit Modern was to create an intellectual climate in which the intellectual disciplines were acknowledged as intrinsically valuable, scholars were set free to do their work, and control of intellectual life and education by religious authorities no longer made sense. But now we are also seeing evidence of a trend in the opposite direction, however, in the number of attempts and movements to present university education as morally formative. Slogans like "education for justice" and "forming men and women for others" signal this trend. Of course the idea that education should be morally formative was part and parcel of the classical Jesuit understanding, so here Jesuit Modern is attempting to retrieve or to reformulate a classic Jesuit theme. But it remains to be seen how far Jesuit universities can go in the direction of moral formation before they start to compromise the autonomy of the disciplines. This issue has not yet been joined, because the moral formation of students still takes place mainly through extracurricular activities. But what if a Jesuit university were to reshape its curriculum, or its faculty, with the goal of moral formation? At what point ought familiarity with Catholic social teaching become a criterion for faculty hiring in business or economics?

A strong focus on administration and governance is an element of continuity between the classical Jesuit view and Jesuit Modern. University administrations periodically assert their authority to re-express the mission of the university and their power to allot the university's resources accordingly. But the modern rhetoric of "mission talk" perhaps developed in the context of military operations and was then transferred to the context of business corporations. Whether mission talk can really apply to universities is open to question. Universities are largely composed of self-perpetuating communities shaped by disciplines—the very disciplines that Jesuit Modern has valorized—and functioning with considerable autonomy. From the point of view of autonomous disciplines and their practitioners, the role of administration is instrumental and subsidiary: give them the resources they need to do their work, do not tell them what to do or how to do it. Thus the Jesuit focus on administration and governance is in tension with one of the basic attitudes of Jesuit Modern.

Jesuit Modern thus attempts to hold together two different understandings of the relationship between the university and the Society of Jesus. The autonomy of the university from any form of external religious control is at the core of Jesuit Modern. But Jesuit universities still like to present themselves as directed or sponsored by the Society, and so, as mentioned, the Jesuit Superior General visits Jesuit universities and delivers statements on the meaning of Jesuit education, as if to suggest that the universities take their mission and direction from him. But the reality on the ground is different. As the number of active Jesuits declines, and especially as lay presidents become more common, the ambiguous relationship between the university and the Society that has characterized Jesuit Modern will be up for renegotiation. Will lay presidents speak for the Society as Jesuit presidents have done? If not, who will?

In any case, successful and influential as it has been, Jesuit Modern is starting to show signs of strain. Perhaps it will find within itself the resources to surmount its internal tensions and external challenges; this is, after all, how a tradition lives and flourishes, by responding to tensions and challenges. But we suspect, more rudely, that it is also an idea whose time came, flourished, and then went. Moving beyond Jesuit Modern in a consciously dialectical moment, *Jesuit Postmodern* hopes to state and accentuate the tensions at issue as we move beyond the modern context into a fresh, interesting, and unpredictable era of the Postmodern, an era that both shapes scholarship and thrives on the questions scholars ask.

Such is our working understanding of Jesuit Modern, as the background to *Jesuit Postmodern*, and we are grateful that our readers have stayed with us through a long but necessary aside. But the test of our project is in the individual voices to follow, so let us now turn to the essays, introducing them in the order in which they appear in the pages to follow—an order (as envisioned in my editorial mind, though I cannot be sure I speak for my colleagues!) that charts a path from somewhat more comfort with tradition to more acute problematizations of it.

V. Eight Jesuits, Eight Narratives

Arthur Madigan's "Confessions of an Aristotelian Christian" reflects on the Aristotelian heritage that underlies so much of the Catholic and Jesuit tradition. His account of this scholarly bedrock is coupled with his vivid rendering of the perils and joys of personal and institutional commitments to scholarship. Deliberately employing the familiar style of an insider—a Jesuit talking to other Jesuits, while knowing that everyone else is listening in—Madigan thus resists the temptation to move to a level of generalization whereby persons are erased and meanings rooted in conversation and encounter obscured. We are treated to an inside, familiar and familial view of how that heritage was taught and appropriated in the 1960s and 1970s, and what kind of Jesuit life is generated out from it—along with a philosophically rigorous consideration of the constraints and opportunities provided by an unapologetic and undiluted fidelity to Aristotle and his intellectual heritage at the beginning of the twenty-first century.

William E. Stempsey also writes in the realm of philosophy, though from a different starting point, as well from a younger generation of Jesuit formation and study. His "A Philosophical Dissection of a Jesuit Scholar" probes the genesis and multi-layered core of his Jesuit identity. He recounts how he has combined his vocations as physician, priest, and teacher, "careers" that do not neatly blend into one another, yet that also define and constrain one another in a way that Stempsey finds ultimately satisfying. That a physician turned Jesuit and priest becomes professor of philosophy shows us a particular and very distinctive instance of "Jesuit" and "intellectual" that is nonetheless constituted quite differently from the philosophical persona of Madigan, as well as from the personae of the other philosopher Jesuits among us, Bernauer and Anderson, who are introduced below.

Bruce T. Morrill's "What Difference Does It Make for Me as a Liturgist to Be a Jesuit—or Vice Versa?" explores his work as a liturgical theologian in the context of vivid remembrances of growing up Catholic in Maine. He traces for us the path by which early Catholic memories and practices were woven over the decades into a professional study of Catholic liturgy that has richly overflowed into the practice of priestly ministry and into an acutely sensitized awareness of the practices of honest and just living in a world of injustice. Morrill's narrative memories inform the way in which he has come to articulate the nature and function of the liturgy as the primary form of the Church's mysticism, as well as Ignatius's *Spiritual Exercises* as the mystical heritage of the Jesuits. Finding these two forms of Christian mysticism in many ways complementary, his comparison and contrast of the two in terms of body and space, memory and imagination, ritual and power reveal the extent to which he has come to embrace postmodern categories in his theological work.

Roger Haight's "The American Jesuit Theologian" begins by reflecting on the nature and power of autobiographical writing. Haight thereafter explores the meaning of theology in the American context, as he has understood and practiced it in writing and teaching for over a generation, in light of changes in the society and Church around him. Spirituality is now defined in action and constantly reformulated in an American society that is increasingly complex and global in reach, and in particular in relation to three defining issues of our time: the necessarily growing role of women in the Church, pluralism in and around the Church, and the transfer of energy and leadership from the clergy to the laity. Haight captures a feature common to most of the essays in noting the role of the Jesuit scholar in noting and then crossing boundaries—moving back and forth between faith and reason, the universal and particular. Our autobiographical acts matter, because they tell us more about the subject in the complex situation where we all live today.

James Bernauer's "Philosophizing after the Holocaust," in part also a reflection on the Jesuit learning of philosophy, plays itself out in a strikingly different way. Jesuit intellectual training is pondered in light of the broader frame of Jesuit formation, and even more broadly in terms of how institutions shape their members to act and think in certain ways; "discipline" is at stake as formative of persons, religious societies such as the Jesuits, and whole cultures such as contemporary America or Nazi Germany. His scholarly work connects to the Catholic Church's recent penitential voice regarding Christian conduct during the period of the Holocaust. Study of the German culture out of which Nazi violence exploded may point to more subtle responsibilities borne by Catholic moral and spiritual formation in accounting for that violence. As a consequence of the sometimes-dreadful history between Jesuits and Jews, Jesuit scholars have a special responsibility in the reconciliation of Jews and Christians, and yet too often it seems easier to look the other way. In reminding us that both questions and their evasion are political, Bernauer brings a new urgency to our sense, mentioned above, that the particular questions arising in Jesuit scholarship seem often to be marginal, smoothly forgotten, in the course of the wider life of the Society.

Ronald Anderson too is a philosopher, with a background in science, and expertise in the history of science. His "Studying Physics and Jesuit Life: Worldliness and Life as an Immigrant," draws us into the complexity of a moving world wherein physics, history, philosophy—all self-consciously circumscribed by particular and shifting acts of language—converge, during a life journey that has literally traversed the globe. Most striking in his "Studying the History and Philosophy of Physics as a Jesuit" is the turn to the specificity and complex modes of science's descriptions of nature, the underlying features of the world engaged and understood through the technicalities of modern physics and mathematics. While science and philosophy (and religion) may seem to be moving apart, the Jesuit scholar able to peer deeply into such multiple worlds finds inevitable points of connection that press issues of foundations, ones secure yet always receding, woven into the autobiographical.

Francis X. Clooney's "Francis Xavier, and the World/s We (Don't Quite) Share" pairs Jesuit mission history in India with his personal history as a scholar of theology and Hindu studies at Boston College, somewhat fancifully tracing a path from the pioneering arrival of Saint Francis Xavier to south India in 1544 to his own travel to India, as the most recent foreign Francis Xavier, S.J., to be deeply linked to south India. Clooney aligns side by side, without unifying them, two Jesuit journeys in encounter with other religions: on the left, that of the Society from its early years when Jesuits often pioneered encounter with other cultures and religions; on the right, his own journey, personal and scholarly, as he has studied and learned from Hindu traditions and Hindus today. His account, composed in parallel columns and echoing a style made familiar by postmodern writers such as Jacques Derrida and Julia Kristeva, includes long passages from essays he had written over the years: our words do not have single, fixed meanings and uses, but can usefully recur in new contexts. Perhaps too, Clooney's conceit of writing in columns uncovers a dimension of *Jesuit Postmodern* as a whole: all eight essays and our response essay stand in parallel columns, alongside and near to one another, yet never converging into a single meaning or final conclusion. In any case, Clooney also writes from an unexpectedly liminal position, reflecting on twenty-one years of teaching at Boston College even as he takes up a new position at Harvard University.

Thomas J. Brennan's "A Tale of Two Comings Out: Priest and Gay on a Catholic Campus" is our final essay. In it he vividly charts the interplay between teaching, scholarship, and autobiographical telling and self-construction, all in terms of his location on campus as a gay Jesuit, teacher, and scholar of literature. Richly told and richly elusive, his account weaves into a single text traditional and stable starting points in the Jesuit and university culture, fictions, intended communication and surprising receptions of what is communicated. As in James Bernauer's essay, here too the body is brought to the fore as vulnerable to discipline, acts of language, and recomposition in conversations where both understanding and its absence have their voice. Perhaps the most postmodern of our essays, it fittingly concludes the set by highlighting the Jesuit fictionalization operative in the preceding essays as well.

We refined our essays repeatedly, in conversation with one another and by way of critiques of each other's drafts, yet without seeking to remove all the dissonances and fissures that have marked our personal experiences and those conversations. Tensions will thus be manifest in the individual essays and among them as a group. Fault lines are everywhere: reverence for tradition sits alongside a sense of its receding into an elusive past; admiration for full humanity, Christian identity, Jesuit virtues, rigorous scholarship is tempered by a sense that all these are liable to fragmentation, transgression, and disagreement. Our essays suggest a coherence across the particular instances and a recognition of this flourishing in the lives of others, including fellow Jesuits. We also sense that the pieces do not cohere, that unity cannot be taken for granted; who we are and what we do as Christian, Jesuit, and religious intellectuals must rather be explained again from the ground up. We write together, yet we write as it were in parallel columns that never quite converge into a single cohesive story.

VI. Individual Stories—For a Wider Audience?

Insider conversations can be intense, rich, and worthwhile for their participants—and, we hope, for others who are welcomed to join in later, along the way. Such conversations are necessarily limited in size and membership at any given point. Several confessions are therefore in order. First, we gladly admit that numerous Jesuit scholars—many more than appear in this volume—have helped us along the way; such Jesuits, many of whom live in the Boston area and others only in Boston for a semester or a year, have reflected on the topics addressed here and spoken eloquently to some of the points we make, and many were part of our conversations over the years. It was only our page limit, plus an inevitable narrowing of the lead-up conversations to these essays, that limited us to the current participants. We remain grateful to the many other Jesuits, local and visiting, who helped shaped our conversations over the years. *Jesuit Postmodern* is the fruit of conversations we shared with many fellow Jesuits, conversations appearing only implicitly in this volume.

Second, although this book recalls an inquiry and argument occurring among Jesuits, we also very much hope that a still wider audience of readers, especially our colleagues at Jesuit and other universities, will find it worth their time to read and think their way into the conversation we convene here. In sharing the problematic that faces us as a specific group of Jesuit scholars, we hope to have been specific and concrete enough not to exclude, but rather to provide space for the insights of other scholars who will speak from their equally concrete personal and professional situations. We hope to make the case to our fellow Jesuits and a wider audience of those interested in the intellectual life of Jesuits and of the Catholic community and in the tensions between religious communities, their traditions and institutions, and religious intellectuals within those communities, that only by beginning with the work certain scholars—here, Jesuits—actually live and breathe each day can one really enter their world. As we have stated repeatedly, one begins to understand Jesuit scholarship not by thinking about "Jesuit" and "scholarship," but by reflecting on what Jesuit scholars, as American religious intellectuals within specific working conditions today, actually do.

When all is said and done, however, some readers (Jesuits included) will still consider our approach far too idiosyncratic and insufficiently coherent. Some will fail to see why the old verities—the sturdy umbrella under which we think of ourselves to laboring—are not adequate: why not just talk about "finding God in all things," "union of minds and hearts," "the search for truth as the search for God," and so on? Why not? Our answer is simple: it is because we have more to say, rooted in greater concreteness, and not because we have less to say, that we turn to the stories of our scholarly lives. The verities appear in our accounts as events, not truths; as verbs, not nouns. We conceive of *Jesuit Postmodern* as a series of experiments on the basis of which careful inferences may be made. From our work, evidence of our operative Jesuit ideals will arise, partially shared and partially idiosyncratic. Engaging in these inferences will also, we hope, aid our readers in thinking similarly about their own intellectual practices and their motives in pursuing them.

VII. Jesuit Postmodern?

The essays leave behind questions appropriate to our various stages of unfinished Jesuit lives, and we hope our readers experience their force and find analogies amidst their own intellectual inquiry, religious faith, and institutional context. How does a Jesuit theologian manage to continue writing in a Church that very much seems unwilling to hear his voice or notice his written word? Is Jesuit scholarly identity so intertwined with the Thomistic tradition that Aristotle, newly discovered in the wider academe, is ironically beyond the reach of most Jesuits today? Isn't the sad history of the Christian-Jewish relationship and the involvement of Jesuits in some of the worst aspects of Christian anti-Semitism still a darkness overshadowing us because we still barely acknowledge our corporate responsibility? Aren't we all, and not just the actual immigrants, aliens in our own society and Society today? Is it really true that one can maintain continuity of skill and purpose when moving from profession to profession, as if career shifts are all stages in a single story? Will authentic worship, truly responsive to the needs of today's complex broken world, really remain the liturgy of any particular church? Isn't the Jesuit tradition of interreligious mission basically over with, if we can no longer articulate why "our" tradition is better than "theirs"? Can the gay Jesuit really succeed in holding a place, seen and heard, asked and telling, in today's beset and troubled Catholic Church? We answer many questions in the book, but in the end, we hope, questions such as these will be more and not less urgent than at the start.

It is because of these disparities and questions that we chose to highlight "postmodern" as well as "Jesuit" in our title. Above, in section IV, we have already stated our ambivalent feelings about the Jesuit Modern heritage with which we grew up. Here we go a step farther. Granting that "postmodern" has many richly complex, varied, and sometimes contrary meanings, we have been working with a sense of "postmodern" according to which the verities of modern discourse can no longer be taken for granted. We are skeptical about any easy assertions of the following sort: discourse has identifiable, coherent foundations; the universe presumes a single set of stable values; texts have single right meanings fixed by their authors; learning charts a path of progress; spiritual traditions have the power to shape individuals into definitely and definitively formed adherents to a single, articulable code; communities record coherent histories that can be traced unproblematically back to clear starting points; scholarship concludes in determining what things actually mean. We have engaged in our conversation and in *Jesuit Postmodern* with a postmodern expectation that while we have succeeded in speaking and listening and working together, it is not wise to expect a final consensus and common statement as the outcome of the conversation. The book is not "postmodern" because all our scholarship is decidedly postmodern in a uniform fashion or because we have all lined up in support of a recent theory about how to live or how to write. Such a unicity and its essentialist instinct would be surprising among scholars and Jesuits who are scholars, and it would be ironic had we succeeded at crafting a new "postmodern Jesuit" theory to replace old Jesuit theories. As William Rehg's essay (discussed below) very ably illustrates, we do not all agree on what "postmodern" means or how seriously the notion of a "postmodern Jesuit" is to be taken.

Rather, our book is postmodern because we have chosen to return to particularities that cannot be adequately accounted for by even the best of theories, and sought to find meanings in the individual stories of our scholarly production even as these continue to sit somewhat uncomfortably next to one another. We are seeking, by way of example, to make audible not only dominant Jesuit views or our own personal opinions, but also to make room for the array of smaller and quieter voices often muffled in the loud, mainstream conversations about Jesuit identity. We have co-authored a book after years of conversation, and we are confident about the fruits of our collaboration, but do not expect to have discovered or to give evidence of a harmonious, single-minded Jesuit view of the world. We are not disappointed that no such view has been revealed. Rather, it is voices allowed to speak from and toward particularities that can better address the postmodern situation we claim as "Jesuit" today. Stories such as those we tell, in our own ways in our several essays, serve to communicate the living Jesuit scholarly mission—limping, but still on the way—that is ours in the early twenty-first century. It is only in our selves—and in other selves inscribed in similar accounts—that "Jesuit" and "scholar" now exist together.

This postmodern resistance to totalizing theories, essentialization, foundationalism, and settled discourse should not be mistaken for a fiercely or even mildly un-Christian hopelessness. We marginalize, postpone, bracket the standard explanations of Catholic and Jesuit scholarly work, but we do not disown them. We are "Jesuits" and we are "scholars," and we persist in claiming that both terms are important and applicable. We have written this book not to end the conversation about how one can be a Jesuit and a scholar—or a Christian and a scholar, a religious person and a scholar—in today's American universities, but to make use of our experience in order to start a wider conversation that we hope will draw in a wide variety of Jesuits and other like-minded scholars. We attest that our lives and work do succeed in forming a web of partial correspondences and connections, overlapping stories and practices in which the Christian and Jesuit practices and worldviews imperfectly but nonetheless brightly continue to show forth. While there may not be any one thing such as "Jesuit scholarship" or "religious scholarship," there are Jesuit scholars and other scholars who continue to insist that both faith and scholarship really matter, in particular ways—and we are just a few of these scholars. So much the better if *Jesuit Postmodern* prompts other scholars to offer complementary or contrasting personal narratives and, if so inclined, even to restate in convincing terms why the standard histories and institutional accounts about the charism of Jesuit, Catholic and other religious intellectuals do actually manage to get to the core of where scholarship leads us today.

VIII. A Friendly Jesuit Skeptic Responds

Whether our project—a measured complaint about the Modern, and then too a more radical non-essentialist turn—actually makes good sense is a matter to be decided by our readers. As mentioned, William Rehg, a Jesuit philosopher not hitherto part of our conversations, is our very first reader, and in very interesting ways he refuses to embrace our scenario. In his conversations with us, and in "Do Jesuit Scholarly Endeavors Cohere? Self-Reckoning and the Postmodern Challenge," Rehg has steadfastly held his ground in explicating, problematizing, and resisting the trajectory of our essays. He thus introduces into the volume a fresh perspective from outside our conversation, raising questions of the kind we anticipate hearing from other readers as well. Rehg takes our discontent and postmodern complaint very seriously, and like us eschews easy solutions and pat rhetoric about what the Jesuit charism is supposed to mean. His eyes are wide open regarding the problems facing Jesuit scholarly work today. By his close analysis he seeks to draw us back into the realm of more ordinary reflection on Jesuit tradition and charism; he thus initiates a needed second reading of our project. It is only fair that he should do so: if Jesuit sources, strategic choices, and rhetoric are re-read in light of our essays, our essays themselves should be scrutinized in light of familiar and less dramatic Jesuit practices—vows, pieties, virtues—of the kind that have for generations held this Society together. Skeptical of our claim to a postmodern identity that matters more than the continuities of Jesuit tradition, life, and practice, Rehg unpacks the dialogical intention that instigated our project from the start. As our first reader, he may also be anticipating how other readers will react—with interest in our venture, appreciation of the individual accounts, but also some doubts: don't we stop short, say too little, and fail really to explain why our projects should be called "Jesuit," if we seem so reluctant to say what Jesuits normally say? We likewise stand our ground and do not agree entirely with Rehg, since a return to a common ground would be intellectually too hasty; the conversation among Jesuit scholars and educators about what we *think* has broken down, and this situation, even if honestly conceded, is only beginning to create the possibility of real learning. But we are delighted to see his critique inscribed in our volume as essential to it, and are grateful to him for his willingness to become our co-author.

In conclusion, we hope that many readers will find in our essays signs of life, indicators that Jesuits are still Christian religious scholars, perhaps more in continuity with the great Jesuit intellectual heritage than we ourselves notice: respect for tradition, yet also a refusal to rest upon it, and a determination to interrogate the tradition in light of our experience today; a love of the Church, yet also an insistence on prodding all of us to ask questions and think; a commitment to knowing, yet also a conviction that knowledge is a supreme moral force; an awareness of disciplinary and religious boundaries, yet too a willingness to transgress them; a commitment to build and foster communities of inquiry and conversation, though tempered by a suspicion of settled determinations of what things are to mean; a confidence that scholarship and religious vocation go together, even if there is no smooth narrative by which we could take for granted their connection.

Other readers may be dissatisfied, left wondering whether these essays—near one another, but written in parallel lines that never meet—really communicate what is interesting and important about Jesuits and their scholarly commitments: "Sure, the authors are scholars, and they are Jesuits, but do their essays fruitfully illumine 'Jesuit' and 'scholar'?" We are not the ones to dismiss such hard questions posed to us, but we would like to think that readers who return to the standard sources will nonetheless carry with them the questions and particularities of our project, re-reading standard discourses on the Jesuit intellectual life in light of the experience of nine contemporary Jesuit scholars who have worked at sharing a common conversation and have learned much even from disagreeing with one another. We would like to think that the conventional and still dominant ways of talking about Jesuits, scholarship, and religious intellectual inquiry will be unsettled by the contrapuntal display of voices enunciated in *Jesuit Postmodern*—not to end the conversation, but to push us to talk more, and more critically and imaginatively.

2

Confessions of an Aristotelian Christian

Arthur Madigan, S.J.

I N *A NATION UNDER LAWYERS* Mary Ann Glendon tells of a young lawyer's first appearance in a Chicago municipal courtroom:

> Full of himself, he stepped up when his case was called, and began, as we were taught to do in law school: "May it please the court, my name is Edward R. Lev of Mayer, Friedlich, Spiess, Tierney, Brown & Platt and I represent the Continental Illinois National Bank and Trust Company of Chicago." The judge glared down at the unfortunate newcomer and remarked (to the delight of seasoned onlookers): "Well, bully for you!"

This essay was first written for a group of Jesuits who called ourselves "Jesuit Scholars in a Postmodern Age." We were trying to talk about faith and research and Jesuit commitment all in the same breath: how our faith and Jesuit commitments shaped our intellectual work, and how our intellectual commitments and identities shaped us as believers and as Jesuits. We criticized one another vigorously, but each of us was interested in what the others had to say. It is one thing to present a paper in the context of a small self-selected group, something else to present it to a wider public who may respond (perhaps to the delight of seasoned onlookers): "Well, bully for you!"

What can the reader expect from these pages? In the autobiographical part of the essay I talk about people and experiences that have influenced my development as a Jesuit academic. This part complements, and may to some degree offset, the interpretations of American Jesuit life in Joseph Becker's *The Re-Formed Jesuits*, Peter McDonough's *Men Astutely Trained*, and the recent *Passionate Uncertainty* by Peter McDonough and Eugene Bianchi. The latter part of the essay, in which I try to explain why I identify myself as an Aristotelian, is addressed to readers who take some interest in philosophy; but even those who find my Aristotelianism wanting may perhaps find its wants instructive.

I. Where I Am Coming From

I entered the Society in 1963, fresh out of high school, in the earliest phase of Vatican II, a proceeding of whose existence I was only dimly aware. Pope John XXIII had just died, and John Baptist Janssens was still General of the Society of Jesus. Thus the earlier part of my Jesuit course of formation, at St. Andrew-on-Hudson, Poughkeepsie, and Loyola Seminary, Shrub Oak, was only beginning to be transformed by the Council and by the Thirty-first General Congregation. I have never regretted that, because it has helped me to understand and appreciate older Jesuits, both those who embraced their formation and those who reacted against it; and it has kept me from absolutizing more recent developments in the church and the Society.

In my year of juniorate at St. Andrew and in my first year at Shrub Oak, I concentrated on Latin and Greek. In the second and third years at Shrub Oak I felt increasingly drawn to philosophy and especially to Greek philosophy. The idea of an Aristotelian-Thomistic philosophical synthesis was still alive in our time, but its days were clearly numbered. The nearest thing to a standard philosophical doctrine at Shrub Oak was a mix of transcendental Thomism (Maréchal, Rahner, Lonergan) with existential phenomenology. This was not a genuine synthesis, and yet the structure of tract courses and lists of theses to be defended conveyed the aspiration to synthesis. I was (and am) receptive to this aspiration, and yet the single thinker who influenced me the most was, I believe, Robert Johann. Johann introduced us to the pragmatism of Dewey, and I still come back to his saying that the basic philosophical question is not "Why?" but "Why bother?" He also introduced us to Blondel, and taught us that ethics, not metaphysics, is first philosophy. Johann's ethics was really the only kind of ethics on offer at Shrub Oak. Martin Mahoney, who taught ethics and social philosophy, had, like Johann, seen beyond the limits of older scholastic ethics, and he had certain insights into axiology, teleology, and the reciprocity of persons; but Mahoney had difficulty in spelling out the implications of these insights. In any case, I never had an old-fashioned natural law ethics course to react against, which may help to explain why I take natural law ethics, or at least some versions of natural law ethics, seriously.

When we are ready to write (and read) the history of Jesuit formation, John Dinneen's rectorship at Shrub Oak will be an important chapter. Whatever that history may say, however, Jack's introduction to Anglo-American analytic philosophy did me a great service. Jack's central thesis was that linguistic analysis was a philosophical method that involved no commitment to any particular metaphysical, epistemological, or ethical position; thus there is nothing anti-metaphysical, anti-ethical, anti-theistic, or anti-religious about analytic philosophy as such. I have borne that thesis in mind ever since. I don't think I could have gotten through graduate school or worked in ancient philosophy without it. Analysts have their limitations, to be sure; but I have never really understood why some Catholic philosophers, and some Aristotelians, are so closed to the practice of analytic philosophy.

Two other professors had a strong influence on my development in these years: John Heaney, who taught us liturgy, ecclesiology, and Saint Paul; and George Glanzman, with whom I studied Hebrew at Fordham. Both were men of high integrity, but their intellectual personalities were starkly different. Heaney's most definite statements were tinged with hesitation, while Glanzman seemed not to know the meaning of doubt. Heaney was committed to the project of theological understanding, while Glanzman's scriptural positivism left little room for a theological enterprise; once the biblical text had been accurately exegeted, what more was there to do? Glanzman and Heaney stand for two desires that have been strong in my own intellectual work: the desire to break free of unexamined assumptions and come to definite judgments on the basis of solid evidence, and the desire at the same time to be open to the many different kinds of reality and the many ways of understanding them.

In 1969 I left New York to begin an M.A. in philosophy at the University of Toronto. Later I received permission to continue through for the Ph.D. Thus I was in Toronto from 1969 through summer 1973, living, since there was no room in the local Jesuit inns (so much for the niceties of Jesuit formation!), in the seminary of the priests of the Congregation of Saint Basil, a group founded in nineteenth-century France, best known for founding Toronto's Pontifical Institute of Mediaeval Studies. I must often have been a trial to the Basilians and the other religious living at St. Basil's. To them I owe a strong sense that being a Jesuit is but one way of being a religious, and that religious life only makes sense within a broader commitment to Christian life, understood as a life in the church. The years at St. Basil's cured me of the Jesuit temptation to treat commitment to the Society as a substitute for commitment to the church.

It would take too long to discuss all the issues that filled the air at St. Basil's in those days: the Vietnam War, *Humanae Vitae*, the renewal of religious life, the historical-critical approach to scripture, the charismatic movement, the Nixon presidency, and the challenging and purifying movement that went by the name of the Death of God. It was at St. Basil's that I first read John Courtney Murray's *We Hold These Truths: Catholic Reflections on the American Proposition,* and there I began to wrestle with the question that Murray himself never had to face: is there something in the American proposition that leads inevitably to the majority's opinion in *Roe v. Wade?*

I had good friends in Toronto and elsewhere, but the years in graduate school were in many ways desert years. Living at St. Basil's meant living in a Catholic context; but studying at the University of Toronto, I made my first real contact with people who were thoroughly secular and sometimes (behind the veil of Canadian politeness) even anti-religious. If I have passed through a phase that would deserve the name "crisis of faith," it was during those four years of graduate school. Ideological atheism and anti-religious propaganda did not shake me very much, but the mindlessness of so much Christian talk and practice made me sick to the heart. I spent a great deal of time examining deistic and reductionist accounts of religion and Christianity. I was working out how to think about God—the living God, not some reductionist substitute—so that I could continue to pray and worship God without abusing the intelligence that God had given me. I found much help in C. S. Lewis: not in his apologetics, but in the rich psychological and metaphysical insights of "Membership," "The Inner Ring," "Transposition," and "The Weight of Glory." Evensong at St. Thomas on Huron Street and (on visits back to New York) Sunday Mass at Corpus Christi near Columbia were high among the graces of these years.

After an unpredictable chain of events, and by the good offices of Vincent Potter, I had a year of regency teaching philosophy in Fordham College in 1973–1974. I worked hard, had a lot of fun, made a great many mistakes and (I hope) learned from them. I was the only scholastic in the Loyola-Faber community that year, and that led to some lonely spells and some awkward moments; but living with older Jesuits was on the whole a positive experience, and I am grateful for it.

Many Jesuits at the time thought of the Fordham community as a hotbed of conservatism. That was at best imprecise, and one of the things I learned at Fordham was not to let the labels "conservative" and "liberal" do my thinking for me. The community did include a number of articulate and unintimidated supporters of the controverted teaching of *Humanae Vitae,* and a few who sympathized with the Roman Forum that still gathered around Dietrich von Hildebrand; but the Fordham Jesuit community had accepted the decrees of the Second Vatican Council and the Thirty-first General Congregation. There was, to be sure, frank discussion about certain directions that the Society was taking, or seemed to be taking, in its Thirty-second General Congregation.

When I was doing regency, the ink was barely dry on the separate incorporation of Fordham University and the Jesuits of Fordham, Inc. The term "separate incorporation" calls for explanation. Until the late 1960s or early 1970s, the typical Jesuit college or university and its local Jesuit community formed one corporation. When the Jesuit Superior General in Rome appointed someone as rector (religious superior) of a given Jesuit community, he was *eo ipso* appointing him president of the college or university. By the late 1960s the colleges and universities saw the advantages of responsible boards of trustees and freedom from ecclesiastical control. Separate incorporation thus gave rise to a new class of Jesuit: the American Jesuit president, accountable to Jesuit superiors for his personal religious life, but accountable to his board of trustees for the running of his college or university. Once separately incorporated from their Jesuit communities, the colleges and universities generally adopted the conventions of American academic professionalism, such as the tenure system. This gave rise to another new class: the tenured Jesuit professor. Like other Jesuits, presidents and tenured professors may receive new assignments from their Jesuit superiors at any time; but since separate incorporation Jesuit superiors no longer have the power to place their men in college or university positions. While some Jesuits regard separate incorporation as a legal fiction, behind which the Society still directs a Jesuit network of colleges and universities, others see separate incorporation as making a decisive difference in our relationships with the colleges and universities and even with one another.

At Fordham the separate incorporation had come with pain. There were the inevitable cheerleaders ("It's time to let the lay people have their chance," etc.), but many in the community regretted the move ("Why have we given up our university?" etc.). The people I listened to most, and whom I still think of as the realists, were neither elated nor depressed by separate incorporation. They recognized that the religious character of Fordham would depend not on its long Catholic history, but on the activities and strategies of Jesuits and other believers. They recognized that being a Jesuit was not (and had not been for a long time) the ticket to respect and influence at Fordham; that ticket was thoroughgoing academic professionalism. Among many who saw these truths, the one who put them to me most forcefully was the medievalist Edwin Alphonsus Quain. I've taken these insights for granted ever since, and been surprised and disconcerted at how long it has taken for them to be accepted, if indeed they are accepted, among Jesuits even today. But back to the story.

I have sometimes wondered what difference it might have made if I had done theology at Woodstock in New York or at Weston in Cambridge. As it was, I returned to Toronto in fall 1974 to begin theology at Regis College and to finish the dissertation. All sorts of ideas were in the air at Regis: the Thirty-second General Congregation's call for the service of faith and the promotion of justice, which some interpreted as a call for Christian Marxism or liberation theology; the renewal or rediscovery of the *Spiritual Exercises*; the emergence

of clinical pastoral education (CPE) as a major instrument of religious formation; the replacement of the older ascetical vocabulary with a new psychological vocabulary; the vogue of the enneagram; the transition from a large
community at the edge of metropolitan Toronto to a set of small communities downtown; and the manifold influences of Bernard Lonergan.

My classmates were a wonderful group. From its earliest days at Regis, our
year was distinguished from others by a shared contrarian spirit. We were
ready to question all sorts of assumptions: not only the 1950-ish assumptions
that some of our faculty brought to theology and community life, but also the
late 1960-ish assumptions of other faculty, and even (with great discretion!)
the assumptions of that Ignatian renewal associated with the names of John
English and Colin Maloney. I suppose that we said much nonsense—I certainly did—but on balance the result was good: a relativizing of all these
frameworks, new as well as old, and a growing appreciation that each of the
frameworks, old as well as new, had something going for it. Reinforcing this
experience, and a blessing in many other respects as well, was my initiation,
under the tutelage of the late Joseph Barton, into directing religious women in
the *Spiritual Exercises.*

I came back to Toronto in September 1974 thinking that I would need at
most a year to finish the dissertation, and that I could wrap it up while studying theology. How wrong I was! I spent the next two years studying theology,
directing retreats, and writing about Aristotle's *Categories.* Then, one evening
in fall 1976, not long before ordination to the diaconate, I called up my supervisor to ask when we might discuss the draft of the dissertation that I had
given him that summer; and he told me that there was no point in our meeting, because what I had given him had no philosophical significance.

My supervisor and I had not been communicating, and I had overlooked
this or even denied it. I had sent him chapters and we had had meetings, but
I was not getting across to him the philosophical significance of my work (if
indeed it had any). Worse than that, I had not picked up my supervisor's hints
that the pages I had turned in (well over two hundred of them) lacked significance. Worst of all, I had no idea how to take his negative verdict and learn
something from it that I could use to improve the dissertation. I was looking
for my supervisor to take issue with things that I had said, and he did not; he
just didn't think that it all amounted to anything. In retrospect, I can see that
he had some good reasons for this judgment. At the time, though, I didn't
even pick up what his judgment was. I just thought he was being dilatory and
disorganized, which he was.

The moralist Richard Roach once quoted Lonergan to the effect that we
often learn most from our mistakes. One day in the middle of the dissertation
crisis, Dick took me aside and told me first, to finish the dissertation and get

the degree, and then, once that was done, to link up with a good analyst (he meant a psychoanalyst, not a linguistic analyst) and find out why I had made the mistakes that had landed me in this mess. I still haven't linked up with a good analyst, but after several years I did admit to myself that my own mistakes were at the root of the crisis: not mistakes about philosophy, but mistakes about reading people and working with people: my supervisor, other members of my committee, other faculty, and my peers.

Conflicts have a way of making one grow up, and the conflict over the dissertation taught me some important truths about academic life. Leading an academic life is not just a matter of being talented, working hard, and writing up a storm. It requires insight into people (more than I had at the time!), and a readiness to face one's personal limitations (such as my reluctance to confront my supervisor) and to work on them. Disagreement and conflict are to be expected in academe. If something seems obvious and important to me, that does not guarantee that it will seem important to others, or even true. A good academic needs the humility to recognize that he or she can be wrong, even seriously wrong. But by itself, that humility might lead an academic to shy away from saying anything worth saying. A good academic also needs the courage to try to say important things, with no guarantee of getting them right. Further, academic disagreements are not always articulated clearly, and academic conflicts are not always settled rationally. Academic life has a surd dimension, and leading an academic life means living with that surd.

After about a year, and with the help of many people, I was finally able to switch supervisors and work with a man by the name of John Rist, to whom I am indebted in many more ways than I can begin to say here. John Rist deferred to no one and had no interest in being deferred to. From him I began to learn what I should have learned when I studied with George Glanzman but was not ready to learn at that time: the frankness with which human beings should deal with one another. I have been trying, with varying degrees of success, to practice it ever since.

Somehow I finished theology and my "honeymoon" in studies was over. I filled in at Le Moyne College for the winter-spring semester of 1979 and then (courtesy of the academic-political skills of Joseph Flanagan) came to Boston College, where I have been ever since, apart from sabbaticals, fellowships, visiting appointments, and my recent (2002–2005) appointment as rector of the Jesuit community at Le Moyne College. The years at Boston College have been extremely rich and are correspondingly difficult to summarize, but let me begin with two formative experiences.

The first of these was a year away from Boston College in 1985–1986, as a junior fellow at the Institute for Hellenic Studies in Washington. I was working on Alexander of Aphrodisias's commentary on Aristotle's *Metaphysics*, but the formative experience to which I refer was living in the group at the Center (director Zeph Stewart, his wife Diana, the nine junior fellows, and spouses and children—American, Canadian, Irish, British, Welsh, Austrian, and Israeli). Apart from a few forays to visit the Georgetown University Jesuits, these classicists and their families were my community.

That year at the Center was my first contact with the Harvard ethos: urbane, inquiring, confident, and with nothing to prove. I began to appreciate the power, and the attraction, of the shadow that Harvard casts across the Charles. Several of us were believers, though none of us knew very well how to talk about God or religion in the context of our professional work. That year was also my first extended contact with people in whose lives God had no place, and who did not experience that absence as a void that needed filling. I had met people like this in Toronto, but at the end of the day I was always back in a religious community. At the Center I was living with them day by day. Finally, the year at the Center was the first time I had lived in community with women. They were, and are, wonderful women: strong, articulate, fair-minded rather than ideological. Some were believers, but none was Roman Catholic. To this day, when our church comes out with a statement about this or that, I ask myself, "How would I go about explaining it to them?"

When I came back from the Center for Hellenic Studies, Joe Duffy, the rector, and Jim Halpin, the minister, were looking into ways of revitalizing the Boston College Jesuit community. Right at this juncture Ronald Anderson came up with the visionary proposal that the Jesuit community found and run what he called an institute of interdisciplinary studies. The proposal was that the Jesuit community would provide the forum for the study of issues that confront religious believers working in a wide variety of intellectual disciplines. This was a need that neither campus ministry nor regular academic programs were meeting: an intellectually rigorous enterprise that was also experientially religious. Filling this need was to be the focus of the Jesuit community's own interior renewal. Ron Anderson's brainchild was quickly colonized and transformed by others, but not without some stressful discussions in the Jesuit community and between the community and university administration. These discussions are the second formative experience that I need to mention.

The obvious issue was control: would the direction of the institute be in the hands of the community or in the hands of university administration? One way I used to frame the issue at the time was whether the Jesuit community wanted to have a distinct corporate voice or presence of our own to address the intellectual and religious concerns of the campus, or whether we were content to be represented by the university's administration. The deeper issue, I now think, was whether the Jesuit community, or even those Jesuits active in the university, could envision ourselves working together to run a shared intellectual apostolate, with the kinds of discussion and reflection that that would have entailed. From this distance I can see that I was naïve about what our community could have accomplished by way of a corporate apostolate. Still, I think that if we had tried to run an institute ourselves, that attempt would have led us, through much struggle, to levels of intellectual and religious renewal that today we can barely imagine.

As it turned out, our community did not want to develop a voice of its own; and so we went the conventional route of giving money to the university to set up an institute and run it. Our decision to hand the institute idea over to the university for implementation was a decision not to attempt a genuinely corporate apostolate. Since the late 1980s our policy has been to support the work of the university and to provide maximum support for the apostolates of individual Jesuits, as we conceive of those apostolates. I was on the losing side of the discussion about a shared community apostolate, but I have been grateful ever since for the community's generous support for my own intellectual work, to which I now turn.

II. Where I Am Going

My major project since coming to Boston College in 1979 has been to understand Aristotle, in particular his *Metaphysics* and *Nicomachean Ethics*. Translating and annotating Alexander of Aphrodisias's commentaries on *Metaphysics* III and IV and writing my own commentary on *Metaphysics* III have focused my study of the *Metaphysics*. Regular teaching of the *Nicomachean Ethics* and the writing of the occasional paper have kept me in touch with that book. I still have much to learn about Aristotle, but I am fairly confident that I have what you might call his wave-length.

I do not spend all my time on exegesis. Mindful of Joe Flanagan's advice not to be totally immersed in the past but to keep an eye on the present as well, I have also tried to keep up with a range of twentieth-century and now twenty-first-century authors, some of them (Alasdair MacIntyre, Martha Nussbaum) placing themselves in the Aristotelian tradition, others (Pierre Manent, Robert Spaemann, Robert Sokolowski) drawing on the Aristotelian tradition, and still others (Maurice Blondel, John Macmurray, Charles Taylor) coming from outside it.

MacIntyre and Nussbaum are both Aristotelians, but MacIntyre reads Aristotle through the eyes of Aquinas and to some extent of Marx, while Nussbaum reads him through the eyes of Hilary Putnam and John Rawls. Their differences are not simply exegetical; they are issues of philosophical fruitfulness and adequacy to human life. Spaemann interests me because he tries to integrate an Aristotelian conception of human teleology with insights into personhood derived from modernity and especially from Kant. Blondel's philosophy of action points the way to a rich and subtle understanding of human teleology. Macmurray's personalism and Sokolowski's phenomenology offer ways to enrich Aristotle's understandings of human action and human relations. Taylor interests me as an antithesis to MacIntyre, because he articulates a richly humanistic and Christian position that embraces modernity and the Enlightenment, rather than rejecting them as pernicious errors. Manent's interpretation of the transition from classical or premodern politics to modern liberal politics and his reading of the modern liberal mentality stimulate my thought on a wide range of ethical and political issues.

In the last four or five years I have been more and more interested in issues of ethics and political philosophy. I began to implement this ethical-political side of my project in two lectures at Marquette University: "The Future of Aristotelian Politics" (October 1999) and "Making Sense of the Common Good" (March 2000), and in a presentation on Pierre Manent's *The City of Man* and *An Intellectual History of Liberalism* at the Jesuit Philosophical Association in November 2000. I have also begun to teach introductory courses in ethics, as a way of working out my ideas in this area. Lately I have been trying to come to grips with the notion of common good. This topic interests me on several counts: its Aristotelian and other classical roots; its long standing in Catholic tradition; its eclipse in the 1950s and 1960s and its rediscovery in the mid-1980s; and the objections from which it needs to be rescued. I took the invitation to deliver lectures at the Catholic University in Hungary in March 2004 as an occasion to explore the interpretations of the common good offered by Michael Novak and David Hollenbach.

III. My Aristotelianism

It is time to explain what I mean by calling myself an Aristotelian. I accept the basic realism of Aristotle's theory of knowledge. I accept a version of Aristotle's teleological understanding of nature, that is, the view that living beings have inbuilt principles of development and fulfilment, and that an adequate understanding of living beings requires attention to the structures and patterns of their development and fulfilment. I take the broadly Aristotelian view that human nature is neither reducible to its bodily dimension nor intelligible without that bodily dimension. I agree with Aristotle that living in political society is natural to human beings but that concrete social and political arrangements are largely artificial, conventions that are more, or less, in accord with human nature. I accept Aristotle's view that there is no single overarching science of all reality, but rather a variety of distinct sciences and inquiries, each with its own standards of evidence and appropriate degree of certainty and precision. I accept Aristotle's recognition that the dialectical search for the truth, the scientific exposition of the truth, and the rhetorical attempt to persuade are three very different modes of discourse.

That, in a nutshell, is my Aristotelianism. But since the term Aristotelianism comes freighted with centuries of baggage, I need to say what I do not include in my commitment to it. I do not commit myself to the view that Aristotle's logical works give us a perfectly consistent and adequate system of logic. I make no across-the-board commitment to Aristotle's physics, cosmology, biology, and the rest of his natural science. Aristotle's *Metaphysics* offers brilliant insights, but it is not a perfectly worked out system. I recognize that many of Aristotle's views in ethics and politics are defective.

Aristotle may have aspired to produce a consistent and all-encompassing system, but that system is not to be found in the writings that have come down to us. The Aristotle of the writings is a *Problemdenker*, a thinker who focuses on whatever problem he has in view at a given moment, and whose reflections on that problem are not necessarily consistent with his reflections on some other problem, for neither set of reflections is simply a set of deductions from higher and prior principles. Aristotle is richest in insights where he is least consistent, for example, in his discussions of the sources of human action. His philosophy of nature and metaphysics, and even more his ethics and politics, are not positions to be accepted or rejected *en bloc*, but remain sources of insights—insights that often call for transposition into broader frameworks than Aristotle himself managed to work out.

My adoption of the title "Aristotelian" can be read as adversarial, as setting myself up in opposition to other ways of thought, such as modern philosophy or Platonism or Thomism. Insofar as I accept the basic realism of Aristotle's theory of knowledge, I have to treat many ancient and modern problems as non-problems—at least those that arise from the Cartesian and Lockean versions of the "egocentric predicament" and the "epistemological problem." And my experience has been that it is easier to find a place for modern insights, such as Kant's insights into human dignity, in an Aristotelian framework, than to find a place for Aristotelian insights, such as the teleology of nature, in a Kantian or other modern framework.

As an Aristotelian I am inclined to be critical of many aspects of modernity, and one of the reasons that I have felt so comfortable in our Boston College department has been the department's inclination to be critical of modernity. That inclination springs from many different sources: Aristotelian, Thomistic, Nietzschean, Heideggerian, Straussian, Lonerganian, and Foucauldian. Lately I have come to think that we have undervalued modernity, and especially the tradition of Enlightenment liberalism, to the point where we no longer let it challenge us. My reading in modern philosophy, and especially in the Enlightenment, has been too limited. I need to keep in touch with the liberal Aristotelianism of a Martha Nussbaum, with other liberals like John Rawls, and with defenders of the Enlightenment like Peter Gay, if my criticism of modernity is to be more than a criticism of my own caricatures and imaginings. I have much to learn.

My admiration for Plato is vast, and I think that Aristotle took many of his best ideas from Plato, so why not call myself a Platonist? I would not mind being called a Platonist, on many counts, but I don't think that my style of thinking deserves the name. I do not see in myself those powers of imagination and evocation that so distinguish the work of Plato from anything else that I have ever read. I would not object to being called a Neoplatonist, but I do not see in myself either the articulation of mystical experience that I find in Plotinus or the rampant deductivism of a Proclus.

Why an Aristotelian rather than a Thomist? Being a Thomist is one way (roughly, an Augustinian way, or a Christian Neoplatonic way) of being an Aristotelian; and the Thomistic metaphysics of creation is an authentic development of Aristotelian insights, one that goes beyond Aristotle on Aristotelian principles. So my debts to Thomas Aquinas are great, and I do not accept for a moment the view that his thought is passé. If I identify myself as an Aristotelian, rather than as a Thomist, it is for three main reasons.

The first reason is that when I try to come to grips with philosophical and even theological issues, Aristotle's dialectical and aporetic methods help me more than the deductive method of Aquinas's writings. (Even if, as some argue, Aquinas was a dialectical thinker, the literary form of his principal writings remains thoroughly deductive.)

Second, I learn more from differences and arguments among Aristotelians than I do from the differences and arguments that I run into among Thomists. In my limited experience, Thomists tend to be so committed to Thomas that they confound issues of exegesis with issues of substantive philosophy, as though grasping the Angelic Doctor's meaning were the same as grasping the truth. Most Aristotelians, by contrast, know that Aristotle makes mistakes, and so they learn to distinguish exegetical arguments about the meaning of his texts from strictly philosophical arguments about what is true or false.

Third, while Aquinas is a genius and a saint, his grasp of the biblical and patristic traditions suffers from serious limitations. Apart from everything that Aquinas simply did not know about scripture, the church fathers, and the councils, his harmonizing manner of citing these authorities tends to occlude the realities of difference and development that characterize the Christian tradition, even those parts of it that are generally reckoned to be orthodox. I sympathize with calls for a return to Aquinas, but not if the price of this return is to sacrifice two centuries of historical study.

It may be possible to graft a contemporary historical-critical understanding of scripture and tradition into a Thomistic framework. Arguably, that is what Lonergan was trying to do in his Roman lecture courses. For myself, I find it better to start with the biblical and patristic traditions, now better understood than in Aquinas's day, and to confront them with those parts of Aristotle that are still philosophically alive. This is particularly true when it comes to Augustine. It is commonly and correctly said that Aquinas presents a synthesis of Aristotle and Augustine; but I find it more illuminating to go back to Aristotle and Augustine themselves and to work through the points on which they differ, for example, the this-worldliness of Aristotle's ethics and Augustine's insistence on the absolute necessities of grace and faith.

The phrase "Aristotelian tradition" may summon up visions of a philosophical synthesis unchanged since Aristotle's day, championed by zealous disciples against all comers. Away with such chauvinism! When I call myself an Aristotelian, I am not subscribing to that kind of a philosophical creed. I work towards synthesis, but I do not have a synthesis in hand. When I speak of the Aristotelian tradition, I use "tradition" in a sense spelled out by Alasdair MacIntyre: not a protective medium to transmit a philosophy without change, but a social and intellectual form for the pursuit of certain goods, a form that faces up to problems that arise from within the tradition itself, as well the claims of competing traditions, and that supports a continuing argument about how the goods that the tradition stands for can best be pursued.

Let me try to make these ideas of tradition and argument more definite. Since the 1980s, Alasdair MacIntyre and Martha Nussbaum have been exploiting Aristotelian insights that have led them in different and even opposed directions. MacIntyre's Aristotelianism has led him to a renewed appreciation of Thomas Aquinas and the tradition of Thomism promoted by *Aeterni Patris*, to a deep suspicion of the modern nation-state, and to a politics of small local communities. Nussbaum's Aristotelianism has led her to a reexamination and modification of Rawlsian liberalism, and to a political view that she styles Aristotelian social democracy, not to mention her involvement in work for the betterment of oppressed women in Africa and Asia. While Nussbaum's Aristotelianism is more cosmopolitan and MacIntyre's more particularist, there are also signs of convergence. MacIntyre's *Dependent Rational Animals* focuses on the ethical implications of the human life cycle, of the fact that all humans start life helpless but are helped by others, that most of us end our lives helpless and are helped by others, and that all of us are vulnerable to becoming helpless and in need of the help of others. One of Nussbaum's recent book reviews, a deep and sensitive reflection on the situation of physically challenged and mentally disadvantaged children, comes to almost the same point.

Nussbaum and MacIntyre are familiar names, at least to those who read the *New York Review of Books*, the *New York Times Book Review*, and other organs of American intellectual culture. One who looks farther afield will find other forms of Aristotelianism in contention, for example, the Americanizing Aristotelianism of Mortimer Adler, the Aristotelianism (not that it is only an Aristotelianism) of the followers of Leo Strauss, and the quasi-Aristotelian objectivism of Ayn Rand. The two main contemporary versions of natural law theory—the "new natural law theory" of Germain Grisez, Joseph Boyle, and John Finnis, and the revived "old line" natural law theory of their critics—are in important respects Aristotelian. And there are strong Aristotelian resonances in the phenomenological work of Robert Sokolowski.

When I place myself in the Aristotelian tradition, these are the people with whom I place myself. Their names are enough to indicate that contemporary Aristotelianism is neither monolithic nor necessarily antiquarian. I find their insights helpful and congenial; and even their differences with one another I often find more instructive than the differences between them and non-Aristotelians. For example, I have come to think that the differences between MacIntyre's Aristotelian ethics and Nussbaum's Aristotelian ethics are more significant and interesting than, say, the classical modern disputes between Kant and the Utilitarians or between deontologists and consequentialists.

Let us suppose, then, that Aristotelianism is not monolithic or chauvinistic or merely antiquarian. Bob Johann's old question still remains to be faced: why bother? What is attractive, insightful, or challenging about an Aristotelian approach to reality? Let me address this question in two ways: first, by outlining an understanding of Aristotelian philosophical method, and then by instancing some Aristotelian insights and questions about certain present-day concerns.

IV. Aristotelian Inquiry

The *Posterior Analytics* indicates that Aristotle's ideal of scientific knowledge was axiomatic and deductivist and that his model for the presentation of scientific knowledge was geometry. Most of Aristotle's surviving work, however, illustrates a different procedure, a procedure for discovering truths, and for discovering the explanations of these truths. It is this set of procedures for discovery that I think of as the typically Aristotelian method.

Aristotle practices a variety of methods of discovery. One method, which some call dialectic and others the "method of appearances," is to start from the various common and expert opinions in circulation about a given topic, and to try to harmonize them, to show how they reinforce one another. But opinions do not always harmonize, and so Aristotle has a further method, which goes by the name of aporetic. Aporetic is a matter of identifying contradictions, or what appear to be contradictions, among the common and expert opinions, and of trying to resolve them, sometimes by finding for one side over the other, but often by identifying and revising the background assumptions that are responsible for generating the aporia in the first place. A third method goes by the name of peirastic: a set of techniques to test for minimal consistency and grounding in evidence, to help someone who is not an expert in a given field test whether something presented as expert knowledge in that field really is knowledge or not.

Behind and beneath these techniques, none of which is claimed to be strictly scientific, lies Aristotle's commitment to the diversity of reality and the plurality of disciplines. The degree of precision, the level of proof, the possibilities of generalization, differ from one discipline to another. Someone with an Aristotelian habit of mind is continually asking questions like: what kind of an inquiry are we in? are we simply trying to present the facts accurately, or are we also trying to explain them? what counts as evidence in this inquiry? what degree of precision or proof can we reasonably expect? In a world that is interdisciplinary, or at least multidisciplinary, Aristotelian dialectic, or something like it, is a useful medium of inquiry and communication. For someone like myself, who regularly engages with the different mindsets of classicists, philosophers, and theologians, something like Aristotelian dialectic is a practical necessity.

V. Some Aristotelian Provocations

A highly intelligent but quite unphilosophical friend once asked me, "What does Aristotle say that's interesting?" Her question took me aback, as friends' questions sometimes do. No quotation from the Master came to mind, and I felt that her question was somehow unfair, though I could not say how.

Now I think I would tell my friend, "It's not that Aristotle himself has such interesting things to say, but people who study Aristotle can have interesting things to say." For all that Aristotle is one of the founding figures of Western cultural tradition, his world and assumptions are so different from ours that he can also be the outsider who forces us to examine our assumptions. The Aristotelian "angle" on contemporary reality is in many ways the angle of a stranger. The next few paragraphs are an attempt to illustrate this point—not that the observations in them are the whole story about Aristotle, or that the

Aristotelian path is the only path that could have led to them, or that every Aristotelian would have to see things in the same way.

An Aristotelian who listened in on contemporary American politics would be struck by the widespread use of the terms "conservative" and "liberal." He would want to know what the people who use these terms think they mean. He would want to know how being "conservative" came to mean such different things as favoring a free market, opposing abortion, and approving of military interventions overseas; and how being "liberal" came to mean being in favor of affirmative action, humanitarian interventions overseas, and restrictions on certain kinds of speech. He might wonder whether the rhetorics of liberalism and conservatism serve to veil the realities of our situation. (MacIntyre's remark that what we think of as debates between conservatives and liberals are really debates between conservative liberals and liberal liberals would be one way of responding to this question, as would his contention that, despite all the rhetoric about the free market, there simply are no free markets above a very small and local level.) In the spirit of the *Politics*, our Aristotelian would want to have a searching analysis of the American constitution—not the document printed in civics books and displayed at the National Archives, but the real system on which the country actually runs. (MacIntyre's argument that we are living in an oligarchy disguised as a liberal democracy would be one example of such an analysis.)

An Aristotelian who tuned in on the debates about globalization would not be surprised to find powerful nations and cultures exerting influence on less powerful nations and cultures; she would have learned something from Thucydides. She would be biased in favor of political forms in which people who know one another take decisions for their common welfare, but she would understand the economic and political factors that made the city-state obsolete, and those that seem to be making the nation-state, or some traditional features of the nation-state, obsolete as well. Believing that the economic dimension of life ought to serve the political and cultural dimensions, she would regret the erosion of certain cultural and political goods in the global economy; and she would not be impressed by arguments that justify globalization on economic grounds without addressing its political and cultural effects. (Nussbaum's criticism of the oversimplifying use of GNP statistics would be one example.) But she would understand that the nature of economies and cultures and polities is to interact, to change and to be changed. Cultures are not museum pieces.

An Aristotelian who got to know Catholics would not be surprised to find them differing over the meaning of their Vatican Council. Catholics have taken centuries figuring out what to make of modernity, and they are not finished yet. It would be naïve to think that their recent council could settle this complex of issues in a definitive way. A living tradition carries on a continuing argument about the goods of the tradition and how to protect and promote them. That is what Catholics are doing, and if their argument ever stops, it will mean that their tradition is no longer living.

An Aristotelian would not be surprised, either, to find Catholics arguing about their church institutions. Without social form, ideas go nowhere; without institutional embodiment, traditions die out. But tradition and institution are locked in a continuing and inescapable tension. Institutional dynamics often subvert the very goods that traditions stand for and undermine the virtues necessary for the maintenance of those goods. Our Aristotelian would quickly take in that the Catholic church is not a democracy, but she might need time to understand its true political form, its real constitution. Her nearest ancient analogue for the church would be the Persian empire with its bureaucrats and satraps. She might wonder how such a large and centrally controlled entity could also be a community of free human beings. And she might ask whether the church's bureaucratic centralization is an authentic requirement of Christian tradition, or whether it simply represents the church's adopting certain features of the modern nation-state.

An Aristotelian would be sensitive to the many different modes of Catholic discourse, and alert to the interplay of truth claims, rhetorical strategies, and assertions of authority. She would be fascinated by the diversity of theological disciplines, and intrigued to hear how liturgy, canon law, and systematic theology talk about the same realities in different ways. She would want to know what counts as evidence in each of these disciplines, and what degrees of certainty and precision they can attain. She would be interested in the pluralism of theologies, and concerned about the conditions for meaningful conversation among them; she would want to know what their common ground is and isn't.

An Aristotelian might wonder why so many of the issues debated by philosophical ethicians seem remote from the concerns of ordinary men and women, and why the moral theologians seem to be talking past one another, using such different methods that they cannot agree on what counts as evidence. (Perhaps what they need is some dialectical encounters, or a dose of peirastic!) Hearing some moralists wax eloquent about the objectivity of truth and the validity of moral absolutes, the Aristotelian might ask about the level of precision that ethics can attain, and about the workings of practical wisdom. Hearing other moralists talk about autonomy and the rights of conscience, he might ask about the role of upbringing in the development of autonomy and the influence of the passions on the formation of conscience. Aristotle knew, just as well as Plato, that animal passion can distort and corrupt our judgments. Nonetheless he insisted, against Plato, that perception can be more than mere subjective opinion. If the ethicians were to take a break

from their calculi and counterexamples, and the moralists from their wran-
gling over the papal magisterium, they might tell us more about how our per-
ceptions can be educated and refined, disciplined and liberated.

Our Aristotelian would be fascinated by American colleges and universities.
She would be impressed by the extent to which they depend on the largess of
individuals and governments, and she would understand the inevitable gap
between what actually goes on in them and the rhetorical faces that they present to the outside world. While she might initially be put off by all the talk in
universities about the value of diversity, she would be relieved to learn that
American higher education has its diversities well under control. As always,
she would want to know the true constitution of the university. While naturally sympathetic to the teleological question, "What is the university for?" she
would question the kind of "mission talk" that implicitly likens the university
to a military unit or a business corporation. She would be cool to the idea that
a university is a business with shareholders (trustees), executives (administrators), workers (faculty and staff), and customers (students). She might ask: is
it of the essence of a university to be governed by its own members, or to be
governed from outside? and who are the real members of a university anyway?
She would be interested in universities, and perhaps even more interested in
small colleges, as potential political communities: relatively autonomous
groups of people taking decisions together for their common good.

One might contend that the crucial test for any philosophy is whether it has
anything illuminating to say about sex. I am not sure if Aristotle passes this
test. Here again he is an outsider to our culture, or at least to the culture of our
intellectual elites. A visiting Aristotelian would not be too surprised, or too
upset, by the amount of sexual activity going on in our society, or by its variety. Humans are, after all, animals, and animals are sexual beings, whatever
else we may become. What would surprise and puzzle her is the amount of
talk and writing about sex, and the proliferation of abstractions that we use to
talk and write about sex, or, as many prefer to call it, sexuality. As Aristotle was
matter of fact (perhaps too matter of fact) about sex, so our Aristotelian
would be skeptical (perhaps too skeptical) of attempts, whether Christian, Romantic, or postmodern, to make sexual activity, or the renunciation of same,
into something mysterious or spiritual, the bearer of deep meanings.

Aristotle's matter-of-factness about sex may be, from our more advanced
standpoints (Christian, Romantic, postmodern), a deficiency, an instance of
what Aristotle himself calls *anaisthêsia*, insensibility or lack of perception. It is
certainly a problem and a challenge for anyone who wants to be both Aristotelian and Christian. Let us suppose, then, that sex is much more mysterious and significant than Aristotle ever imagined; even so, he may still have
something to tell us. His standard advice is to start from what is clear to us and

then move on to what is not yet clear to us. "If sex, or sexuality, is so deep and mysterious," he might counsel, "then it's not the place to start, when you are trying to make sense of your life. Start by trying to understand friendship." Do we yet understand friendship?

VI. Aristotelianism and Jesuit Commitments

There are questions to face before this essay can end. Can an Aristotelian really be a Jesuit? Can a Jesuit really be an Aristotelian? Simply to say that there are Aristotelian Jesuits or Jesuit Aristotelians ("we're here, get used to it!") straightarms the questions without addressing the legitimate concerns behind them. I see three such concerns, and I will put them into the mouths of three imaginary objectors.

> A Jesuit needs to live in the present and be a man of the present, which means, among other things, being historically conscious. This is difficult for Aristotelians, since their philosophy has no place for history, and their oracle died over 2300 years ago.

Aristotle had little to say about history, and that little includes the notorious remark that poetry is more philosophical and more serious than history, because poetry discloses the universal, whereas history only tells us about particulars. One of the hazards of being an Aristotelian is the temptation to rest in eternal certitudes and to exempt oneself from the work of coming to terms with the contingent particular realities of the past or the present. Arguably, it was neglect of historicity that doomed the old Aristotelian-Thomistic system of Jesuit philosophical training: as theologians became more and more historically conscious, it made less and less sense to insist on an ahistorical Aristotelianism as a necessary propaedeutic for theology.

But Aristotelianism does not have to be ahistorical. Ours is an era of unprecedented historical consciousness; or at least we have an unprecedented opportunity to be historically conscious, whether we take it or not. An Aristotelian today needs to pay attention to history. When the Aristotelian is also a Christian, the need to pay attention to history is if anything more urgent. This is an area where my Christian commitment pushes me beyond Aristotle to the affirmation that certain historical facts have permanent religious and spiritual meaning—and not as instances of general laws or typical patterns, but in all their unrepeatable particularity. How do the particularities of history have philosophical and religious meaning? What kinds of intelligibility is it legitimate to look for in history anyway? These are questions that Aristotelians can and should ask.

Years of work on the history of Greek philosophy have shaped my view of
how to practice history. The reflections of Bernard Lonergan, John Courtney
Murray, Frederick Crowe, and others on the development of doctrine in the
patristic period have also been influential, as have the works of Cardinal Newman and Christopher Dawson. Lately I have been paying attention to work by
MacIntyre, Taylor, and others on the writing of philosophical history, and to
Roger Haight's discussions of history and divine transcendence in his *Dynamics of Theology*. It is becoming clear that I need to come to terms with the
work of Quentin Skinner. If I can ever get back to studying the pagan-
Christian encounters of the patristic period, or the Enlightenment, these will
be additional incentives to reflect on these questions. But Saint Ignatius, we
are told, said that no one ever really does more than one thing.

> A Jesuit needs to be in touch with the diversity of cultures and especially the
> diversity of religious paths in the world today. This is difficult for Aristotelians,
> because their philosophy has its roots in a classical Greek culture that is now
> long extinct, and because that philosophy sheds little or no light on religious
> experience.

It is no one's fault but my own that I have taken no part in the contemporary dialogues with the great religions; and I cannot think of a single prominent Aristotelian who has also been prominent in these dialogues. That said,
Aristotle's distinction of dialectical, scientific, and rhetorical discourse can
usefully be applied to interreligious discourse, even if other distinctions will
also be needed. But an Aristotelian would have to press a question about the
presuppositions of interreligious discourse: does the term "religion"stand for
a genus of which the various religions are different species, or are the religions
so diverse that it is a distortion to think of them as all species of a single genus?

Further, and granting that religion itself occupies a very small niche in Aristotle's thought, an Aristotelian today will have to question where and how the
line should be drawn between religion and philosophy. A sharp distinction between the vanity of human philosophy and the saving wisdom of God is one
of the great commonplaces of Christian rhetoric, and some preachers still get
a fair amount of mileage out of it. But in an era when Catholics are increasingly interested in the great world religions, and when some are asking
whether the religions may be authentic ways of salvation, even without reference to or reliance on Jesus Christ, is a sharp line between religion and philosophy still appropriate?

A colleague once made the point that if we ought to have dialogue between
Christians and Jews, then we ought to have dialogue not only with believing
and observant Jews but with unbelieving and non-religious Jews as well. I
would take that insight further. If we are thinking about a possible plurality of

ways of salvation, we should not neglect those of our fellow human beings for whom "salvation" is not even a meaningful category. We should be in dialogue not only with Hinduism, Buddhism, and Islam, but also with those philosophies and humanisms (religious, non-religious, or anti-religious) upon which many contemporary men and women are trying to build their lives. The Society saw this, and acted on it, in the dialogues with Marxism and existentialism; and the importance of this kind of work was confirmed in Pope Paul VI's mandate to the Society with regard to atheism. We should be making similar efforts today, and Aristotelian techniques of inquiry can be helpful in these dialogues.

> A Jesuit needs to be on the side of the poor in their struggle for justice and human dignity. This is difficult for Aristotelians: for some of them, because their Aristotelianism places them on the side of established elites; for others, because their intellectual detachment holds them back from engaging in the struggle for justice.

I have done little or nothing by way of solidarity with the poor. I have made little or no contribution to their struggle for dignity and justice. I don't think it is my Aristotelianism that has stood in the way, but my weaknesses and limitations. But whatever you think of Alasdair MacIntyre's critique of capitalism and the liberal nation-state, his intention is clearly to empower people who are currently powerless. And whatever you think of Martha Nussbaum's proposals for Aristotelian social democracy, her intention is clearly to bring the disadvantaged to a threshold of capability from which they can go on to lead autonomous lives. As an educational movement, Aristotelianism can make significant contributions to educating people about justice. The Aristotelian conception of practical wisdom offers an alternative to the kind of cost-benefit analysis that so many of our students are taught to regard as the paradigm of rationality. And the Aristotelian conception of political community as focusing on the achievement of common goods offers an alternative to the possessive individualism that pervades so much contemporary thinking. The struggle of and for the poor is ground on which Aristotelians can have something to say.

Back in the 1970s and 1980s, a number of Jesuits thought that our promotion of justice would best be served by a social analysis that drew significantly on Marxism. Perhaps some of us were not sufficiently discriminating in our appropriation of Marxist insights; but at its best (I recall Quentin Lauer's wonderfully careful letter, written at Father General Arrupe's request, on the meanings of the term "Marxist analysis") this was a serious and responsible attempt to arrive at a form of social analysis that could guide Jesuits and others in the promotion of justice. Since about 1990, if not earlier, Marxism has appeared to be intellectually bankrupt, and the idea that there can be any economic alternative to market capitalism now seems untenable. Have we taken sufficient account of these facts? If Jesuits are concerned with the promotion of justice, and if the promotion of justice requires some form of social analysis, what is our current Jesuit form of social analysis? What is our overall approach to understanding socio-economic realities and political situations? What should it be?

I am not suggesting that the answers lie buried in Aristotle or in some preconciliar synthesis. But those who intend to promote justice together need some sort of social analysis, or at least some sort of common language in which to communicate. As the Society tries to develop a social analysis that recognizes both the positives and the negatives in market capitalism, the new information technologies, and globalization, I hope that there are some Aristotelians at the table.

A phrase that sticks in my mind, from the days when we first met as the Jesuit Scholars in a Postmodern Age, is "my current project and what gives it its intellectual energy." It is axiomatic that Jesuits derive their energy from the experience of the *Spiritual Exercises*, but I have not had much to say about the *Exercises* in the course of this essay. My recent task of trying to guide a Jesuit community in line with the *Constitutions* and the recent grace of guiding a colleague through the *Exercises* have made me more conscious of debts to Ignatius than I had been for a long time. I think I have internalized, or rather received as graces, something of Ignatius's great meditations on the Foundation, the Kingdom, the Two Standards, the Modes of Submission, and the Contemplation to Obtain Love of God. I suppose I could have written about how these meditations, or rather the contacts with God that come through these meditations, inspire and support my philosophical work; but I have not felt the need to do that here, any more than I have felt the need to write about all the friends who have helped me along the way.

3

A Philosophical Dissection
of a Jesuit Scholar

William E. Stempsey, S.J.

I. Introduction

IN 1998, I WROTE AN ARTICLE for the weekly journal *America*. The article, entitled "The Battle for Medical Marijuana in the War on Drugs," argued that the use of marijuana for medical purposes ought to be legalized. I puzzled about why the federal government would not allow states to legalize such use. After all, marijuana does have useful medical purposes, and it is not more harmful than many other drugs that are legal. I did not argue that marijuana should be legalized for non-medical purposes. My point was simply that the medical use of marijuana is being held hostage because of its significant symbolic role in the war on drugs being waged by the United States government.

One day, three years later, I was sorting my e-mail and came upon a message from an undergraduate student at a state university in the Midwest. The student was preparing a class presentation on the medical use of marijuana. He said that my article had a lot of useful information, but that he could not use it unless he knew my political perspective. He asked, "Would you consider yourself a liberal or conservative or libertarian or what?"

The student was disappointed, I suspect, when he received my reply. I answered that I really did not know what political perspective my article represented. Was it liberal, or perhaps libertarian, in arguing for marijuana use? Or was it conservative, or perhaps libertarian, in arguing that physicians ought to be able to prescribe drugs in the way they see fit without government interference?

People like to put other people in boxes. When you have me in a ready-made box, or even a box that you have constructed especially for me, you think that you know how to deal with me. That may seem to make your life a lot easier, but it creates a problem. The trouble is that our mental boxes are never exactly the right shapes to contain actual persons. Real people will not exactly fit the preconceived categories of others. Often they do not even fit neatly into categories that are presumed to be given by nature. Race is a good example.

I usually resist attempts of other people to put me into their boxes. This is only partly because I find that my thought, as in the medical marijuana case, does not always fit into standard boxes. It is probably more due to my feeling that there are no standard issue boxes that fit persons. Even those who have tried consciously to make themselves fit into some box, that of a particular political party, for example, will not fit the box precisely unless they are willing to abandon their true complexity and become mere caricatures of some ideal.

The reader who is hoping to discover the Jesuit-intellectual-shaped box from the essays in this book may be disappointed, for Jesuit intellectuals resist, or ought to resist, such uniform characterization. They are complex individuals, each and every one. When I try to put an individual Jesuit into a box, I inevitably leave something out.

One might argue that this is a reflection of the postmodern condition in which today's Jesuits find themselves; that Jesuits are not immune from postmodern influences; and that this is either good or bad, depending upon the perspective of the observer. According to this postmodern viewpoint, there is no "essence" of the Jesuit scholar today. This may or may not be true, depending upon how robust one's sense of essence is. I believe that there is an essence of the Jesuit scholar, and that is first to be a Jesuit: to live the common life of Jesuits. This is a prescriptive claim—about what a Jesuit scholar *should* be. But I also believe that this Jesuit essence has many more manifestations than most people would think. So, I do not presume to present any claims about the universal essence of Jesuit scholarship except that it is done by Jesuits. It is better just to let each Jesuit describe his life and work, and leave judgments about the existence or essence of the Jesuit scholar to the reader.

The various parts of my life and work interact in a way that would not be possible if they were simply sorted into boxes and stacked together in a bigger box. An adequate description of my life and work requires a more organic image. Consider the cells that compose our bodies. They provide both structural and functional integrity. They are the physical stuff that is the body. But the cells also work together in ways that are not immediately obvious in order to make our bodies function. Our bones consist of many types of cells. Some provide the structure we need to keep from collapsing into a formless blob;

others are the stem cells that give rise to our blood cells. The pituitary gland consists of many different kinds of cells. Consider just a few examples. Some secrete hormones that control our growth. Others secrete hormones that stimulate the thyroid gland to make its own hormones. Others secrete hormones that induce the adrenal gland to make its hormones. Complex feedback loops allow the levels of some hormones to turn the pituitary cells off and on in order to regulate the levels of those hormones. Such complex cell interactions are a metaphor for the complexity of the various facets of my life as a Jesuit involved in the intellectual apostolate. This essay is a philosophical dissection of the scholarly system that I am and an attempt to show how the individual cells interact to form an integrated whole.

II. My Metaphorical Cells

Let me list just of few of my metaphorical cells. I am a physician. I am a philosopher. (Now, *everyone* is a philosopher, but only a few of us are paid for it.) I am a college professor. I am a Roman Catholic priest. I am a Jesuit. I have listed these things roughly in order of ascending importance to me at this time in my life, although it is hard to separate and rank some of these things. There are other cells, of course. I am Polish-American. I am an only child. I am left-handed. But here I focus only on the cells that are most important for the functioning of a Jesuit intellectual.

The philosopher cell and the college professor cell go very much together for me. (If they did not, I would just be an unpaid philosopher like everyone else.) The priest cell and the Jesuit cell also go together, although they are separable in a way. I know how to be a Jesuit without being a priest, but I do not know how to be a priest without being a Jesuit. That can be done, of course; many priests do it. It is just that *I* do not know how to do it; my entire life as a priest has been as a *Jesuit* priest. The physician cell is what makes me interesting to a lot of people. Although it is probably least important in my daily functioning right now, it has had a big influence on the person I have become. Let me describe these cells and how the "hormones" they produce have mutually influenced one another.

1. Physician Becomes Jesuit

I went to college wanting to become a physician. My reasons were vague, but as good as any of the reasons I have heard from the current crop of premedical students. I was interested in science, especially the biological and social sciences. I wanted to help people. I had grades good enough to make it. I had had good experiences with doctors who helped me feel better when I got sick, who sewed my finger back together after an unfortunate encounter with a lawn mower, and so forth. I had had opportunity to work in a hospital and I enjoyed being around the place. Most pre-medical students dream grand dreams, and that is a good thing. But one needs some grounding in reality as well. I had about as much as could be expected. None of this preparation *really* prepares a person, however. No one really knows what it is like to be a doctor until one *is* a doctor.

So, I gritted my teeth and got to the work of medical school. No one breezes through medical school. It is hard work—always fascinating, sometimes enjoyable, often a miserable grind, and never less than a total challenge to one's intellectual, moral, and physical strength. I somehow survived through four winters, often buried deep in the recesses of hospital wards and operating rooms, not seeing natural daylight for a week at time, and emerging only to find myself buried again, but now in snow. Finally, clutching a diploma that coupled my own name and the title "Doctor of Medicine," I prepared to enter into the strange world of residency in pathology.

Why pathology, of all things in the world of medicine? Why would I choose to devote myself to life in a laboratory, dissecting cadavers, and examining tissue and blood samples, devoting myself to diagnosis rather than to treatment? Role models were probably most important. I liked the pathologists I knew. That was not true of all the physicians I had met. I did get along well with many surgeons, who were not at all like their stereotypes, but I did not feel that I had the capacity to stand on my feet for long operations and the dexterity under pressure that surgery requires. Pathology offered an intellectual challenge. It is one of the few specialties that allows one to be reflective, and, although it sometimes requires important judgments under pressure, it usually affords some time to think.

An odd thing happened, though. The work was interesting enough but a sort of existential angst was developing within me. For so long, I had dreamed of becoming a doctor. For so long, I had worked at becoming a doctor. Now, I had actually done it. I was a doctor. But something was missing. Inwardly, I was singing along with Peggy Lee, "Is that all there is?"

Soul-searching, contact with Jesuits from college days and many new Jesuit acquaintances, beginning attempts at mature prayer, and much conversation resulted in my entering the Jesuit novitiate three years later, at the age of thirty. I skip over the details, the winding roads and the dead ends, but the result was a realization that God was calling me to be a Jesuit. That meant, for at least a while, abandoning the practice of medicine. That did not really bother me, for I had come to know that I did not want to spend my life in a pathology laboratory. Just what I would do as a Jesuit, however, remained an open question.

Should I consider, as a Jesuit, going back to residency in some other specialty? Or should I look to something else altogether?

2. Jesuit Becomes Philosopher

Such questions occupied my prayer and reflection for several years. But now they were different questions. They were no longer just my questions, but questions of my relation to the Society of Jesus. Jesuits vow obedience to their superiors, especially in terms of being available for any mission anywhere in the world. This is not just a blind obedience, but is essentially a discernment of what work is for the greater glory of God. It depends on both the individual Jesuit and his superior understanding of the individual's particular talents and desires and the needs of the people of God whom the Society of Jesus is called to serve. How would I best be able to contribute to the overall mission of the Jesuits?

Perhaps the biggest challenge of being a Jesuit novice was to lay aside professional aspirations, and even more, professional identity. As a physician, that is hard to do. It is even hard to explain to someone who has not been in the situation. Being a physician is different from being a bank teller, a carpenter, or a teacher. Being incorporated into the medical profession gives one an identity that is all-consuming. It is not a job in which you put on a hard hat for your shift and then take it off at the end and forget about it until the next shift. It is not even like other professions. Professors have an identity and can go through extended periods in which they are consumed in thought about one idea or another. But professors are not expected to be prepared to teach anything, anytime, anywhere, on the spur of the moment. Physicians, on the other hand, are expected to be ever ready to render universal service. This, along with many other complex factors, has a profound effect on one's identity, and it creates a bond between physicians. What I would come to discover is that being a Jesuit brought me to acquire another identity that was peculiarly similar. Now I had two all-consuming identities.

This is not my unique problem. There are other Jesuit physicians. Most of them are actively practicing medicine, and so face the dual-identity issue in an even stronger way than I do. They cope with this issue in varying ways, and with varying success. I have been privileged to come to know these Jesuit physicians, to be accepted as one of them, and to learn from them as I struggled to learn how my physician cell and my Jesuit cell could function together without destroying each other. They have taught me much about being a physician and being a Jesuit.

I gradually came to realize that being a Jesuit and being a physician are both important but distinct cells within me. The Jesuit cell is the one that contributes most to my day-to-day living, but the physician cell, even though I have stopped practicing medicine, is still alive and functioning. These are not just historical accomplishments, but elements of true identity—things that make me who I am.

As I proceeded with my Jesuit studies, I continued to question what I would do after ordination. I realized that I no longer had a desire to be a pathologist, but there was a lingering question in my own mind about whether I might go back to residency and pursue some other specialty. As time went on, however, the thought of my advancing age and the rigors of residency made me question whether I really wanted to start over again in post-graduate medical training. As I did my philosophy studies after the novitiate, I came to the exhilarating realization that I really like philosophy. I even realized that many of my childhood questions, which up until then I had been interpreting as scientific questions, were really philosophical questions. It was exciting in a way that the intellectual challenges of pathology were not. I became interested in medical ethics, which, at the time, was said to be the only "growth industry" in philosophy.

Theology studies were a time to consider even more seriously what I would do after ordination. After much consultation with my superiors and with some of the top people in the field of medical ethics, I realized that if I really wanted to do something significant in medical ethics, I should get a doctorate in an appropriate field. Philosophy was appropriate. Theology was appropriate. But I felt drawn to philosophy.

So, I set out to pursue, as my dissertation title page eventually said, the degree of "Doctor of Philosophy in Philosophy." It was every bit as challenging as getting a medical degree. The emotional strains, although of a different sort, were equally significant. The physical fatigue, although largely self-induced, was as real. The intellectual challenge was even greater. I often tell my students, especially the ones who begin to approximate the excessively smug pre-medical stereotype, that getting a degree in philosophy was harder than getting a degree in medicine. While there is a vast amount of information to learn about medicine, there is just as much to learn about philosophy—and many of the philosophical concepts are harder to grasp.

As it became apparent that I was actually going to finish this course of studies, it became time to look for a source of meaningful and gainful employment. When I had started, the Jesuits and I had both thought that I would end up working in a hospital, advising physicians about ethical matters and perhaps guiding them on their spiritual journeys as well. Jesuits do not, or at least should not, pursue studies just for the sake of knowledge. We are, after all, supposed to be on a mission having something to do with giving glory to God. St. Ignatius of Loyola never envisioned the personal accumulation of knowledge to be a proper mission for the members of his company. He recognized the value of education, but he always had a vision of education as a means to the mission of helping souls. Hospital work seemed to fit the mission, and seemed to be what I was obviously suited to do. God's call, however, is sometimes more subtle.

3. Philosopher Becomes College Professor

As I was finishing my studies, I began to visit Jesuit institutions of higher education for job interviews. I ended up with offers to go to a couple of medical centers to do exactly what we had envisioned. But there were also a couple of opportunities to teach undergraduates in liberal arts colleges. Why would I choose to become a lowly college professor, teaching undergraduates, when all signs were pointing toward doing ethics consultations in major medical centers?

The answer is rooted in the Jesuit concept of the *magis*. What would be for the greater glory of God? It is not just what would give glory to God. Working in a hospital could do that; even going back to pathology might have done that. The issue is what would be for the *greater* glory of God.

In fact, I had enjoyed teaching medical students and working with physicians during my time in graduate school. What I realized, however, is that they were very busy. I understood that. Taking time to consider philosophical issues was interesting to them. It was even important. But they were often preoccupied with the more immediate tasks of taking care of their patients, and rightly so. How much of an effect could I have on these people?

On the other hand, if I were to work with pre-medical students, before they got into the grind of medical school, might I have a greater influence on them? Might I get them to think philosophically about their medical studies from the very beginning, rather than trying to convert them later on? That seemed to me to be a greater challenge. And so, after conferring with my superiors, I was sent to become a college professor. It is a good life, one that presents interesting colleagues, many eager students, constant challenges, and new ideas. My greatest satisfaction comes when I see a light bulb go on in the head of a student struggling with a difficult concept.

The teaching and trying to influence future physicians even before they get to medical school is not the whole of my work, of course. Most of the students I teach are not going to become doctors. My work is to get all my students to think philosophically about whatever they do.

There is also the solitary research in libraries and, increasingly, in front of computer screens, and the writing, editing, and lecture preparation. All this is done to advance knowledge. That is what scholarship is all about. But it is of a single piece with what I do as a teacher. Teaching and research inform one another. I have written about teaching, and I have taught what I write about.

Teaching and scholarship are no less God's work than feeding the hungry and visiting those in prison. The work that I do sometimes focuses on rather abstract issues, such as the concepts of health and disease. Such fundamental philosophical reflection is essential, though. How can we visit the sick or bury the dead unless we know what it means to be sick or dead? Such questions may seem silly at first, but when one becomes involved in health care in more than a superficial way, one realizes that such questions are essential and difficult. It is not obvious when life begins and ends, and it is not always obvious when one is sick or healthy. Trying to bring clarity to such questions may not be glamorous, but it is important. Seeing undergraduates become aware of such issues for the first time and seeing the eagerness with which many tackle such difficult problems makes my life as a college professor exciting. It is a ministry.

The route to where I am now has not been a straight one. It is not a journey that I would have mapped out for myself. I remain convinced, however, that God has led me and the Society of Jesus in its assigning me to this work and I have tried to respond in the best way I know. This takes a degree of humility and not a small amount of faith that God gives us particular talents and directs our desires in order to accomplish good that we might not even imagine ourselves doing.

4. Cells and Organization

Cells do not function independently. They are organized into organs and systems, which have coherent functions. Just as there are different ways of conceiving the organization of the body, there are different ways of conceiving the organization of the metaphorical cells of an individual. For me, the most obvious and useful organizational conception links the priest cell with the Jesuit cell and the philosopher cell with the professor cell. I will call these, for convenience, the religious organ and the intellectual organ. Sometimes it seems that academia wants to keep these organs from having anything to do with one another. Faith and religious practice are either relegated to the realm of one's personal life or made into objects of study for sociologists or psychologists. Perhaps one of the primary marks of the Jesuit academic is the resolve to hold these two organs together in a system, like the cardio-pulmonary system, in which both heart and lungs are jointly necessary for the proper distribution of oxygen throughout the body.

I am reminded of the story of Martha and Mary (Luke 10: 38–42). The two sisters invite Jesus into their home. Mary sits at the feet of Jesus and listens to what he has to say. Martha, however, is busy with all the details of hospitality. She becomes indignant that Mary has left her to do all the work. Jesus tells

Martha that she is being distracted by extraneous things; it is Mary who has chosen the better part.

This is not an indictment of manual labor. What kind of hospitality would have been shown Jesus if Martha had refused to do the cooking? The contrast, rather, is in the attitudes of the sisters. Mary found contentment and consolation in listening to Jesus. Martha chose to let distraction and indignation overcome her, even though she might have found contentment and consolation simply in cooking for Jesus. As Saint Teresa of Avila said, we should remember that if obedience to our religious superiors sends us to the kitchen, "the Lord walks among the pots and pans."[1]

It is tempting to see Mary as representing the religious person and Martha as representing the intellectual who lets scholarship take precedence over faith, but this cannot be; the Church has always valued scholarship. Scholarship is not to be abandoned for the sake of religion, the "better part." One of the most striking characteristics of Catholicism has been the insistence that faith and reason are not in conflict, but go hand in hand. The tension lies in finding consolation and contentment in both these things.

This is just the sort of tension I find in being a Jesuit, a contemplative in action. Here, a double tension is manifested. The contemplative side and the active side exist in each Jesuit, although each Jesuit tends to have a particular tendency—a Mary tendency or a Martha tendency. This is particularly true of the Jesuit intellectual. We are called to do research and writing. That is a contemplative and solitary pursuit. Yet at the same time, we are called to be teachers. That is an action-oriented and social pursuit. Notice, however, that already the Mary and Martha roles have been jumbled. The intellectual side has both a contemplative, quasi-religious aspect and an action-oriented aspect. Yet this aspect of the life of the Jesuit intellectual is scarcely different from the life of any other intellectual in higher education. What makes Jesuit intellectual life distinct is another tension—a tension manifested at a higher level, in the Jesuit order, as a whole. The Society of Jesus has both Marys and Marthas. There are social activists and solitary scholars, charismatic preachers and shy but sagacious spiritual directors. This can give rise to tensions, not unlike the tension between Mary and Martha, but it also creates a marvelous and creative force of ministers for the Church.

For me as a Jesuit, the Mary-Martha tension is not just the typical academic tension between research and teaching. The more difficult tension is between teaching and mission. My teaching is my mission, but why? How does my teaching as mission differ from the excellent teaching of my non-Jesuit, non-Catholic, or even non-believing colleagues?

The Jesuit has aptly been characterized as a man on a mission. My mission, as an intellectual, is not my own. I have been sent to teach at an institution founded and still sponsored by the Society of Jesus. Certainly, I have been sent on this mission because I have some aptitude for it and much interest in it. Still, the mission is not just mine but is the mission of the entire Society of Jesus, and this makes my mission unlike the mission of my non-Jesuit colleagues.

What I do is done in the name of the Society of Jesus, just as the work of the Jesuit social activist or spiritual director is done in the name of the Society of Jesus. Inasmuch as all Jesuits are brothers in the same Society of Jesus, all Jesuits share in the work of the Society. The work of the social activist and the spiritual director is mine, just as my work in research and writing on the concepts of health and disease is theirs. We do not often recognize or admit this. In fact, Jesuits often find themselves disagreeing about the direction of their ministries. Some may think that I am wasting my time trying to figure out the philosophical nature of disease; they may want no part in identifying with my mission. I have to admit that I sometimes feel that way about some of the work of others. We are not unlike Mary and Martha. Remember Martha's resentment of Mary. But remember also that without Martha's work, Jesus would not have been fed. Mary and Martha are a team. Each performs a proper function. So it is with the Society of Jesus. From the early days of the Society of Jesus, Jesuits were sent to preach and hear confessions. But Jesuits were also sent to establish and teach in schools. The intellectual life has always been a characteristic Jesuit mission.

Much has been written about church-related higher education. George Marsden argues that the Christian scholar is somehow doing something different from what the non-Christian scholar working in the same field is doing.[2] Many scholars would completely divorce their academic pursuits from their religious faith. Sometimes even Jesuits might fall into this way of thinking. But, if Marsden is right, one's religious faith ought to have important implications for many areas of thought, scholarship, and teaching. If we believe that the world is created by a God who cares for us, then our moral values must be more than arbitrary social constructions. If we seriously reflect on this, we must come to the realization that our faith importantly influences our scholarship.

By now, it should be evident why it is so hard to pack all these features of the Jesuit scholar into one box. My story is not unique; it is just particular. All Jesuit scholars, perhaps by virtue of the long and complex formation that we go through, are complex beings. The parts of any Jesuit scholar are just not that neat. The cells and organs of which they are composed are living, organic things. They are in constant flux and they continually influence each other. They are fluid. They would always tend to spill out of any sort of box constructed to try to hold them. Understanding the Jesuit intellectual requires that one try to imagine the living dynamism that incorporates these many cells into one system.

III. The Shape of the System

Discussing some of my work might help to illuminate what I have said so far. Writing on ethical issues in medicine is such an obvious way of bringing the religious and intellectual together that it hardly needs comment. My primary research interests, however, lie in the general philosophy of medicine, which encompasses the metaphysical, epistemological, and aesthetic dimensions of medicine as well as the ethical. While there is nothing overtly religious in much of what I write about, I am still conscious of bringing all of who I am to what I write. Let me illustrate this with three examples from past and current work.

1. Medical Diagnosis and Values

While I was a resident in clinical pathology, I came to realize that laboratory test results did not simply reflect "truth" about patients. There are many factors that go into the design, usage, and interpretation of laboratory tests; these factors make laboratory tests more than simple objective observations by a neutral observer. Take the example of measuring the level of sodium in the blood serum and determining that it is low. There are different technical methods of measuring sodium, and these different methods might give slightly different ranges of "normal." Furthermore, determining just what a normal range is depends on judgments about the concept of normality and about the mathematical models used to determine normality once it is defined. The laboratory report only indicates a level, say 125 milliequivalents of sodium per liter of serum, and labels that number as low. It gives no indication of the sorts of judgments that went into making that report.

I never disputed the validity and usefulness of what we were doing in the lab, but I did realize that more went into the practice than most physicians realized. I wondered about the precise epistemological status of laboratory test results. At the time, I had enough philosophical sophistication to realize that I was asking a philosophical and not a scientific question, but I did not have the philosophical tools necessary to address my question adequately.

The question continued to percolate in the back of my mind for years, but it was not until I was sent by the Society of Jesus to graduate studies that I had the time to think about it more systematically, and from a new philosophical perspective. This became the topic of my doctoral dissertation, and took me more into the philosophical theory of medicine, as opposed to the more "practical" realm of bioethics. This turn itself led me to an improbable academic dispute, which is worth relating as a bit of an aside, although one relevant to my overall topic.

Prompted by an article arguing that the philosophy of medicine does not exist as a field,[3] a vigorous scholarly debate has ensued. Some have responded that if the field does not exist, it is puzzling just what it is that they are doing when they are writing about and debating philosophical matters related to medicine. The heart of the debate has been concerned with what constitutes a field, discipline, or sub-discipline, but many other interesting issues have also been raised. The subjects proper to the philosophy of medicine; whether the philosophy of medicine belongs more properly to medicine or philosophy; and whether the field has a canon and what works belong to the canon are among the most important. It seems to me that the philosophy of medicine is an emerging sub-discipline, and that it is more closely related to philosophy than it is to medicine. However, I have also proposed that in the future the philosophy of medicine may evolve in the way that the philosophy of science has evolved.[4] "Science Studies" incorporates not only the philosophy of science, but also the history and sociology of science. Understanding science requires an appreciation of how these various disciplines interact. Some day, we may come to appreciate "Medicine Studies" in a similar way. I mention this because the debate about the identity of a discipline parallels my struggle with my own identity as Jesuit scholar. Just as I struggle to hold together the various cells, organs, and systems that constitute my own identity, some who work in the philosophy of medicine struggle to hold together the various aspects of its practice in one discipline.

Let us return now to my questions about the philosophy of diagnosis. In my dissertation, later turned into a book,[5] I attempted to reconcile the social construction that goes into making a diagnosis with the view that there are objective facts about disease. I had come to believe that the social constructivists, who are often seen as relativists, and the scientific realists, the objectivists, both make important points, and that the usual strategy of separating objective fact from subjective judgment has been a barrier to such a reconciliation. I argued that values are at the root of all facts that are discovered in diagnosis. The values here are not all moral values; there are many types of value involved, including epistemic, social, economic, and religious. Although facts about disease are independent of our theorizing about them, our expressions of those facts are inherently value-laden at several levels.

First, specifying any fact in the diagnostic process depends upon judgments involving values. What values determine just what we are willing to call a fact? Epistemic values are especially important here. For example, value judgments are involved in something as basic as delineating the scope of a field of inquiry and establishing the standards of communication in the field. The choice of a particular technical language to describe observations determines what we are able to say about what we observe. To choose one language as better than another language involves a value judgment. These sorts of values are what I call *foundational* values.

Second, *conceptual* values enter the diagnostic process when we begin to speak about diseases. Diagnosis is the discovery of disease, but understanding the concept of disease is a thorny philosophical problem that is a central issue in the philosophy of medicine. While some would say that disease is a value-free concept, being defined simply as the failure of a normal biological function, I believe that even the notion of normal biological function is inherently value-laden. Human organs generally can perform several functions, each of which has a particular goal. How one describes the function of an organ depends on which goal one considers most important. Judging relative importance involves values. A further indication of the importance of values in the concept of disease is this. Some people are reluctant to admit that certain diseases are really diseases—eczema and some other skin diseases are good examples. They resort to euphemisms such as "condition" to describe such diseases. "Disease," for most of us, connotes something bad and unwanted. People resist admitting that part of them is bad, and so they maintain that they have a "skin condition." Yet sometimes diseases can be beneficial, such as when a soldier becomes ill and is unavailable for a dangerous mission, or when an individual has a certain enzyme deficiency that is harmful to some extent but is also protective against an even more serious disease. Having the sickle cell trait, which is protective against malaria, is a good example of the latter. What we take to be a disease depends upon the values that we use to construct our notions of normality and sickness.

Third, *nosological* values affect the way we classify certain experiences of illness as diseases. One might construct a disease classification, or nosology, for purely theoretical reasons, as a botanist might classify plants. Physicians, however, classify diseases in various ways largely for pragmatic reasons. They are interested primarily in helping their patient to heal and not merely in classifying the set of diseases. The choice of one way of classifying diseases over another—by etiologic agent as opposed to anatomic site, for example—reflects the reasons for making the classification, and these reasons will necessarily incorporate some values. One nosology might see the site of disease as most important, while another sees the cause of the disease as most important. Such choices depend on one's goals and purposes for constructing the classification, and these goals and purposes carry value judgments.

Fourth, *diagnostic* values come into play when physicians carry out diagnostic tests on their patients. Here it is evident that moral values are involved. Physicians must make judgments about how much risk to a patient a diagnostic fact is worth. Does the information potentially gained from a series of x-rays, for instance, justify exposing the patient to potentially damaging radiation? In addition, other values are involved in interpreting laboratory test results. Establishing a normal range for any test requires that lines be drawn to separate what is normal from what is abnormal. The range of results of tests done in both healthy and diseased people and the mathematics of distribution curves make it impossible to avoid all errors in matching abnormal test results with truly abnormal patients. Where we draw the lines between normal and abnormal should depend upon whether it is more important to avoid false negative results or false positive results. If some disease carries a great social stigma, but is non-curable and non-contagious, more damage will likely be done by falsely labeling a normal person as having the disease than by missing the diagnosis in a person with the disease. In deciding where to draw the line we have to make value judgments about whether it is more serious to err on the side of labeling some normal people as diseased or labeling some diseased people as normal.

Diagnosis, then, is a social construction that depends importantly on values. However, this need not destroy objectivity, for values are not necessarily only subjective. There are, I argue in the book, objective values that serve as the basis for our construction of diagnoses. Hence, although all our statements about facts in medicine include values, we can still hold a robust realism about the objectivity of the facts that we assert.

While there may seem to be nothing overtly religious in this, I believe that such theoretical reflection on a fundamental practice of medicine shows how many different facets of human experience are bundled together in just one seemingly simple practice of diagnosis. This scholarship shows how intellectual cells interact with one another, spill their contents, and ultimately cooperate in forming larger organs and systems.

2. Theoretical Medicine and *Harmonia*

Just as my experience in medicine has affected my philosophizing, so has my experience in a liberal arts college philosophy department with a strong emphasis on the history of philosophy affected my philosophizing about medicine. I have begun more and more to wonder about medicine and philosophy in the way that the ancients saw them.[6] Classical thinkers saw medicine as a science, but a special kind of science. Plato recognized that knowledge of health does not by itself produce health. In order to heal, the practitioner must also know the art of medicine. Plato and Aristotle were fond of using medicine as an example of an art, or *techne*, an activity that produces something. In the *Philebus*, Plato distinguishes the exact arts, such as numbering and measuring, from the empirical arts, such as navigation, agriculture, military science, and medicine.[7] For Aristotle, medicine is unlike the purely theoretical sciences, which study what necessarily is. Medicine is an art associated with *poiesis*. Medicine aims to produce something—health—and the discipline of medicine is the formal cause of health.[8]

Modern thinkers draw a dichotomy between the theoretical and the practical. The influence of this dichotomy may lead us to read these thoughts of Plato and Aristotle in a similar vein. However, Christopher Dustin has argued that *techne* and *theoria* are more intimately related than we ordinarily take them to be.[9] *Theoria* is rooted in "reverent" seeing of and wondering at beautiful things. *Theoria* begins with an attentive gaze upon the outward appearances of things, but in the true contemplation that is *theoria*, the inner nature of things is made visible.[10]

Theoria begins with a wondering gaze and *techne* aims to complete what *theoria* has begun—not as the *telos* of *theoria*, to be sure, but nonetheless a concrete end that might well serve as a proper object of further wondering gaze. Practitioners of an art allow *kosmos* (order, form, and arrangement) to be revealed and discovered through the activity that is the art.[11] The order that *techne* makes visible is *harmonia*. An art finely done produces something functional, but also something that reveals on its surface the inner beauty and form that the activity of the art has allowed to become manifest. The skilled practitioner of an art, then, is a sort of *theoros*. What the artisan produces provides an occasion for the contemplative gaze.[12] Michel Foucault has argued that with the rise of the academic hospital, the "gaze" of the physician shifted from outward bodily symptoms to the inner pathology of the body's organs.[13] The inner gaze that is necessary for healing, however, must go even deeper than looking at the body's inner organs.

Medicine as *techne* aims at producing health, but the modern notion of medicine as an applied science is not adequate. Medicine has always been considered both science and art. The "art" of medicine is aptly understood as *techne* when *techne* is understood as I have described it. Physicians do not "produce" health in their patients according to a modern understanding of production, but rather, the *kosmos* of health is revealed through the interaction between doctor and patient. It is the healing of nature, or God, if one is a person of faith, that is revealed in the activity of the art of medicine. Furthermore, the activity of *techne* forms the artisan as much as it forms the artifact.[14] Just as the minister of the sacraments is transformed by the liturgy, so is the physician transformed in healing relationships with patients.

The activity of medical practice, then, necessarily incorporates theory. The various elements of theory and practice intermingle to form the fullness of the practice. Philosophy can bring one to appreciate the depth of medicine. This recapitulates on a broader social level the kind of interaction between the various metaphorical cells and organs that constitute my self-identity as a Jesuit scholar of the philosophy of medicine.

3. Partial Incommensurability and Reconciliation

Thomas Kuhn's notion of incommensurability[15] seems to have become a hallmark of postmodernity, even though it is often misunderstood. Incommensurability is the idea that concepts in different paradigms have such radically different meanings that they cannot be adequately understood across paradigms. "Paradigm," by which Kuhn meant a particular scientific world view, has become somewhat of a buzzword, and is often trivialized by reducing it to mean nothing more than a particular viewpoint in any realm of human experience. The classic paradigm shift is the supplanting of Newtonian physics by Einsteinian physics. Such paradigms are said to be incommensurable and this is used to support relativism. Although much in his writings suggests such a radical relativism, Kuhn, in fact, often describes himself as a realist. In response to critics of the notion of incommensurability, Kuhn has explained that there is only "local" or partial incommensurability between many scientific paradigms.[16]

Robert Veatch and I have used this idea to explain some important aspects of the physician-patient relationship.[17] In some respects, the patient and physician have very different world views. Patients have an experience of illness, which affects them on physical, psychological, emotional, and spiritual levels. The physician's task is to translate the patient's experience into the biomedical language that will provide the basis for treatment. While physicians may have an appreciation of what disease does to a patient, they do not experience the patient's disease as illness in the way that patients do. Because of this, when physicians and patients enter into a therapeutic relationship, they speak somewhat different languages. This is not to say that physicians are inhumane or that they cannot appreciate the suffering of an ill person. Rather, the problem lies in the partial incommensurability between the medical scientist's language and the layperson's language. This partial incommensurability arises at four levels.

First, there are disputes among those who are actually doing medical science. Scientific disputes may be nothing more than disagreements over ambiguous data. But they may be deeper; they may reflect disagreements about fundamental concepts such as causality and standards of proof. Two groups of scientists might have quite different world views and formulate research questions differently, conduct tests differently, evaluate data differently, and come to different conclusions. Even if each group agrees that the other is practicing modern science, they may still be engaged in partially incommensurable activities.

Second, the data of medical science must be translated into clinical settings. Clinicians with different world views might tend to read data differently. Moral values might indeed influence the way one sorts through a vast and sometimes conflicting body of data. For example, various studies have come to different conclusions about a possible link between contraceptive pills and breast cancer. The differences may arise when different clinicians look at different bits of data to support a position they favor. Deciding which data among thousands are relevant and which are irrelevant will depend in significant ways upon one's general world view. A clinician who is morally opposed to contraception, for instance, may tend, even unconsciously, to favor studies that show a link between contraception and cancer. This may not be so much a reflection of bias, but rather a genuine difference in understanding causality and standards of proof. A clinician's understanding of the medical facts may turn out to be partially incommensurable with the understanding of the scientist who produced the facts.

Third, medical facts must be communicated to the patient by the clinician. Patients and physicians will often have different understandings of the nature of causation and probability and the proper interpretation of evidence. They may have very different understandings of the fundamental reality of disease. Hence, it is likely that even if there is no dispute between scientist and clinician about the medical facts, differences may arise between clinician and patient.

Fourth, patients rightly expect physicians to make recommendations about courses of treatment. Even if patient and physician agree on probable outcomes, there may still be significant differences between them about which treatment would be best. What is best is obviously a value judgment. Whether one year of life in a wheelchair is better than six years confined to bed is not a question that can ultimately be decided by appealing to data. Partial incommensurability may surreptitiously give rise to many sorts of disagreements in the physician-patient encounter. Values may lie hidden in talk that on the surface appears to be about purely objective facts.

While this analysis might appear to support a typical postmodern type of relativism, it does not imply such a view. The incommensurability thesis is just as compatible with a realist world view in both the scientific and ethical spheres. While it may be difficult or even impossible to specify which one of competing accounts of physical or ethical reality is true, it is often possible to establish some accounts as false. Over time, we reach more certainty about some of our claims. It becomes obvious that some accounts of medical reality are objectively better than others.

This work, like my work on diagnosis, is an attempt to reconcile important postmodern insights with the more traditional view that science aims to discover an order that exists prior to our invention of theories to describe it. It is also a good illustration of what I see as an important part of Jesuit ministry—reconciling what seems to be irreconcilable. The "service of faith and the promotion of justice," the formulation of the heart of Jesuit mission for the past thirty years or so, involves the reconciliation of the natural and the supernatural realms. This mission is carried out no less by the tradition of Jesuit scholarship than by social or pastoral ministry.

Jesuit colleges and universities strive to provide an integrated Jesuit education to their students. The idea of various cells coming together in an individual Jesuit scholar to form an integrated and unique system might also provide a fruitful image for these institutions. It is too easy for the institution of higher education to lose a sense of corporate mission in the complexity of its various departments, institutes, and levels of administration. The level of complexity must be higher in institutions than in individuals, of course, but trying to see how the various systems of an institution work together for mutual support to form a super-system with an overall mission might prove useful for the self-understanding of Jesuit colleges and universities.

IV. Conclusion

While my research interests do not directly address the question of the identity of Jesuit scholars in the postmodern age, much of my work does reflect major issues implicit in the question. Furthermore, my own personal development has itself been a model of bringing together several possibly conflicting spheres in an attempt to bridge some of the gaps that are seen as characteristic of postmodernity.

Sometimes I think that I have already lived more lives than can reasonably be expected of one human being, but I cannot see how I could do what I am now doing without having had all of these experiences. The various parts of my life have come together to lead me into the Jesuit intellectual apostolate, and that is to me perhaps the greatest sign of a vocation from God. While my current work has come about only after a great deal of rigorous training, I never really planned to be where I am today. I suspect that it is more the work of the Holy Spirit that the various metaphorical cells that constitute my identity somehow function together as a coherent system.

Jesuit scholars are complex beings. Jesuit scholars cannot be put into one box that characterizes them as a group. Neither can any single Jesuit scholar be conveniently put into a prefabricated box. We are all organic beings, composed of various cells that interact in unique ways to form unique organs and unique systems. As Jesuits, though, we share a particular religious heritage that ought to make our systems look distinctive in the body of all intellectuals.

Notes

1. St. Teresa of Jesus, *Book of the Foundations*, ch. 5, in *The Complete Works of St. Teresa of Jesus*, ed. E. A. Peers, vol. 3 (London: Sheed and Ward, 1946), 19–26.

2. George L. Marsden, *The Outrageous Idea of Christian Scholarship* (New York: Oxford University Press, 1997).

3. Arthur L. Caplan, "Does the Philosophy of Medicine Exist?" *Theoretical Medicine* 13 (1992): 67–77.

4. William E. Stempsey, S.J., "The Philosophy of Medicine: Development of a Discipline," *Medicine, Health Care and Philosophy* 7 (2004): 243–51.

5. William E. Stempsey, S.J., *Disease and Diagnosis: Value-Dependent Realism* (Dordrecht, Boston and London: Kluwer Academic Publishers, 2000).

6. This section is adapted from William E. Stempsey, S.J., "The Medicine of Philosophy," in *Practicing Catholic: Ritual, Body, and Contestation in Catholic Faith*, ed. Bruce T. Morrill, S.J., Susan Rodgers, and Joanna E. Ziegler (New York: Palgrave Macmillan, forthcoming 2006).

7. Plato, *Philebus*, 56a–c.

8. Aristotle, *Metaphysics*, 1070a.

9. Christopher A. Dustin, "The Liturgy of Theory," in *Practicing Catholic: Ritual, Body, and Contestation in Catholic Faith*, ed. Bruce T. Morrill, S.J., Susan Rodgers, and Joanna E. Ziegler (New York: Palgrave Macmillan, forthcoming 2006).

10. Josef Pieper, *Only the Lover Sings: Art and Contemplation* (San Francisco: Ignatius Press, 1990), 34.

11. Indra Kagis McEwen, *Socrates' Ancestor: An Essay on Architectural Beginnings* (Cambridge, Mass.: MIT Press, 1993), 41–47.

12. Dustin, "The Liturgy of Theory."

13. Michel Foucault, *The Birth of the Clinic: An Archaeology of Medical Perception* (New York: Vintage Books, 1975).

14. Dustin, "The Liturgy of Theory."

15. Thomas S. Kuhn, *The Structure of Scientific Revolutions*, 2nd ed. (Chicago: University of Chicago Press, 1970).

16. Thomas S. Kuhn, "Commensurability, Comparability, Communicability," in *PSA 1982: Proceedings of the 1982 Biennial Meeting of the Philosophy of Science Association*, ed. P. D. Asquith and T. Nickles, vol. 2 (East Lansing, Mich.: Philosophy of Science Association, 1983), 670–71.

17. This section is a summary of Robert M. Veatch and William E. Stempsey, S.J., "Incommensurability: Its Implications for the Physician/Patient Relationship," *Journal of Medicine and Philosophy* 20 (1995): 253–69.

4

What Difference Does It Make for Me as a Liturgist To Be a Jesuit—or Vice Versa?

Bruce T. Morrill, S.J.

I. Introduction: Recalling a First Attempt at the Question

THE QUESTION ENTITLING THIS ESSAY was first posed to me five years ago as a member of an international group of Jesuit liturgists that met regularly on the eve of the Annual Meeting of the North American Academy of Liturgy, an ecumenical association of liturgical academicians, artists, and architects. The group's leader asked us to compose short essays of one to two pages, duplicate them for distribution to the twenty or so confreres attending, and plan on briefly presenting and commenting on our own and each other's statements, with a view to possible publication. I do not now recall much from the actual meeting, which was amicable and mutually supportive, as always. Notable, however, was the lack of enthusiasm for working on a joint publication. The day passed pleasantly enough, and that was that.

A friend of mine in that group often laments our failure to pursue a common publishing project. The situation, I believe, touches on at least two dynamics. First, one can observe the contemporary struggles of North American Jesuits with individualism and professional isolation, characteristic of not only late-modernity in general but also higher education in particular. Second is the malaise in Roman Catholic liturgics and liturgical theology at the turn of this new century fueled, in part, by an ever-increasing dissonance between official Vatican liturgical documents and the scholarship and pastoral findings of liturgists, but also, in part, by an ever-increasing dissonance between contemporary social-cultural patterns of behavior and traditional liturgical forms. These dynamics provide already a certain glimpse at the state of Jesuit theological scholarship in the postmodern era, but I shall not do more than note the phenomenon here at the outset. I turn, rather, to the few paragraphs I wrote some years ago, quoting them in full, so as to provide an introduction, both affective and conceptual, from which to build this present chapter.

What difference does it make for me as a liturgist to be a Jesuit and vice versa? Try as I might, when thinking about this question I cannot get an old saying out of my head, the description of a confused person being "as lost as a Jesuit in Holy Week." My family's pastor, a man now in his late seventies, used to lay the joke on me during my first few years in the Society every time I was back home, visiting my family. He did so each time with such fresh delight and zeal that I always found myself wondering whether the old man was unaware of repeating himself or whether this was a conscious ritual performance, the repetition of which helped to keep the cosmos in order. I tend to think the latter was the case, especially since the cosmos for this imposing cleric is synonymous with the Roman Catholic Church. An alumnus of the College of the Holy Cross, Class of 1942, the now-retired pastor has enduring affection for the "Jebbies," but this carries the expectation that they continue to perform their proper role in the church as the bookish schoolmasters and strong disciplinarians for whom either the practicalities or sublime mysteries of the Church's ritual are not a concern. Having now spent nearly twenty years in the Society, I assure him that, however tenuous the Jesuits' grip on their educational institutions, they for the most part fall far behind the vanguard of liturgical renewal.

Living in the Society has had a strong impact on my experience of the Church's primary theology, of actually celebrating the liturgy, whether as a member of the assembly or as its president. The impact is variably positive and negative, supportive and stressful. The genius of Ignatian spirituality, I find, can both enhance and hinder the practice of liturgy. On the positive side, the *Spiritual Exercises* form a believer in a personal, imaginatively engaging relationship with God, fostering a generous interpretation of the world, the expectation of "finding God in all things." This attitude has the potential to make the Jesuit really "own" the liturgy, in one of its truest senses, as the symbolic celebration of the world as God envisions it, as a way of coming to know ourselves and all around us to some real extent as God knows us.

On the other hand, the seemingly individualistic character of the contemporary engagement of the *Exercises*, which are, of course, contemplative in nature, can hinder a Jesuit's being disposed to liturgy as a *corporate* action of the assembled body of Christ. I cannot help but wonder if there is not some connection between the way U.S. Jesuits practice their spirituality and the way in which they, by and large, seem to resist reform of the practical attitudes whereby they "say Mass." As a liturgist, I find the latter to be a grating problem amidst the Company[1] I keep, but one which also inspires my work to help the contemporary Church discover the fundamentally corporate and corporeal qualities of the Church's worship that carry the promise of God's epiphany to us therein.

Looking at those paragraphs now, some five years later, I recognize in them qualities representative of Jesuits in general: a passionate yet critical love for the Church; genuine gratitude for the Society of Jesus and my part therein marked, nonetheless, by a sharp edge of mutual- and self-criticism; a deep desire to seek what Ignatian tradition calls the *magis*, the greater good to be done for the greater glory of God; a concern for just order and relationships in the world fueled by an optimistic expectation of finding God in the quest for such justice. An additional feature, specific to many of my generation of Jesuits in higher education in the United States, would seem to be a penchant for analysis drawing upon various forms of critical theory—literary, social, philosophical—for deconstructing various modern symbols, narratives, and systems (both theoretical and practical). In the case of my development as a sacramental and liturgical theologian, I acquired such critical theoretical capacities by means of a master's degree in cultural anthropology, as well as extensive coursework in philosophical theology and ritual studies in pursuit of my Ph.D. in theology.

The critical dimension of my liturgical-theological scholarship is, nevertheless, in service and grateful devotion to the Gospel, with the conviction that its redemptive promise for humanity invites a worthy vocation for one's (my) life. This affective embrace of the Christian faith requires at the same time a realistic recognition, and indeed acceptance, of the ever-increasing challenges—both negative *and* positive—that late modernity poses to the practice of religious tradition and, specifically in my case, to Roman Catholic tradition.[2] This requires theology to be both descriptive and prescriptive. The theologian must take account of the history and current state of both official church teachings, rituals, and laws, as well as local practices (clerical and lay, popular and official) of the faith, while also arguing for what *should* be the case if the tradition is to continue in a way that is both true to its sources *and* constructively viable in the lives of believers today in service to the wider world. A further complication for me personally is the need to distinguish between my own special disposition toward and specific talents for leading an assembled community in worship and what can be more widely proposed for and generally expected of liturgical participation and leadership for the present and near future in the Church, as well as more specifically in the Society of Jesus and its apostolates.

With these introductory comments in mind, I can glean from my earlier testimony as a Jesuit liturgical theologian an itinerary for expanding upon several of the dynamics operative in my vocation, at once scholarly and ecclesial, theoretical and pastoral. I shall begin the next section with a general description of how I, as a theologian, understand the nature and function of the Church's liturgy, elaborating especially upon the notion of "corporate and corporeal" with which I concluded my earlier testimony (above). Such attention to the communal, bodily experience and knowledge entailed in this primary form of Christian mysticism will invite some consideration of the mystical practice at the heart of Jesuit tradition, the *Spiritual Exercises* of Saint Ignatius, followed by a theoretical inquiry, through comparison and contrast, into the relationship between the practice of the Church's liturgy and the practice of Jesuit spirituality. This theoretical exercise, especially in its attention to body and practice, necessitates some attention to narrative, and so in the subsequent section I shall offer some further autobiographical reflections as a contributing source to my evolving theological view of liturgy in Church and society. In the concluding section I shall briefly articulate some of the challenges—societal, ecclesial, and academic—as well as something of the promise that lies immediately ahead for the sort of liturgical theology I find myself attempting at the start of the twenty-first century.

II. Liturgy and the *Spiritual Exercises*:
Mystical Practices Nourishing Lives of Service

Strongly influenced by fundamental theologians Edward Schillebeeckx and Johann Baptist Metz, I have come to think of Christianity as a praxis of mysticism and ethics, that is, practices of prayer, liturgy, and contemplation in an ongoing, mutually informing relationship with interpersonal, social, and political patterns and decisions for living in this world. From the perspective of liturgical theology, especially as articulated by the late Russian Orthodox theologian Alexander Schmemann, this is to say that there is no place for religious business-as-usual in the practice of Christian faith. Dividing the world we experience into sacred and profane categories is illegitimate in the light of the Gospel.[3] When Christians compartmentalize their religious life into certain holy objects, actions, personages, and precincts, they tend likewise to consider the everyday, ethical, social aspects of their lives as that which they have to work out on their own, whether in tough perseverance or blissful indifference or, more likely, somewhere in between. Here I would like to spell out a bit what I, with the help of such prominent theologians, am arguing for as a comprehensive view of the Christian life so as, subsequently, to correlate it to elements of Ignatian tradition and, thus, my Jesuit life.

  Christian faith, no mere assent to ideas, is only genuinely known as a way of life, a praxis, an ongoing immersion in the paschal mystery. This practical-theological proposition has as its sources and center the always de-centering, paradoxical revelation of God's love for humanity and all creation in the death and resurrection of Jesus. While such reference to the cross might seem, at the outset, to amount to a Christian truism, making Christ's death and resurrection the primary focus of the faith is not necessarily obvious. I am thinking here, specifically, of the largely popular contemporary theological notion that the "sacramental imagination" is what characterizes Roman Catholic faith and this, moreover, as founded on the doctrine of the incarnation. Perhaps partially in reaction to what so many American Catholics experienced as a condemnatory and guilt-ridden theology prior to the Second Vatican Council, this sacramental-incarnational Catholicism tends, in language one regularly encounters in pastoral and even academic circles, to celebrate the goodness of our bodily human *experience*. To my observation, however, this current theological trend (as found, at least, in the middle-to-upper-middle-class context of the Jesuit university where I teach, as well as the suburban parish where I assist on weekends) is largely based on an *idea* or *concept*, namely, that God became human and, in so doing, confirmed the goodness of all things creaturely. But not all things, after all, at least not when we find ourselves struck by the harsh reality of sin and evil in our world. Many Roman Catholics then take recourse to a theology of satisfaction or atonement for sin, the settling of a debt with a God who demanded a form of payment human beings could not produce.

This sort of conceptual notion of sacramental incarnation ends up leaving contemporary believers adrift between two religious images, the nativity and the crucifixion, life-affirming wonder at God's tender love taking form in a baby cradled in his mother's arms and personal-sin-forgiving wonder at God's mercy for *me* ("no matter what I've done") in the outstretched arms of the executed Jesus. The believer works out his or her life, the unfolding story of decisions, actions, and reflections, in the personal space between these two ideas of divine acceptance and judgment, in front of the images of nativity and crucifixion. Years of conversations with undergraduates, as well as with adults in the context of pastoral ministry courses and parish courtyards, have led me to conclude that the easy language of incarnation (I am not, of course, in any way discounting the formal doctrine of incarnation) does not serve us believers as well as its immediate sense of warm goodness might lead one to think.

The work of French sacramental theologian Louis-Marie Chauvet has persuaded me that starting from the notion of incarnation is a misplaced act of wonder: "Rather than '*How* can God (it being understood that *we know who God is*) do such and such?' would it not be more in keeping with biblical revelation and especially with the 'scandal of the cross' to ask '*Of what God* are we speaking when we say that we have seen God in Jesus?'"[4] Chauvet argues against the sacramental theology found in the Scholastic manuals, which took the incarnation as their starting point, focusing on the question of the hypostatic union, the question of how the divine Word could appropriate and sanctify human nature. Philosophically, the sacraments thereby came to be approached as metaphysical and ontological problems concerning the presence and action of divine Being in material elements. To the extent that they were also considered as practice, the sacraments came to be understood as "the prolongation of the redeeming incarnation," the liturgy as celebrating "the various 'anniversaries' of Jesus' destiny," and the church year as "a sort of immense socio-drama in which one would somehow mime the events that have punctuated this destiny."[5]

The problem with all of this is that the action of liturgy becomes a matter of watching the *completed* drama of Christ's life, rather than of entering into the mystery of the Father's call and the Spirit's empowerment of Jesus for a self-emptying mission of service unto death and, finally, into life. That mission is a dynamic salvific process that, while definitively inaugurated, has yet to reach its final completion. In this far more biblically informed (as opposed to philosophically formulated) view, the liturgy takes on a more dynamic and ethically challenging quality. It calls and empowers Christians to participate in what has not yet been completed, namely Christ's proclamation of the Kingdom of God. True to that gospel vision, such an understanding and practice of liturgy prohibits any compartmentalization of faith (as sacred beliefs and rituals) from the decisions and actions of life in this world. In adopting the latter perspective, the reformed Rites of the Roman Catholic Church, based on Vatican II's *Constitution on the Liturgy*, as well as contemporary theologians like Chauvet, have recovered a far more ancient tradition of the Church's sacramental liturgy, the *paschal mystery*. This concept has biblical and patristic roots in theological reflection on the Church's ritual celebrations of the mystery of faith that came through two lines of development, one emphasizing the sacraments as *participation in* the definitive event of salvation that was Jesus' death and resurrection, the other emphasizing how the sacraments immerse believers in the work of salvation that Christ's death and resurrection continues to realize in their lives and, ultimately, for the life of the world.

The salvific content of the paschal mystery is most fully revealed in the Church's celebration of its liturgy, especially the sacraments of Eucharist and baptism. The performance of liturgical worship, however, far from being an end in itself, is for the purpose of revealing our entire lives as an ongoing act of worship, of glorifying God by sharing in God's creative and redemptive action in our world. Perhaps the most prominent metaphor for our entrance into the life of faith is Saint Paul's description of baptism as our being buried with Christ in death, "so that, just as Christ was raised from the dead by the glory of the Father, so we too might walk in newness of life" (Rom 6:4).[6] Having no sooner made this indicative proclamation of our death to sin in Christ, Paul immediately goes on to exhort believers not to allow sin to have any power over us (Rom 6:14). This is but one way of describing the mystery that is the Christian life of faith, a life patterned on Christ's God-given mission of redemptive solidarity with a suffering world. For his having faithfully carried out that mission even to death, God raised Jesus from the dead, making him the source of life for all who would embrace faith in him as a praxis of following him.

What prevents a Christian life patterned on redemptive suffering from being an exercise in divine-human sadomasochism[7] is our ongoing surrender to the paschal mystery, a tragically beautiful dialectic of mysticism and ethics.[8] If what sustained Jesus of Nazareth in his mission—especially as its social-ethical implications caused increasing conflict with religious and governmental authorities—was his mystical relationship with God, so too Christians sustain lives of solidarity with the suffering by their mystical practices of prayer and liturgy. The Eucharist, most importantly as celebrated on the Lord's Day, is the source and summit of the Christian life,[9] the enacted, lived proclamation of the Lord's death as the very revelation of God's life for the world. What so often threatens the possibility of knowing the joyful character of such a life is the loss of the tensive quality of the paschal mystery, the awareness that Christ's suffering and death are only redemptive because of the revelation of who he is—and, therefore, who God is for us—in his life and resurrection. Hence, the centrality of eucharistic worship as the weekly revelation in word and sacrament of ourselves and our world as the ongoing story of God's redemptive presence and action among us, especially in those who suffer. The Sunday Eucharist, the original Christian feast,[10] draws together into one body, the living body of Christ, all of our lives of prayer and service in union with all the world's struggling search for and unnamed encounters with God.

When Paul teaches, "For just as the body is one and has many members, and all the members of the body, though many, are one body, so it is with Christ" (1 Cor 12:12), he wants believers to understand that their lives are now bound in solidarity with all Christ's members: "If one member suffers, all suffer together with it; if one member is honored, all rejoice together with it" (1 Cor 12:26). The challenge for Christians in the late-modern world lies in comprehending the scope of this one body of Christ, with its many members. Following the dogmatic ecclesiology of the Second Vatican Council, we know that Christ's members, the Church, cannot be limited to the Roman Catholic Church (even as it subsists therein), nor merely to Christian ecclesial bodies but, rather, encompass the breadth of humanity in this world.[11] The mission of the Church, the mission of all its members, is a compassionate solidarity with the joys and hopes of all people, especially the poor and suffering.[12] This means that ethics, that is, the Christian way of living one's faith in the world, cannot be restricted or isolated to the personal or interpersonal contexts, nor merely to some immediate community, let alone one national group but, rather, must pursue a vision that keeps all these circles of action in dialogue with one another. And that is what the Church's liturgical worship is primarily about, albeit in a different mode, namely, enacting symbolically the vision of God's kingdom for the life of the world, for every precious creature participating in it.

This liturgically formed vision of each unique individual ultimately arriving at his or her value in the communal context of all creation has an undeniable grandeur. The practice of the Church's liturgical worship can only avoid sacral isolation if there are other ways of prayer and action in daily Christian life resonating with it. This is precisely where my formation in Jesuit tradition comes into play. In the *Spiritual Exercises*, at the beginning of the Second Week, Ignatius invites the retreatant to join the Triune God in surveying the entire scope of struggling humanity in the world and to hear the divine persons consider what they can do to save it. This big dream of God, a dream that promises the redemption of all creation, nonetheless works through the retreatant. The Spirit of Jesus moves the retreatant to reflect on the stories from his or her own experience, so as to perceive them in the company of Jesus, in the perspective of his story. The Spirit draws one into such exercises not for their own sake, not for the experiences of consolation (whose characteristics change across the four weeks) *in themselves*, but for the purpose of reaching a moment of decision, the free response to follow the Suffering Servant on the paradoxical path that *is* God's glory. One ends up falling in love with the God of Jesus who, in turn, elicits great desires in the person to love God in God's people, according to the same pattern of Jesus' life unto death. The genius of the *Spiritual Exercises* is the way in which the disclosure of the irreducible value of the retreatant before God opens out into a life of loving service with God, with and for God's people and, indeed, all creation. This might be considered the Ignatian practical solution to the philosophical problem of the one and the many. To the extent that it is, however, it is only insofar as Ignatian spirituality is evangelical, an entrance into the life of following the Jesus of the gospels.

The Jesuit life is a movement between exercises of prayer that highly engage the human imagination and a life seeking to realize something of God's reign concretely in the world: a life of contemplation in action, of mysticism and ethics. Those parallel phrases reach from the present context of the Church in a postmodern world back to the Christendom of the fifteenth century but, ultimately, further back to the earliest centuries of Christianity, when in their homilies the Fathers of the Church expounded an understanding of Christian worship as the glorification of God through the sanctification of people.[13] It is those patristic roots that the Second Vatican Council identified as the key resource for reforming and renewing the Church's liturgy for our present time.[14] If there is any merit to the lineage I have just drawn, then it should not be surprising to observe the sizeable number of Jesuits who have served the liturgical renewal over the past century or so through their publications, teaching in seminaries and universities, and service on commissions of the Vatican and to local bishops.[15] On the other hand, there is also the clearly evident phenomenon of the overall Society's general slowness, if not in some places failure, to embrace the reformed liturgical rites of the Church, let alone exploit their utterly evangelical potential.[16] This is something that pains me deeply about the present life of the Society of Jesus in the United States.

Liturgy (I think here primarily of the Mass) is not a didactic exercise in hearing what a priest "got out of the readings" and then consecrating, adoring, and receiving the host. The extent to which so many priests in the Roman Catholic Church today, Jesuit or otherwise, practically understand and perform it as such cannot but be a contributing factor to the ongoing decline in Mass attendance in American churches and collegiate chapels. As long as the operative word is attendance, and not participation, the continued demise is assured. The Council, on the contrary, teaches that the liturgy is a corporate activity in which the faithful together encounter Jesus the Christ present through the fourfold *ritual symbols* of the assembled community, the presiding minister, the proclaimed word, and the sacramental elements.[17] Ritual symbolism, of which the proclaimed word comprises a constitutive part, is the key to unlocking what liturgy is and, therefore, to understanding its proper, irreducible role in the life of the Church in its mission to the world. In the liturgy believers obtain a kind of experiential knowledge not otherwise accessible yet utterly essential for their living out the Gospel's mission now in history. The affective encounter with the crucified and risen Jesus in the liturgy is the paramount form of mysticism that grounds a believer's response to the circumstances and events in life, raising a cry of protest to all that contradicts the truth of God's reign revealed in the liturgy's enactment,[18] sighing a word of gratitude for moments when goodness, beauty, and justice break forth.

In these late-modern times, however, the ability to engage robustly in symbolism, that is, in a world of symbols such as the one that Christian liturgy entails, is difficult for most well-educated, financially well-off believers (such as we Jesuits, our colleagues, and students in our schools). It requires *imagination*, an imaginative leap, a giving oneself over to the eschatological new creation of which the liturgy is a foretaste, a surrender to symbols in the sort of second naiveté that Paul Ricoeur so persuasively defined. The ritually engaged imagination, furthermore, needs a *space* to leap into, a ritual space (as Chauvet defines it) comprised not only of the physical meeting place, with its permanent and moveable fixtures, appointments, and furnishings, but also the people themselves assembled, the music they sing, the gestures they perform, and silences they keep together.[19] Liturgical space, then, is all about *bodiliness*—the body of each individual believer, the assembly as the body of the risen Jesus, the worship environment (including all its sights, sounds, smells, and movements) as the microcosmic body of that new world God has yet to bring about in the parousia. The divine counterpart to all this human, created bodiliness is the Holy Spirit (epiclesis). The fundamental work of this multivalent body of worship, this fourfold liturgical presence of Christ in the power of the Spirit, is *remembrance* (anamnesis), keeping memory with God and one another, through Word and Sacrament, of what God has done for us in Christ, what God is doing now in Christ, and what God has promised yet to bring to completion when Christ returns. The corporate celebration of the liturgy keeps us aware of ourselves as part of a larger eschatological reality, gives us an experiential knowledge that we are not merely individual souls migrating to our final ends but, rather, participants in God's ever-coming reign of a justice and peace whose truth, as Metz has so prophetically argued, is only viable if true finally for all, living and dead.[20]

Space and body, memory and imagination, faith and justice: Are these fundamental elements of the liturgy's mysticism not congruent with elements crucial to the mysticism of Saint Ignatius's *Spiritual Exercises*, especially in the manner the Society of Jesus has rediscovered them as central to our mission in the late-modern context? To provide but a sketch of that correlation, one might consider in Ignatius's spiritual method the fundamental role of the composition of place (space), the necessity of paying close attention to one's feelings and holistic reactions as one practices the discernment of spirits (body), the great amount of time and energy expended in repeatedly visiting narratives from the gospels and the *Exercises'* meditations in a way that integrates these with one's own life story (memory), and the pervasive assumption throughout the *Exercises* that the retreatant is willing and able to enter into a mode of contemplation whereby one inserts oneself in the scriptural narratives and converses with God in their wake (imagination).

While liturgy and the *Spiritual Exercises* are two highly distinct genres of mystical activity, still one would think that there would be an affinity among Jesuits for the robust practice of the former given their fundamental and ongoing formation in the latter. Perhaps one crucial factor essential to realizing something of that correlation, and this for the apostolic potential therein, is the Jesuit priest's being both aware of and eager to engage the fundamental principles of the liturgy I have expounded in these few pages. This would seem to entail the desire to get beyond "saying Mass" by merely "getting through" its seemingly disjointed series of words and actions, to resist (in the face of the daunting task of presiding over *ritual*) falling back on the forms of group leadership and religious formation most familiar to Jesuits, namely, teaching a class or giving instructions, and instead to explore the inner logic of the rites so as to conduct them in such a way that all involved—presider and assembly— end up sensing that the liturgy really *does* us, not we, it.[21] But that would, I suppose, require Jesuits becoming as convinced of the evangelical potential of the (post-Vatican II) reformed rites of the Roman Catholic Church as so many of us are of the renewed contemporary engagement of the *Spiritual Exercises*. Once engaged, of course, either form of renewal requires a significant commitment of time, energy, study, practice, and supervisory feedback.

I am well aware, however, that the generalizations in which I am writing here leave my argument open to a sizeable range of objections. First among the limits is the fact that I am indeed exploring a correlation, a sort of "apples and oranges" affair, both fruit but not the same flavor or consistency or color. Correlations are like the analogy I just utilized in the preceding sentence: they give insight into two different things on the basis of crucial similarities, while a significant measure of difference between the two entities nonetheless persists. Liturgy and the *Spiritual Exercises* are both forms of Christian spirituality and, as I have argued above, both engage space, body, imagination, and memory; however, they are likewise significantly different forms of practice. To take just one example: The reformed sacramental rites of the Church take as fundamental the assembling of a group of believers in a common, corporate ritual action, that is, in a collective pattern of sound, silence, and space wherein the God of Jesus is encountered. The *Spiritual Exercises*, in contrast, take as fundamental the individual imaginative work of a retreatant, with the help of a director, pursued largely in silence and according to bodily conditions conducive to each individual's pursuit of interior reflection and prayer. Thus, in drawing the correlation between the genius of the Church's reformed liturgy and Ignatius's renewed *Exercises*, I must not fall into the very trap against which we liturgical theologians so regularly rail, namely, a reduction of the practices of faith to ideas, to the neglect of the highly significant role that bodily aspects (and here, differences in bodily engagement) play therein.

A second objection, moreover, can lead to a perhaps more helpful, because more specific, "move" in this essay, that is to say, an autobiographical move. I can easily see a legitimate and formidable objection running along the following lines: Yes, it is all well and good that you, Bruce, have a certain set of intellectual, artistic, and personal talents that dispose you (and others who are called Jesuit liturgists) to such enthusiasm for the theory and practice of liturgy, but it is hardly reasonable to expect that all Jesuits would be so inclined. The point would be readily well taken, although I would still want to insist upon a certain responsibility on the part of all of us who are ordained presbyters to seek to understand and animate the liturgy of the Church, as reformed for its contemporary renewal,[22] so as to make it more adequately available to the faithful, for whom it is their (baptismal) birthright. And so I am going to change the genre of discourse in the next part of this chapter, setting aside the form of theological argument I have attempted over the preceding pages and turning, instead, to narrative, a narrative that might shed some light on how it is that this particular Jesuit has come to bear these theological convictions.

III. Autobiographical Underpinnings of This Jesuit's Liturgical Theology

How does one say something cogent about one's self, one's life-project, one's vocation in a way that does not come off as self-aggrandizing or, in the case of a "religious vocation," obnoxiously pious? I must admit at the outset here that I find taking the autobiographical turn in this essay very difficult to negotiate. Perhaps this is due to my being in the early phase of midlife (I am forty-four years old); it just does not seem like a good time for clear introspection. Or, perhaps, another contributing factor is my having only a little less than two years ago attained tenure on the faculty of my university; I feel like I have had to explain, defend, justify, account for my theological writing, teaching, and service to the academy at great length, awaiting a final judgment, not so very long ago. Or, perhaps more positively, I have come to be a Jesuit liturgical theologian so integrally, that is to say, the two terms "Jesuit" and "liturgical theologian" seem so intertwined in me, that parsing these elements and analyzing them along the lines of events or periods of my life seems somehow artificial. But analyze I must, and so here I shall start from the perspective of my being a liturgical theologian, even as I know quite well that the Jesuit aspect will insist on being heard early and often.

A person can only succeed in obtaining a Ph.D. in some subject, let alone turn around immediately and press oneself into publishing a number of books and articles in the next six years in the pursuit of tenure, if he or she has nothing short of a driving passion for the material. In my case, I cannot help but state that my love for the Church's liturgy has come to me as a vocation from God, as an offer and a gift. If pressed, I would trace my awareness of this gift to my teenage years when I found myself, perhaps typically for a teenager, questioning the merit of attending Mass each weekend. In my case this was not an act of protest against an activity that I found boring or oppressive in some way. On the contrary, I found going to Mass with my father and older sister each Saturday evening a basically comfortable, regular, and regulating experience. We went to a church where we were not registered parishioners, and I note this fact because it indicates that participation at liturgy was a quite personal, individual exercise for us, a matter of fulfilling religious obligation and spiritual need. But that was what became problematic for me in my sophomore year in high school. I came to recognize that we did not seem really to be listening much to the readings from Scripture during the Mass, especially as I became increasingly aware of their dissonance with my experience of the world around me. I think that a reading from one of the household-code passages of the letters of Saint Paul (the "children be obedient to your fathers" type of material—again, not surprising in the case of a teenager) contributed significantly to my sense that I needed either to accept the Word of God being proclaimed as *being proclaimed to me* or else I should quit being present for the proclamation at all.

And I did not want to quit being present. For lack of a more sufficient human explanation, I would note that by that point in my young life I had benefited from several years of private lessons each at piano and studio art. In high school I also was developing as a public speaker, participating in regional and statewide competitions. I mention these three interests (if not talents) because they may give a hint into why the genre of liturgy in general would be appealing to me, as well as why I found participating at Mass at Saint John's Church in Bangor, Maine, in particular so agreeable. It is not that the liturgy there was done exceptionally well; indeed, one would have to say quite the opposite. The perhaps one hundred people scattered through pews that could accommodate more than one thousand did not much sense themselves as forming an assembly or community, nor was the preaching or presiding or even the musicianship of the organist of particularly high quality. Still, two things remain prominent in my memory: first, that we people were *there*, which is to say that, for whatever personal reasons (and these are, I believe, always to be respected) being at this Mass each week mattered to all involved. Second, I recall that among the reasons I personally liked being there was the environment of that church's interior. Saint John's, a massive 1850s neo-gothic structure built of modest materials by Irish immigrants, was at the time in very poor repair, yet it housed two remarkable artistic treasures: one of the very few remaining complete sets of soaring, lancet-shaped stained glass windows designed by the famed Viennese artist Franz Xavier Pernlochner and executed by the Tyroler Glasmalerie of Innsbruck, and one of the largest tracker-action pipe organs by the historically important E. & G. G. Hook company of Boston. Even though the organ was in very poor condition (some years later it would be restored and acclaimed a national treasure), it still made a beautiful, warm sound from the rear gallery through the vaulted space and around the people.

Looking back on that period of my life, some thirty years ago, I interpret the artistic aura of Saint John's interior, even in its decrepit condition, as helping to charge my nascent faith-life with a sense of tragic beauty. To this very day, tragedy and beauty characterize how I experience the life of the Gospel sounding through the world, revealing itself in the liturgy I celebrate and study, as well as in the stories of human struggle and triumph I am privileged to share. At that time in my life, as I started to mature intellectually and psychologically, becoming critically cognizant of my immediate circumstances but also the events and conditions of the wider world, I also began to pray more earnestly. The prayer was characterized by honest words to God about how unfair— because unfulfilled—God's words seemed to me as a result of the instances of suffering I had come to experience personally or through the mass media. This never, however, amounted to a rejection of the Word. I think that at that time I was being grasped by the proclaimed word of Scripture as invitation, a life-giving call to do what the incarnate Word (Christ) does and, thus, to know something of the very life of God. Mass was the catalyzing occasion for encountering that Word and, gradually, knowing that call. By my senior year I was quite active in the parish where my family had subsequently moved and settled, serving as a lector but also participating in the programming offered to high school students. The ethical imperative of such affective and spiritual formation continued to grow in me as well, taking forms of service to local elderly folks but also concern about social-political issues. And so I guess it is not all that surprising that I ended up enrolling at the Jesuit College of the Holy Cross in Worcester, Massachusetts, following my graduation from high school.

Holy Cross had at that time a strong reputation as a Catholic undergraduate school consciously committed to the Jesuits' emerging commitment, in the wake of the Thirty-second General Congregation,[23] to the faith that does justice. The campus ministry was well staffed and financed, priding itself on both its extensive liturgical programming and panoply of social and religious outreach programs in the greater Worcester area. It was a "feeder school" for the Jesuit Volunteer Corps (JVC)[24]; indeed, I remember hearing about the JVC from my very first week on that campus. Four years later, upon graduating, I found myself heading for the JVC: Northwest, where I would work in a tiny Eskimo village on the Bering Seacoast of Western Alaska, along with a Holy Cross classmate, for one year. The college extracurricular experiences that led to that rather daunting commitment included increasing involvement in the campus ministry's liturgical programming, retreats based on the *Spiritual Exercises*, volunteering as a religious education teacher in inner-city parishes as well as on a service trip to Appalachia—in a word, a combination of prayer, liturgy, and social action. Academically I chose to major in religious studies, while also taking a large number of courses in philosophy and classical languages, with my selection of courses and immersion in the material often motivated by my burgeoning religious praxis.

The studies, however, certainly informed the praxis, as well. During the last two years my passion for theology as an intellectual discipline sparked and ignited under the tutelage of Bill Reiser, S.J., newly arrived from Vanderbilt University, a most engaging and demanding professor of systematic theology; Piet Schoonenberg, S.J., a prominent Dutch philosophical theologian, who was for three fall terms a visiting professor on campus; and Bernard Cooke, one of the more creative and influential American theologians of his generation, who joined the faculty at that time. As I reached the end of my senior year and mused over ideas of eventually pursuing doctoral studies in sacramental theology, Cooke advised me first to get a degree in one of the social sciences, as these, he averred, were proving the cutting edge tools for the discipline, new means for understanding the psychological, social, and anthropological dimensions of the Church's sacramental rites. Down the line, the advice proved invaluable.

Four very important years intervened between my commencement from Holy Cross and matriculation in the masters program in cultural anthropology at Columbia University. The year in Emmonak, Alaska (pop. 650), an isolated Yup'ik Eskimo village accessible only by small aircraft, was once again an experience of tragic beauty. The poverty there was not a question of food and shelter, although both were rough by any modern standard; rather, during that year I experienced, painfully as an outsider, the poverty of an indigenous people caught between two worlds—the native culture of subsistence hunting, fishing, dancing, and storytelling, and the speedily overpowering world of consumer goods, multimedia entertainment, and chemical addictions. The liturgical and catechetical life of the mission parish was strong at that time, and my work therein, along with my primary responsibility as co-director of a youth center, afforded me a succession of contrasting experiences of light and darkness, of God's presence and absence, of the Gospel's as yet unfulfilled but life-inspiring promise, experienced as a foretaste in liturgy and prayer.

I moved from that humbling year (I was no great human success in much of anything there, but it was nonetheless a wondrous year) into the novitiate of the New England Province of the Jesuits. As Saint Ignatius would expect, making the thirty-day *Spiritual Exercises* was undoubtedly the highlight of those two years. There was, however, a real genius in the pattern of the first year, whereby George Murphy, the novice master, sent us almost immediately after the Thirty Day Retreat to third world (for lack of a better term) countries for a several months' pilgrimage experiment. The contrast between the four silent wintry weeks of January in Gloucester, Massachusetts, and my subsequent four months in sultry Guyana, South America, could not have been more profound or rewarding. Serving for most of the time as a youth minister in one of the parishes in the poverty-stricken capital of Georgetown, but also for three weeks among the Amerindians in the interior, I was granted a sustained view into how people struggling under political, economic, and racial tyranny share life, faith, and hope freely. I experienced how important liturgy and prayer were to those people in those contexts, how aching the laments, how confident the petitions, how exuberant the joy. I came to realize more than ever that God "speaks" through the lives of the poor and suffering, indeed, through the stories of all our lives, in at times remarkably clear ways when those stories are contemplated in prayer and celebrated in sacramental worship, with Scripture integral to all.

I have only touched here on the very first year of my life in the Society of Jesus. I could for many pages describe the spiritual formation (through spiritual direction, annual retreats, etc.) and the types of apostolic work the Society has called me to do over the past two decades, but the lesson for my life has pretty much been consistent throughout: the discovery over and again that God is always already ahead of us in the world, inviting us to know something of the love of the Trinity if we but dispose ourselves to the abundance of faith and hunger for justice all around us. What I want briefly to note here is the challenging nature of both types of practices, as these were given to me in the Society. In the case of spirituality, the various spiritual directors I had over the years, as well as directors on retreats, were by and large people who listened very carefully to what was happening in me and did not hesitate both to affirm consolations (whether these were enjoyable or distressing) and to push me lovingly but firmly into exploring further with God memories, feelings, or dreams from which I might otherwise shy away. Likewise, in the matter of my apostolic assignments, various superiors and supervisors in my formation considered carefully the young man before them and missioned me to work with youth in the South Bronx or as a chaplain on the cardiac floor of a university hospital. Perhaps most important about these apostolates was the experience of being with people in the messy situations of life that cannot be solved adequately by the standards of human ambition or personal longing and, yet, repeatedly proved themselves to be intensely cogent moments, often in retrospect, of when the Spirit of the God of Jesus was present in action. But there again I find evidence of the mutual influence of mysticism and ethics, liturgy and life, as it were: the possibility of discerning God's presence and action in situations where humans would consider God to be absent depends, I have found, on continuously encountering the God of biblical faith in the Church's liturgy along with, for me, Jesuit spirituality.

The primary apostolic mission I have, nonetheless, received and developed as a Jesuit over the past two decades has been in the intellectual field. While the forms of contemplation and action I have described in the previous paragraph have all contributed to the motivation for and content of my academic endeavors, my studies have in turn impacted upon my life of faith, lived as a Jesuit. Those apostolic activities, along with spiritual and liturgical practices, have largely generated my theological questions. For me theology has always been a work done in the interest of serving the Gospel, an ardent search for theoretical methods adequate to not only understanding but teaching about—indeed, advancing—the content and practice of the faith. I have never, however, been comfortable for too long exclusively in front of my books and computer, not only because of my personal limits for sustaining such intellectual concentration but also because, over and again, the material I have found myself studying has motivated me to return constantly to the field of pastoral practice.

The Society of Jesus has over the years shown great trust in my desire and potential for doing academic work, especially by supporting my pursuit of studies in fields and at institutions located outside the conventional patterns of Jesuit studies at the time. The first such experience I had was my petitioning to do not two but one year of philosophical studies after the novitiate so as to be able to pursue immediately a master's degree in anthropology. By the early to middle 1980s, Jesuit formation superiors had an agenda to establish greater uniformity in American scholastics' philosophical training, both in terms of a limited number of Jesuit universities and a standard number of course credits to be earned. I was able to convince those in charge of me at the time to accept many of the credits I had earned as an undergraduate so as to be able to do just one full year of philosophy at Fordham University before moving on to the study of anthropology. The year at Fordham was helpful to me in a somewhat ironic way, insofar as the manual-style, Transcendental Thomism still regnant there gave me a solid background in the way theology had been approached over the previous century, as well as the tools for actually reading Saint Thomas and other primary sources later as a graduate student in theology.

After one year I abandoned the Bronx for Manhattan, matriculating in the master's program in the Department of Anthropology at Columbia University. With youthful zeal I threw myself into five courses each semester while also researching and writing a thesis, completing the degree in just one academic year. I pursued courses in the anthropology of religion, kinship systems, linguistics, American society, Marxist theory, archaeology, ritual, and more, hungrily taking in the array of methods this eclectic social science has generated for describing and analyzing human social and cultural life. For my thesis I did several months of fieldwork in a local Roman Catholic parish's RCIA program,[25] eventually analyzing the abundance of observations I had made by means of various theories of rites of passage. By the end of my writing for that project I could already recognize some strong benefits but also the significant limits of such theories for addressing the subject of Christian initiation in the contemporary North American context. The limits were not only in terms of the discipline of anthropology itself—for example, in terms of the applicability of theories founded on fieldwork among pre-industrial or pre-modern peoples to American Catholic parish life—but also in terms of the "insider" sort of questions I brought to the material as a believer. My studies at Columbia sharpened my critical analytical skills as well as the breadth of my intellectual knowledge immensely. One specific lesson I have taken from that year's work for my theological endeavors concerns the complex nature of religious tradition, a cautionary note about the always historically conditioned character of religious beliefs and practices, of the ideological blinders hindering people's abilities to perceive the origins, motivations, and practical implications of the power their religious practices and institutions wield in all dimensions of social life. But as negative as that evaluation may sound, I also have carried from that year into my theological studies and subsequent scholarly career a profound respect for the irreducibly bodily and social nature of religious faith and practice. This respect sounds a cautionary note against any language—popular or academic—about immediate experiences of the divine.

After two years of teaching high school religion for regency[26] back in New England, the vice-provincial for formation moved me along to theological studies at the Jesuit School of Theology in Berkeley, California. I found the courses there largely exhilarating. Likewise exhilarating was the great deal of experience I obtained in the theory and practice of liturgy, working constantly on the preparation of liturgies for the community and school, serving regularly as organist and pianist, and learning much about ritual creativity and historically informed tradition from the two Jesuit liturgists on the faculty, Jake Empereur and John Baldovin. By the beginning of my third year I was able to articulate to my superiors my case for wanting to do a doctorate in systematic theology with a focus on liturgy. Two other Jesuit professors, Hal Sanks and David Stagaman, had encouraged me to do my studies in a full-blown systematics program (as opposed to liturgics), and I shall always be further in Stagaman's debt for suggesting that I seriously look into Emory University, whose theology faculty he said was coming into a particularly strong, creative moment. This I did and, after visiting the school, found myself coming away with an abundance of new ideas for how I might constructively work in my chosen field of specialization.

During my second year at Emory two specific courses catalyzed the shape that my approach to systematic and liturgical theology would take in my dissertation and beyond. Philosophical theologian Walter Lowe introduced me to the prophetic critical philosophy of the Early Frankfurt School, assigning me to study how German Catholic theologian Johann Baptist Metz had appropriated that theory in his rather enigmatic fundamental theology. At the same time liturgical theologian Don Saliers was introducing me to the body of Alexander Schmemann's work on liturgy. Schmemann, I found, was a brilliant rhetorician with a deep love for the Gospel as revealed in sacramental worship, emphasizing the dissonances between the Church's liturgical tradition and the social-cultural context in which it is currently practiced in the Northern Hemisphere. Both Schmemann, with his emphasis on the formative potential of Christian worship, and Metz, with his insistence on remembering the suffering and dead, dazzled me with their restless insights into modernity's resistance to and yet desperate human need for the Gospel. Their passion took hold of me, really, and has never let go since. I wrote a dissertation exploring the similarities in their two significantly different theological projects, attempting a further contribution by highlighting what each lacked, as well as proposing how the liturgical concept of *anamnesis* (or ritual memory), especially in its eschatological character, could help. Several years later, the revised version was published as a Pueblo Book with The Liturgical Press, *Anamnesis as Dangerous Memory: Political and Liturgical Theology in Dialogue*. In the intervening years, as well as those since, my liturgical theological work has been characterized by a concern for the critically redemptive capacity of liturgical practice, that is, for arguing how the ongoing practice of liturgical tradition comprises a singular contribution to the life of the Church in service to the world if done in mutual, critical dialogue with the social, ethical, and political contexts in which the faithful practice it.

IV. Conclusion: Continuing Life as a Jesuit Professor and Priest

Perhaps the strongest challenge I find myself facing now as a Jesuit professor of theology and ordained pastoral minister in the Church lies in the tension I experience between trusting and honoring people's experiences of life, and thus faith, and anxiously hearing the prophetic word resounding from our faith's heritage of Scripture and tradition, a word that is critical of whatever degrades humanity and creation even as it bears hope in the very act of criticism. Christian faith does so because it acts out of a love at once divine and human, revealing the human face of God especially where humanity would not tend to be looking—the suffering, the poor, and the dead. While there is indeed much to celebrate in the goodness of life in our world, especially in the light of the Gospel, my concern nonetheless runs in the direction of how quickly people, in no matter what circumstances, can tend to marginalize and even victimize others, slipping into subtle and not so subtle forms of triumphalism, that is, misplaced assertions of our goodness based on our being better than others. As liturgical theologian Gordon Lathrop is fond of saying: draw a line to circumscribe who is in and who is out, and you will find Jesus

Christ on the outside every time.[27] I wholeheartedly agree with Lathrop that
the liturgical practices of the Church exist to glorify God by continuously re-
orienting us humans to recognize the scope of the God of Jesus' love for creation, no matter whom, no matter what. This comes as an invitation to see
creation and history with the hungering eyes of God, to taste the divine presence in the Sacrament of the liturgy, to hear the Word in everyday life. This requires a constructive, traditionally grounded practice of the Church's sacramental worship as an irreducible source for knowing, that is to say,
participating in, life as inaugurated by the God of the executed and risen Jesus.

As a professor of theology in a university, as well as a priest serving people
not only in that context but also in local parishes and even once again, after so
many years, on a periodic basis in the Yup'ik villages of western Alaska,[28] I
have no delusions about the great challenges—interpersonal, economic, social, ethical—that late modernity poses for the thriving of human life. Much
about the human condition is changing due to the ever-increasing proliferation of sophisticated, economically and technologically accessible forms of
electronic communication and mass media, functioning integrally in a rapidly
expanding global consumer culture. A little more than a decade ago David
Power, O.M.I, one of the foremost sacramental-liturgical theologians of the
generation preceding my own, argued that the Church currently practices its
liturgy amidst "ruins," both the ruins of pre–Vatican II cultural Catholicism
and the ruins of a modernity that in the twentieth century realized unprecedented global warfare, economic marginalization of entire peoples, and an increasing threat to the planet as a habitable environment. Noting the increasing disparity between the liturgical vision of Vatican documents and the local
dispositions of the faithful, Power argued at the outset of *The Eucharistic Mystery* that the current practice of the church's liturgy is done amidst those
ruins.[29] The social-ethical collapse of modernity, according to Power, would
have had its serious epochal impact on the religious sphere, and thus Catholicism, no less than in all other areas of life at the end of the twentieth century
whether or not Vatican II had happened. Power was right, and I believe he
would also be the first to agree that sacramental-liturgical theologians must
become more attentive to the further turns such social change has taken more
recently, questioning what is beneficial and what is detrimental to the possibilities for celebrating the Church's liturgy as a pastoral contribution to current personal, interpersonal, and social needs.

Such, in any case, is my own conviction, even as I find myself at moments
immobilized by the dissonance between the individualistic, technocentric,
and antisocial aspects of our evolving postmodern culture and the communal,
aesthetically oriented, and tradition-honoring characteristics of liturgically
practiced evangelical faith. With Power and Schillebeeckx and other exem-

plary theologians of the recent generations preceding me, I see the treasures of two millennia of Christian and Roman Catholic tradition ready to serve the human cause as God's cause if only we believers, *as Church*, embrace them in new, critical, yet reverent ways. Only too painfully aware of the present internal ecclesial problems concerning the shape and practice of hierarchical authority, pastoral ministry in local cultures, and personal and social ethics (to name just a few of the major challenges within Roman Catholicism today), I nonetheless want to argue that we late-modern believers must find a way to allow the tradition to *embrace us*. It is this sense of being able to give ourselves over, albeit critically, to the authority still inherent in the Church's tradition that, I believe, distinguishes believers' practical task today and thereby places us in contradiction to the postmodern ethics and aesthetics of pastiche. The trust that I as a Roman Catholic and Jesuit still have in the God revealed in the liturgy (in word and sacrament) and the *Spiritual Exercises* grounds this counter-cultural commitment. The actual practice of each, as well as ongoing contemplative integration of the two with the unfolding story of life in this world, enacts the very possibility of that trust.

Notes

1. In English, the official name of the Jesuits is rendered "The Society of Jesus." The term "Company of Jesus," nonetheless, can be used at times, especially as it evokes the Latin original.

2. See Terrence W. Tilley, *Inventing Catholic Tradition* (Maryknoll, N.Y.: Orbis Books, 2000); John E. Thiel, *Senses of Tradition: Continuity and Development in Catholic Faith* (New York: Oxford University Press, 2000); and Yves Congar, *Tradition and Traditions: An Historical and a Theological Essay* (New York: Macmillan Books, 1966).

3. See Alexander Schmemann, *Introduction to Liturgical Theology*, trans. Asheleigh Moorhouse (Crestwood, N.Y.: St. Vladimir's Seminary Press, 1966, 1986), 182–84; and *For the Life of the World: Sacraments and Orthodoxy*, 2nd ed. (Crestwood, N.Y.: St. Vladimir's Seminary Press, 1973), 120–22, 133.

4. Louis-Marie Chauvet, *The Sacraments: The Word of God at the Mercy of the Body* (Collegeville, Minn.: The Liturgical Press, 2001), 156.

5. Chauvet, *The Sacraments*, 156, 158.

6. Biblical quotes are taken from *The New Revised Standard Version*.

7. See Dorothee Soelle, "A Critique of Christian Masochism," in *Suffering* (Philadelphia: Fortress, 1975), 9–32.

8. See Johann Baptist Metz, *Faith in History and Society: Toward a Practical Fundamental Theology* (New York: Crossroad/Seabury, 1980), 70–77; and Edward Schillebeeckx, *Church: The Human Story of God* (New York: Crossroad, 1991), 66–99.

9. See *Sacrosanctum concilium*: Constitution on the Sacred Liturgy, no. 10.

10. See *Sacrosanctum concilium,* no. 106.

11. See *Lumen gentium:* Dogmatic Constitution on the Church, nos. 14–16.

12. See *Gaudium et spes:* Pastoral Constitution on the Church in the Modern World, no. 1.

13. See *Sacrosanctum concilium,* no. 10.

14. See *Sacrosanctum concilium,* no. 50.

15. Indeed, Joyce Ann Zimmerman, C.P.P.S., editor of *Liturgical Ministry,* states with some regularity her wish that somebody would write a dissertation exploring why it is that so many Jesuits, despite their being members of an order known for its indifferent approach to the church's liturgy, have contributed so prominently to the modern liturgical movement and the more recent efforts to implement the reformed rites of Vatican II.

16. The current, often problematic, role of liturgy in Jesuit life was one of the primary concerns of the first International Meeting on Jesuit Liturgy, a gathering of scores of Jesuit liturgists and a few other clerical and lay colleagues in Rome, during June 2002. For the published papers, see *Liturgy in a Postmodern World,* ed. Keith Pecklers, S.J. (New York: Continuum, 2003), especially the chapter by Robert Taft, S.J., "Liturgy in Life and Mission."

17. See *Sacrosanctum concilium,* no. 7. For a recent treatment of each of these symbolic modes of dominical presence, see the entire thematic issue, "The Place of Christ in the Liturgy," *Liturgical Ministry* 11 (Winter 2002).

18. I am thinking here of Schillebeeckx's theory of the negative contrast experience. See Edward Schillebeeckx, *The Schillebeeckx Reader,* ed. Robert J. Schreiter (New York: Crossroad, 1984), 272–74; and Schillebeeckx, *Church,* 5–6. See also Bruce T. Morrill, "Practicing Political Holiness: The Call to a Life of Contrasts in the Work of Edward Schillebeeckx," *Doxology* 18 (2001): 70–94.

19. See Louis-Marie Chauvet, "The Liturgy in its Symbolic Space," in *Liturgy and the Body,* ed. Louis-Marie Chauvet and François Kabasele Lumbala, *Concilium* 1995/3 (London/Maryknoll, N.Y.: SCM/Orbis, 1995), 29–39.

20. See Metz, *Faith in History and Society,* 113, 177–78.

21. This is one of Schmemann's key insights, to which I am indebted. See Alexander Schmemann, "Symbols and Symbolism in the Byzantine Liturgy: Liturgical Symbols and Their Theological Interpretation," in *Liturgy and Tradition: Theological Reflections of Alexander Schmemann,* ed. Thomas Fisch (Crestwood, N.Y.: St. Vladimir's Seminary Press, 1990), 126–27.

22. See *Sacrosanctum concilium,* no. 4.

23. In the Society of Jesus, general congregations are occasional convocations of representatives from every Jesuit province in the world for the purpose of evaluating and setting the course of the Society's mission and governance.

24. Founded in 1956, The Jesuit Volunteer Corps has one-year placements (renewable up to three years) in various locations across the United States. Volunteers work in church-related institutions and other social service contexts in an effort to live the faith that does justice, while living together on very limited financial means. A popular motto for the organization, one bespeaking the experience of its members, is "Ruined for Life."

25. The Rite of Christian Initiation of Adults (RCIA) has been since 1972 the official pastoral-ritual process whereby individuals become full members of the Roman Catholic Church. Executed in parishes and other local communities, the RCIA follows a series of liturgically marked stages of faith formation, with the celebration of baptism, confirmation, and first Eucharist composing the climax, normally at the annual Easter Vigil.

26. Regency is the third stage in a Jesuit scholastic's formation, a time to step away from academic studies and become immersed full-time in one of the works of the Society of Jesus, usually for a period of one to three years.

27. For a full development of the carefully reasoned thought behind this adage, see Gordon Lathrop, "'O Taste and See': The Geography of Liturgical Ethics," in *Liturgy and the Moral Self: Humanity at Full Stretch Before God*, ed. E. Byron Anderson and Bruce T. Morrill (Collegeville, Minn.: The Liturgical Press, 1998), 41–53. See also his *Holy Ground: A Liturgical Cosmology* (Minneapolis: Fortress Press, 2003).

28. In the summer of 2000 I returned for the first time to Alaska where, among other things, I made my annual eight-day retreat. During those days I found God inviting me to imagine serving the native villages of Southwestern Alaska once again, now as a Jesuit priest. This I have done semi-annually for the past three years, finding myself inexpressibly grateful to the Yup'ik people and the Jesuit community in that region for the opportunity to share something of the struggles and joys of their lives, which they live in a context so sharply contrasting from my primary location at Boston College.

29. See David N. Power, *The Eucharistic Mystery: Revitalizing the Tradition* (New York: Crossroad Publishing, 1992), vii–viii, 9–13.

5

The American Jesuit Theologian

Roger Haight, S.J.

E VERY AGE SEEMS TO BE OVERLY CONSCIOUS of its distinctiveness. Writers across the centuries consistently respond to the crisis of their time; no one thinks of his or her age as more of the same. Postmoderns by definition try to characterize and respond to a period with qualities that distinguish it from the modern.[1] I intend this essay as part of this always contemporaneous project, and I give it a contentious title to mark its intrinsic ambiguity: a single portrait, drawn from an individual's experience, of the North American Jesuit theologian. I do this, first, by explicitly analyzing the dynamics of an autobiographical method and explaining why it fits the task. I will then lay out the spirituality underlying this portrait of a theologian as American, Catholic, and Jesuit. And I will conclude with requirements of being a North American Jesuit theologian today under the theme of loyalty.

I. An Autobiographical Statement

Generally speaking, the appeal to biographical evidence is often represented as carrying little weight as an argument. One person's experience is hardly a proof. But then who can deny the power, effectiveness, and classic quality of Augustine's *Confessions*? Whereas demonstrated abstract truth tends to rise and then float away, personal testimony stays on the ground and at least commands attention. What is going on in this tension?

An interpretation of texts from the perspective of the biography of their authors rarely gives ultimate satisfaction. Biographical interpretation can beg the question of truth by reducing meaning to a function of an individual's experience. Assertions in the first person, the humblest of all, lose their strength in the measure in which they depart from objective evidence. In situations of argument, debate, and most surely polemics the contention that "I think something," or that "my experience tells me so," bears no inner necessity. But in situations where pluralism reigns, where relativity and difference define the context and the suppositions of the discussion, biography can contribute. Autobiographical reference, by so specifying the source with limitation, provides freedom for strong affirmation and, by relativizing the context, depolemicizes the argument and encourages sympathetic listeners. In any case, everyone today implicitly presupposes that the situation of all authors contributes in no small degree to why they hold what they do. An appeal to the autobiographical, therefore, allows one to make general claims about what the present situation demands of the theologian, all the while allowing other views.

An autobiographical method does not lack altogether an appeal to evidence and to truth. One cannot simply reduce the recounting of experience to the eccentric and bizarre; most chronicling or description of experience, when genuinely communicative action, appeals to what humans share in common. When an author can provide a reflective archaeology of a given experience, or a critical analysis of it, the result may function as an appeal to evidence found within the reader. Moreover, all experience has a history and bears a developmental character. Thus a biographical accounting for why someone proffers a position, how it came to be, and why it appears coherent, may be more clearly and convincingly laid out by biographical narrative than by logical argument.

The development of positions can be explained by any number of different theories. But two distinct types of theory each bring out a facet of how a narrative biographical method can represent the developmental character of all theological stances. On the one hand, modern, prospective theories of development seem to share a certain "organic" structure; they show how deep comprehensive experiences that defy complete or adequate expression in either word or practice can remain continuous or constant at some level of depth while they undergo growth, change, revision, and reformulation in theology, doctrine, and practice. On the other hand, a retrospective and more postmodern theory of development, such as the one espoused by John Thiel, explains how a single tradition, and by analogy a single depth experience, can paradoxically include the stripping away of old and the addition of new affirmations.[2] Development is not organic, but by addition and subtraction, and creative reinterpretation of where real continuity with the past lies. This happens when current experience builds explicit bridges between a past and a present that seem antithetical and finds paths between the two that were not there before.

I offer Edward Schillebeeckx's later thought as an example of a theology in which reference to the narrative of his experience increases its credibility.[3] Schillebeeckx was trained as a neo-scholastic, or more precisely a neo-Thomist theologian, and the theology he generated up to and throughout the course of Vatican II represented the best of that tradition. But from the time of the council through to the early 1970s, Schillebeeckx's theology underwent a deep structural change of presupposition and method. In the face of an encounter with secularization, an experience of the historicity and sociality of knowledge, the oppressive character of society for those at its margins, he literally abandoned his neo-classical scholastic imaginative framework, and he reconstructed a historical, critical, socially conscious, hermeneutical method of theology. Schillebeeckx documents this transition in his writings during this period, and in so doing provides an analogous description of the transition that occurred so extensively among Catholic theologians that one may take it as a rough description of a development that marked Catholic theology itself. Schillebeeckx's theological career thus exemplifies by some large analogy how an appeal to biographical experience can open up entry into common experiences that may be persuasive.[4]

To situate this essay with respect to the example of Schillebeeckx, I believe that the theologian today meets a challenge in pluralism analogous to what he encountered in secularization and historicity. I do not mean that pluralism provides an alternative set of questions to address, but that pluralism compounds and provides a new accent to the problems raised by secularization and historicity, and that all three loci of experiences open up new positive ways in which Christianity can understand itself as it slowly moves into the twenty-first century and the ever deeper recognition of how open the future really is. Like Schillebeeckx, I believe that the questions raised within the context of this new experience touch most directly central doctrines for Christian self-understanding: Jesus Christ and the church.

In sum, then, I assume an autobiographical method here in order to free myself from the burden of objective argumentation and to relativize what may appear as overly strong generalization, while at the same time hoping that the autobiographical reference may not appear idiosyncratic but analogously representative. In each of the following sections, therefore, I begin with description of the situations, the experiential sources, and the teachers from whom I have drawn the positions I take.

II. A Spirituality of Action

I turn to the category of "spirituality" as a framework for developing conceptions of the Jesuit theologian. Several reasons dictate the move, but one stands out. Spirituality can be understood as the theological locus which most closely defines the person in concrete terms, as distinct from a generalized theological anthropology. Although not every conception of spirituality will support this claim, I will turn to a specific meaning of the category that will justify the central role that spirituality, whether it be Ignatian or more specifically Jesuit, has always played in the discussion of a Jesuit self.

In the late 1960s and early 1970s I took up the task of writing a doctoral dissertation which included a close study of the early work of Maurice Blondel, the French Catholic philosopher and sometimes theologian. Born in 1861, Blondel published his doctoral thesis which proved to be his master work, *L'Action*, in 1893.[5] A variety of different characterizations describe this original work: "Christian existentialism" points to its focus on dynamic human existence as it primary reference; "metaphysical pragmatism" brings out the empirical and practical focus on everyday action while at the same time noting the comprehensive depth of the analysis; "transcendental phenomenology" recalls what Blondel called a method of immanence, a dialectical analysis of the logic or implicit motives of human action, that inevitably lead at every turn toward transcendence. In Blondelian philosophy, "action" plays the role of "existence" or "human existence." "Action" is an analogous term that shares a range of meanings: it refers most broadly to human existing, giving existence a dynamic sense; it refers most narrowly to concrete practices, doing this or that. It can also refer to sets of practices and social behaviors as in the action of a community.

The dynamic understanding of human existence as action entails some distinct emphases in the arrangement of human functions and goals. For example, the role of human willing receives a certain emphasis: Blondel's pragmatism posits an interaction between knowing and willing and being. Human knowing functions in service of human willing and action; human desire and willing affect human knowing. Action draws up into itself knowing and willing, and mediates a kind of possessive knowledge that forms and shapes the being of a person. The maxim, "we are what we do," describes a holistic self-constructing subject that utterly transcends every shallow utilitarianism. What Blondel calls "possessive knowledge" occurs when, through commitment and action that engages what is known, the object known becomes so internalized to the knowing subject that he or she not only possesses it, but becomes "possessed" by it.[6]

With Blondel's philosophy of action as a background theory, one can construe spirituality as pointing to the foundational dimension of human existence itself, a conception which embraces all aspects of life and integrates them. The following definition of spirituality on two distinct levels exemplifies this. First of all, on an existential level, spirituality refers to the actual way in which each person lives. It encompasses the logic of one's action as played out in one's concrete actions. Spirituality, on this level at which one actually lives it, points to the pattern of behavior, with its motives and goals, its presuppositions, choices of means, and immediate ends, all combining to form a more or less coherent logic or direction of life.[7] This first meaning and reference for spirituality has the advantage of highlighting the fact that all human beings have a spirituality; the category transcends the explicitly religious. Since the distinctive character of human existence lies in its spiritual dimension, one can only conceive of all specifically human existence in terms of some spirituality. This apologetic move of rescuing the term "spirituality" from an exclusively religious usage gives it in turn an anthropological grounding. It also accounts for a bewilderingly broad usage today.[8] What makes spirituality explicitly religious and theological lies in the issue of union with God. Religious spirituality inserts the concrete logic of life into the horizon of transcendent reality and ultimate concern.

Spirituality on a second reflective level refers to various formulations, or theories, or explanations of spirituality on the lived level. Spirituality in this sense roughly corresponds to the discipline of spirituality, the rationalization or analysis of its various dimensions and their integral union. Such a reflective account may be descriptive or critically analytical; it both grows out of existential historical spirituality and reflects back to shape and form it. No existential spirituality exists without some intentionality, some more or less coherent rationale, however implicit it may remain in practice. This reflective side, therefore, should not be understood in separate terms, but always in relation to the kind of life it generates.

Having constructed a conception of spirituality around the category of action, I now want to suggest that intellectual activity is action, and that participation in an intellectual discipline constitutes a spirituality. A moment's reflection yields the self-evident character of the first proposition. Only superficial stereotypical language contrasts the acts of knowing and doing as inaction and action; whole groups of people spend the greater part of their waking hours engaged in the action of thinking and searching and trying to know. But the further step reveals still more: such a life's activity rests on or constitutes a spirituality in act. And frequently enough a reflective second-level theoretical spirituality accompanies this pattern of life as a rationale of motives and aspirations, means and ends, methods and goals. Indeed, one can often find at the bottom of the life-work of a scholar, particularly when a career exhibits a certain consistency, a spirituality that defines and can account for the fundamental direction of the life-work.[9]

Intellectual activity can also contain a religious spirituality. Here I am not referring to the obvious fact that religious people have been engaged in intellectual activity of all sorts for religious reasons. When that occurs, the particular life of the whole person draws up his or her activity into the religious ends that unify the whole life. But one can find deeper ways in which intellectual activity itself carries within itself implicit references to transcendence. Transcendence manifests itself when intellectual activity is driven by a deep inner desire to find the truth, or where truth subsists as a value marked with absoluteness and ultimacy. In this case the searcher dedicates or commits the self to transcendent value; respecting evidence bears a moral claim; truth functions in such a spirituality as absolute Truth. A transcendental analysis of the human quest for truth, and the communication of truth as in the life of teaching, yield implicitly religious (in the sense of "transcendent") values which exert a claim upon human life "from above."[10]

The conclusion of this first probe into the life of the Jesuit theologian may be drawn along several lines which I can verify in my own experience. First, and this applies to any relatively stable activity, but especially an intellectual calling, as a scholar and teacher I feel at home within my discipline. The activity of theology itself goes a long way in shaping my spirituality. Second, in the quest for and communication of what I take to be true or at least appreciations of the real, such activity of itself does not deflect me from God but draws me toward union with God. This activity provides no substitute for prayer; as formally different activities they may compete for time. But such spiritual activity is never seen as distraction from union with God, because all action dedicated to God's values helps to cement union with God in a stable, possessive, and ontological way. Blondel's philosophy helps me to bring out a deep dimension of contemplation in the action of a quest for knowledge and meaning. It is rooted in transcendence and in return draws me toward transcendence.

III. An American Catholic Identity

I'm a Catholic because I was born into a stable Catholic family. One can never quite get over the sense of contingency imbedded in that proposition, no matter how absolute the claims attached to the status. But just when one realizes the historical and ontological arbitrariness of one's deepest commitments, the iron hold of social conditioning compounds the experience. I went to a Catholic grammar school and was taught by Dominican Sisters. Then I spent four years in a Jesuit high school. Add to this the years of Jesuit formation. Catholicism has become so all-encompassing and has so deeply seeped into cartilage and synapse that I have never really considered being anything else. Today this particular route into Catholic theology, typical two generations ago, is so rare that its statistical oddity needs to be underscored.

What does it mean to be a Catholic today? In responding to this I fix my eye on American Catholicism and point to some of the elements of Catholicism that have shaped me and that I find attractive. But the selection is arbitrary, and though all of these qualities may have a shadow side, I paint them in a somewhat idealized way.

1.The Incarnational Principle

Newman thought that "incarnation" might be the central Catholic idea.[11] The root metaphor extends from the incarnation of the Divine Word in Jesus to the general metaphysical principle of the joining of creation, especially humanity, with the divine. From there it reaches out into sacraments and a generous use of physical things to stir the concrete imagination into feelings of the presence of transcendence. The outsider will say of the fully vested bishop, "That man has more religion on him than in him," but the Catholic enjoys the pageant and ritual as somehow related to an incarnational availability of the divine.

2. Geographical Universality

Geographical universality is the translation of catholicity in spacial terms. It impressed Augustine, and he used it as a club with which to hit the local Donatists over the head. Being Catholic includes a sense of belonging to a far-flung organization that is really held together as one. That sense of geographical unity can go to extremes, as when the church leaders argued for retaining Latin in the liturgy so that throughout the whole world it would be equally and uniformly unintelligible. But at its best it can allow the church to mediate a connectedness with people beyond group and nation.

3. The Big Tent

With this metaphor I allude to both the tent and the bigness. The tent stands for the inclusive covering. In the parade of people represented by religions, with Catholicism "here comes everybody": it cuts across nationality, cultures, and class. The American Catholic church continues to grow, if not by conversion, by immigration. But bigness and display are also Catholic traits: like rallying for the home team. A good example was the international Eucharistic Congress held in Chicago in June 1926. Jay Dolan describes the arrival by motorcade of nine cardinals, from France, Germany, Ireland, Spain, Austria, Hungary, and Italy. They were seated in open-top cars and dressed in their brightly colored robes and strange-looking hats; they rode solemnly along a three-mile stretch including Michigan Avenue for an hour and twenty minutes, cheered by 150,000 people, to be greeted by Cardinal Mundelein at the Cathedral.[12] This is "Catholic Big" in its purest form asserting itself for the first time nationally in a Protestant country. It still lingers as a memory, and some young Catholics hanker for it.

4. Social Teaching and Spirituality

These two do not always, but always should, travel together. The Catholic church has been interested in society since the realization that the second coming was delayed, but the commitment became intentional and extensive in the early fourth century. More interesting are the wide variety of different ways in which this relationship to society has been formulated and acted out in different times and places. Likewise, the sheer variety of spiritualities over the centuries can only astonish the investigator. Catholic history and the church at any given time are strewn with a whole array of different techniques and rationales for mediating union with God. The way these two concerns relate and interact within the community provides a barometer of its health.

5. Taking Theology Seriously

I can attest to the fact that the Catholic Church takes theology seriously. Beliefs count; it makes a difference what you believe; there is a tradition to be guarded and protected. All of these beliefs and values need interpretation, and they can be implemented in diverse ways. Sometimes theology gets confused with catechism; fundamental faith commitments can wrongly be identified with doctrinal formulas, and so on. But these misunderstandings are the price for a church which protects its inheritance and resists the proposition that Catholics can publicly proclaim anything they want in the name of the church.

But perhaps I place more importance for American Catholic identity on the potential gifts that it might offer to the universal church. One of these has already been inscribed in the church's formal documents: religious freedom. Learned from the American experience of the separation of church and state through which American Catholicism rose to maturity, the principles involved there were translated into doctrine and accepted by the whole church at Vatican II. But American Catholicism is actively engaging other challenges that may lead us along analogous paths. Three of these stand out.

The first has to do with women in the church. The women's movement in the United States, with roots back in the nineteenth century, reached a peak in the last third of the twentieth century in various forms of feminism. This in turn has deeply affected women in the American Catholic Church and has produced a corps of theologians, a whole body of theology, and a common corporate consciousness among a huge constituency. The movement has spread globally and continues gradually to shape the consciousness of Christians everywhere. In time the themes of equality which so essentially characterize the Christian message will be extended to women within the church and thus help to make its witness credible.

The second theme arising out of American culture revolves around pluralism as a fact, a value, and a challenge to corporate consciousness and action. North America developed as a continent of immigrants. Waves of immigrants mainly from European nations built the United States through the nineteenth and into the twentieth century. These people constituted the pre–World War II American Catholic Church into a pluralistic church. During the last third of the twentieth century a new wave of immigration is introducing a host of non-western peoples, many of whom are Christian, into American life. But instead of building their own churches, the new Americans are joining established parishes, thus creating pluralistic communities. Many of these new immigrants who are not Christian are bringing their own religions with them where they hope to thrive, as did the Catholic Church, in a society where religion enjoys freedom and protection. These latest immigrants have made the United States the most religiously plural nation in the world.

Another instance of how pluralism has come to mark American Catholic consciousness has been mediated by the rise in the educational level of the children of the immigrant church and their subsequent move to the suburbs after World War II. The suburbs are more than a place; they represent a culture. Inculturation has meant that the patterns of behavior, values, and in some cases beliefs of those Catholics hardly differ from those of American Protestants. This inculturation entails a sense of openness to the other that manifests itself in various ways. One example can be seen in the fact that fifty percent of Catholics in Generation X have spouses who belong to other churches. Another is the fact that Catholics are church members by choice and not social necessity, making the church a voluntary association. Members of the American Catholic church may or may not follow the church's authority on any given point of morals and, to a lesser degree, may question a given doctrine. Education and inculturation in American pluralistic society has created a positive valuation of pluralism and openness to the other among Catholic laity that far exceeds the views of the leadership of the church. In time, this positive appropriation of pluralism and difference may help the world church to adjust to the increasing and deepening sense of "the other" and of "difference" in a globalized world.

A third distinctive element of American Catholicism, although analogous experiences may be felt around the world, is the decline of religious and clerics as the responsible agents of ministry and the rise of the laity. One is witnessing a direct reversal of the development that occurred in the first three or four generations of the church. Then ministry gradually passed *from* being provided by a variety of leaders in various capacities according to their position or talents, *to* being provided by a professional class of ministers: bishops, presbyters, deacons, and other lesser orders. Today the professional ministry of apostolic sisters is heading toward extinction in a relatively short period of time, the number of clerics continues to tumble, and as the office of bishop becomes more exigent, the talent pool of candidates for bishop shrinks dramatically. And yet the life of the majority of parishes in the United States is thriving, as the ministry of the laity not only takes up the slack but bears the burden, and in the process becomes more and more expert and specialized. The number of programs for the training of lay ministers has expanded exponentially. Here the educational level of the American church has given the whole church a sense of organic participation that has a potential for overcoming remnants of clericalism. Can this expansion of lay responsibility for the church be institutionalized and exported to the world church?

As a Christian theologian I am right at home as a member of a worldwide church organization that finds God in all things and tries to include everybody, not without some failures. I appreciate Catholicism's social concern, which in its American tradition consistently fought against an individualism that bypassed those at the margins of the social order.[13] I revere the tradition enough to try to mediate by interpretation its meanings and values to an expanding group of educated people who, in quickly changing times, do not experience its relevance. I am especially proud of the story of American Catholicism as one of vitality and creativity. This is not the story of a single leader, a Patrick or Boniface or Charlemagne, but of many groups of squabbling immigrants from a variety of cultures united in a common faith who gradually reached an accommodation with the American reality. But that story is hardly over and the future is full of promise. As a theologian I hope I can contribute to the dialogue and mediation between the church and the laity in general, women in particular, and other Christian churches and world religions.

To conclude this part, American Catholicism has three more potential gifts that it might offer to the world church: a feminist perspective and set of values, openness to pluralism, and the rise of the laity. Being a part of this church marks the identity of the American Jesuit theologian. The possibilities and potential of specifically American Catholic experience give American theology a distinctive sense of mission. But Americans must also be careful to guard against messianism, which often conceals an imperialistic spirit.

The American Jesuit Theologian

IV. A Jesuit Mission

The third element of this portrait of a Jesuit self embraces the Jesuit mission. The Second Vatican Council stimulated a quest for the original charism of the Society of Jesus, and the decline of members in the industrial west occasioned another period of introspection which continues. All know that religious life in the postmodern western world has to change, but no one as yet knows just how to do it. These decades have thus generated an enormous body of literature in all the European languages on Ignatius and the Jesuits, yesterday and today. North America has not been left behind in the study of American Jesuit spirituality, the *Exercises*, and general Jesuit life.

I refer to this literature to heighten the confessional character of the single point that I wish to make in this brief section; I shall not appeal to this literature, but rely only on personal convictions without explicit reference to the many sources which have nurtured these sentiments. I am drawing upon fifty years of life as a Jesuit lived in a variety of countries. An experience of this kind constitutes a resource from which every Jesuit draws. Such experiences work their way into every formulation of an objective argument drawn from Jesuit sources.

To begin, when I think of the specifically Jesuit mission in and for the church, I instinctively and spontaneously turn to the metaphor of a boundary. I situate the Jesuit on that boundary, as between two places or facing opposing forces, with the task of mediating between them in both directions. As I conceive it, Jesuits straddle many boundaries, because they engage so many issues in a wide variety of ministries. But two sets of boundaries bear particular relevance for the Jesuit theologian: ideological boundaries and various boundaries between inside and outside.

The metaphor of the boundary may be applied first of all to the arena of ideology and ideas. Here being on the boundary refers to a state of mind. A whole range of ideological polarities structure the way we organize material. These provide sets of extremes at the ends of spectrums of different views on any given issue. On every issue groups divide into the right and left; relative to tradition or the status quo, every issue elicits conservative and progressive response. Being on the boundary, therefore, always requires dialectical thinking, a weighing of the pros and cons on both sides and measuring them against each other.

Relative to the issues of theology, two sets of polarities today call for the Jesuit to be on the boundary, hold in tension the counterforces, and negotiate between them. One of these is the classic tension between faith and reason. The Jesuit who lives too comfortably on either side of this tension fails in the

Jesuit mission continually to negotiate between them: faith as an act of an intelligent being must be reasonable; reason cannot be reduced to rational functions on controllable data. Another classic polarity might be considered as a subset of the tension between faith and reason, but in our historically conscious intellectual culture, it unfolds according to its own logic. I refer to the tension between the particular and the universal, a tension in human consciousness that has accompanied globalization. For example, in terms of christology, I do not see how one can participate in postmodern culture today and rest secure in traditional christological belief without raising the question of the relation of Jesus to other centers of religious mediation and consciousness. In relation to the church, one cannot participate in the western societies that were once Christian and not wonder what has happened. Before there were few boundaries separating church and society; today the connections are growing thin. Where and how should the boundary between church and world be drawn? How should the church relate to non-church? Someone or some group must explicitly engage the dialectical activity along these boundaries, and I believe this mission has been given, not exclusively of course, to the Jesuits in the modern church. The Jesuit theologian, then, internalizes and lives out ideologically the dialectical interaction between faith and reason as the church moves forward in history.

I envisage a second sphere in which the metaphor of interaction across boundaries describes the work of the Jesuit theologian. Here the metaphor has a spacial connotation of inside and outside, but I refer it symbolically to the community of the church in tension with the world "outside" the church. Although these are closely related to the ideological tensions addressed in the first point, I conceive of this tension as involving much more negotiating between groups or constituencies. From inside the church, the tension arises out of the mission of the church to the world. The success of such a mission depends on a knowledge of the church, a knowledge of the world on its own terms, and the building of bridges that can connect the two. From the perspective of the outside, of the world in which the church in fact exists, as an autonomous social system and culture the world bears its own truth and wisdom which continually enriches the church, unconsciously by symbiosis and less often in other dramatic ways. This is what it means to be on the boundary. These spacial boundaries relate to the first set the way practical reason relates to theoretical reason, and interaction between the two sets of boundaries operates continually. In regard to both I understand the mission of the Jesuit consists in being a catalytic agent. I accept the fact that secularists will consider what I write as a theologian too pious; and that Catholics on the right will judge it too secular. Sometimes Jesuits get into trouble, on either side of the boundary, but if that never occurred, Jesuits would not be fulfilling their corporate responsibility.[14] This leads me to the next point.

V. The Theologian's Loyalty

Thus far I have addressed a spirituality of intellectual activity, within a Catholic and an American context, structured by dialectical correlation between tensively related worlds of meaning, in both of which the theologian lives and assumes responsibility. I now want to ask about where the theologian's loyalty ultimately lies. Can these various strands that bristle with tensions find some integrated cohesion? I will suggest that they can when they are considered developmentally, that is, not in the formal categories of static relationships but in developmental terms of process.

I propose that the context for the discussion of the center of gravity of the theologian today must be understood in developmental terms. It makes little sense today to speak of what should or should not define fundamental conscious attitudes without taking into consideration the life condition of the subject. Here I make a loose appeal to the large body of work that has been done in developmental psychology: Erik Erikson's effort to chart formal transcultural structures of psychological development, Lawrence Kohlberg's analysis of the development of the structure of moral reasoning and responsibility (along with its critique from a feminist perspective), James Fowler's application of developmental psychology to faith and more particularly belief, and Robert Kegan's appreciation of the development of cognitive frameworks. In this appeal to developmental psychology I want to avoid both psychological reductionism and a complete reliance on any of these theories. But at the same time consideration of the fundamental loyalty of the theologian that prescinded from social and psychological context would at best walk with a limp. I borrow from these theories, therefore, only two points commonly shared among them, for to go more deeply would breech the limits of my knowledge: first, that development does occur and, second, that it transpires along the axis of expanding horizons of experience. In the light of these principles I want briefly to allude to how my own experience has gradually expanded my horizons.

After reviewing the experiences or events that have occasioned growth in fundamental attitudes, that is to say, not so much a learning of content, but a shaping of more generalized suppositions and convictions that interpret what is learned, I fix on three series of events. I take it that everyone could point to analogous experiences.

The first relates to my life in the Philippines as a Jesuit early in the formation process: a first period of six years, a period of two years later on, and a total of more than fifteen years being attached to the Philippine Province of the Jesuits. This experience entailed more than living in and learning another culture; it also stimulated questions about cross-cultural communication, inculturation, identity, and sameness of theological and doctrinal meaning when internalized in new cultural forms different from the western standards. It demanded and prompted attitudes of learning and openness to the new and unfamiliar, a respect for differences, and so on.

A second experience, probably the most formative of all, was provided by the University of Chicago. Key words and phrases can characterize the education offered there, but hardly capture the depth of its impression: ecumenical, open, critical, methodologically self-conscious, constructive, pluralistic, broad in the sense of multidisciplinary, exacting, collegial. Much of one's internalized identity is brought to consciousness by contrast. People who have not studied in such an environment may find it hard to appreciate how it stimulates one to internalize more deeply because more critically one's own confessional identity. At the same time role models for emulation were plentiful at The Divinity School: Langdon Gilkey, Joseph Haratounian, Joseph Sittler, Mircea Eliade, David Tracy, Brian Gerrish, Bernard McGuinn, Schubert Ogden, Paul Ricoeur, Martin Marty, Norman Perrin. As students know, these figures sometimes appeared larger than life, but they were also colleagues and friends.

The third formative educational experience has been negotiated through teaching over a period of time in which concern for critical appropriation, for the presuppositions and method of the discipline of theology itself, were always placed to the fore. Over the years the foundations of the discipline themselves have changed through engagement of new problems, in new situations, with new methods.

When I look back on this route, I can discern in the most general of terms three streams of thought in which horizons were continually being pushed open and expanded. In none of these cases did the expanding horizon result in disorientation; in each case it happened so gradually that, although the distance between the earliest point and the last appeared considerable, the development took on the character of spontaneous or natural development into an always deeper appreciation of the way things are.

The first expanding horizon has to do with the institutional framework of life and thought. By this I mean institutional boundaries that form the limits to the range of data that one considers. For example, as a child and boy I viewed the sphere of the religious as entirely contained within the limits of the Catholic Church as I knew it in parish and school. Catholicism in a Jesuit novitiate ran deeper; Catholicism in the Philippines was an utterly different version of the same Catholicism. At the University of Chicago I learned to think Catholicism within the horizon of Christianity; as a christologist today, one has to think of Jesus Christ realistically within the context of the world's religions. And, finally, one must at some point take a critical look at the religious itself to see it as a particular human behavior. As a human being with others, it is more and more difficult to affirm *homo naturaliter religiosus*. The maxim may still carry deep meaning relative to the human, but one can hardly presuppose it. Thus the first expansion runs along the line of Catholicism, Christianity, religions of the world, human truth. These do not replace each other in turn, but the earlier are sublated in the latter, that is, drawn up into a new framework and preserved with new, richer, and deeper meaning.

The second line where an expanding horizon or framework gradually transformed earlier understanding progressed along the line of religious epistemology. Surely as a child I had a literal, imaginative understanding of transcendence and religious reference. The accounts of religious experience and knowledge across western intellectual history alone and in a variety of different disciplines would fill libraries. One has to keep at the task of developing one's own theory of religious knowing and theology of faith in the face of new problems, new cross-disciplinary reference, and a delicate balance with a workable method in theological reflection. I have arrived at the notion of the religious symbol and symbolic mediation as a center for thinking about faith knowledge. But it is an open framework that serves as a clearing house for a variety of eclectic considerations of religious encounter with transcendence. This term of development appears distant from the child's literalist point of departure, but it shares the original realism of reference. In the end, comic-book Catholicism and Christianity are entirely left behind as theological options, but not as folk-practice for a large segment of Christians.

Still a third line of where the framework for appreciating religious symbols has deepened and broadened follows a postmodern trajectory into pluralism and apophaticism. This says very little in itself, but it points a direction, and a series of stations mark the journey along the way. Appreciation of pluralism can come in many different qualities and degrees. Simple recognition of truth in the positions of others requires certain criteria for truth and levels at which it is assessed, if one does not simply yield to relativism. But these criteria must be opened wider to accommodate the other. For me, when such appreciation became extended ever further, I became more impressed by what we do not know about transcendent reality than by what we do. But this, I believe, corresponds with one of those basic truths always affirmed in the Christian tradition concerning the absolute and incomprehensible mystery of God. Recognition of this ignorance reaches different depths of appropriation which, ironically, have to be learned.

This dynamic becomes specific in the analysis of how globalization has expanded the horizons of thinking and how theologians are adjusting to it. Globalization has provided a wider horizon and framework for measuring moral and religious truth. What happens when Jesus Christ, who has been understood to communicate absolute truth because he is God's own truth, is placed in a pluralistic context? What happens when historical consciousness and the sociology of knowledge intrinsically relativize all knowledge and all revelations? At the least, one has new perspectives on God from other religions, or counter perspectives when whole cultures relate to ultimate reality in terms that do not correspond with theism. One still appreciates Jesus Christ on the basis of Christian source material and tradition, but placing him in a context of other religions and religious mediators opens up perspectives, questions, and appropriations of the tradition that shed new light. Indeed, the repetition or vocalization of the affirmations of tradition can take on startlingly new meanings in a new context, while sometimes repetition contradicts the intended meaning of the tradition. Placing the church and consideration of its nature and mission in the context of historicity and deep respect for the autonomy and integrity of other ancient religious traditions both relativizes absolute claims and deepens appreciation for its unique identity and relevance.

In the end, developmental growth of the religious consciousness of the Christian theologian comes from placing the object of study in an ever broader horizon or framework. In my case, the new horizon transcends parochial, literal, and exclusive or competitive notions of truth. These have yielded in a postmodern context to a broader historically understood anthropological basis, a symbolic understanding of how religious truth is mediated, a strong sense of humility before the unknown, and a reserve about stating my own tradition as absolute.

How then would I characterize the loyalty of the Christian theologian in a postmodern context? Surely loyalty finds its center in Christianity itself: the definition of Christianity and thus of the Christian theologian places Jesus Christ at the center of the corporate religious imagination. Christian theology will always be christomorphic and involve interpreting reality through Christian symbols. But Jesus Christ and Christian faith mediate human consciousness into transcendence, and that theocentrism itself leads beyond and provides leverage against tribalism. Imperialism is no longer a possibility. The postmodern Christian theologian appreciates pluralism, is open to the new and surprising, is committed to conversation in a quest for truth, and loyal to Jesus Christ and the church as guarantors of *these* transcendent values.

VI. The American Jesuit Theologian

I have drawn this characterization of the American Jesuit theologian by looking in the mirror and, by adding lines one after the other, portraying the face that I see. Its validity beyond self-portrait rests entirely on the possibility that the experiences that have characterized the development represented here possess resonances in the experiences of others. I do not understand these experiences as idiosyncratic, but as analogous to the itinerary taken by theologians like Edward Schillebeeckx, Johann Baptist Metz, and certain liberation theologians whom I understand to be responding to the signs of the times. This experience passes through the turn to the world with its suffering, hopes, and joys that was mandated by Vatican II; becomes conditioned by the world's historicity, interdependence, and pluralism; opens itself up to coexisting and interacting with the otherness and difference that mark the situation of one race occupying one planet; reappropriates its own tradition now recognized as limited and in dialogue with others; and risks new interpretations of the world and the Christian tradition itself so that these may make sense to those who also inhabit a postmodern world.

Notes

1. I use the term *postmodernity* to point to a culture, a loose set of experiences, values, and ideas, as distinct from a body of truths. I am familiar with five experiences that can be measured over against modernity. First, enlightened modernity admired the universal reason of classical consciousness, whereas postmodernity perceives that all ideas and values are tied to a particular time in history. Second, modern philosophy found the human as such in the individual subject, whereas postmodernity attends to the lessons of the sociology of knowledge and group bias. Third, moderns produced many grand schemes encompassing the real; the postmodern respects perspective and observes how universal schemes ignore differences. Fourth, whereas Newton's relatively small mechanical world led to modern disenchantment, contemporary micro and macro physics provide a vision of the universe that is both awesome and decentering of the human. Fifth, globalization begun in the modern period has so brought traditional cultures up against each other that local standards and norms are deeply threatened.

2. I am appealing here to the work of John E. Thiel, *Senses of Tradition: Continuity and Development in Catholic Faith* (Oxford: University Press, 2000), 56–99, where he contrasts modern, organic, prospective theories of development and a postmodern retrospective theory.

3. While not excluding the various places where Schillebeeckx has explicitly engaged through interview in recounting the relationship of his thought to various experiences in his life, I am more interested in the large shift in theological method that Schillebeeckx underwent in the course and wake of Vatican II. In other words, I presume that new experience within life experiences caused the shift. I cite three works as representative of three stages of his development: *Christ the Sacrament of the Encounter with God* (New York: Sheed & Ward, 1963); *The Understanding of Faith: Interpretation and Criticism* (New York: Seabury Press, 1974); *Jesus: An Experiment in Christology* (New York: Seabury Press, 1979).

4. By contrast, Karl Rahner, ten years older than Schillebeeckx and already in possession of a broad transcendental method in theology that was open to and could

account for change, did not radically alter his theological framework or method. In a more direct contrast to Rahner, however, Johann Baptist Metz displays a theological framework that bears deep resemblances to that of Schillebeeckx and with explicit biographical references at its source. James Matthew Ashley, in his *Interruptions: Mysticism, Politics, and Theology in the Work of Johann Baptist Metz* (Notre Dame, Ind.: University of Notre Dame Press, 1998), sorts out some of the sources of the differences between Rahner's and Metz's theologies.

5. Maurice Blondel, *Action (1893): Essay on a Critique of Life and a Science of Practice,* trans. Oliva Blanchette (Notre Dame, Ind.: University of Notre Dame Press, 1984).

6. I have outlined some of Blondel's philosophical conceptions and applied them to the *Spiritual Exercises* of St. Ignatius in "Foundational Issues in Jesuit Spirituality," *Studies in the Spirituality of Jesuits* 19 (St. Louis: Seminar in Jesuit Spirituality, 1987). Blondel's "pragmatism" differs from American pragmatism while retaining analogies with it. I retain sympathy for Blondel's connection with transcendental analysis of a universal human subject and his metaphysical claims, but perhaps more tentatively and tensively from within postmodern culture. Thus I want to keep this Blondelian impulse in dialogue with the more empiricist and historicist imagination of the American tradition. I applaud the work of thinkers like Donald Gelpi, S.J., who are forging closer alliance between American theology and American philosophy.

7. The idea of "lifestyle" forms a part of this logic of life but, in itself, "lifestyle" seems to convey "life at the surface." Frequently enough one's lifestyle does not at all reflect the deeper intentionality of the whole of one's life.

8. I take it that the postmodern cliché "I'm not religious, but I am spiritual" is not a bad development; it suggests a certain depth of reflection on life and suggests that the problem of religious affiliation may lie with the churches.

9. Ashley's analysis of the logic of Metz's theology, in contrast to Rahner's, leads him back to the differences between their life experiences and their spiritualities. Ashley, *Interruptions*, 171–91.

10. These themes of an ascent toward transcendence in following the lure of Truth are common enough in the religious philosophy of the west from the neo-Platonist Augustine through Aquinas to such transcendental thinkers as Lonergan and Rahner. A striking analysis of the transcendent dimension of scholarly life is found in H. Richard Niebuhr, *Radical Monotheism and Western Culture, with Supplementary Essays* (New York: Harper and Brothers, 1960), 83–89.

11. John Henry Newman, *An Essay on the Development of Christian Doctrine* (New York: Longmans, Green, 1949), 302.

12. Jay P. Dolan, *The American Catholic Experience: A History from Colonial Times to the Present* (Garden City, N.Y.: Doubleday, 1985), 349.

13. This aspect of the story is traced by John T. McGreevy, *Catholicism and American Freedom: A History* (New York: W. W. Norton, 2003).

14. When a theologian becomes the subject of an investigation in the Roman Church, he or she is usually asked not to speak of the process publicly. One can get a good idea of the content of the discussion over the book *Jesus: Symbol of God* (Maryknoll, N.Y.: Orbis Books, 1999) from the epilogue of Roger Haight, *The Future of Christology* (New York: Continuum, 2005), 196–216.

6

Philosophizing after the Holocaust

James Bernauer, S.J.

M Y EXPERIENCE OF THE PHILOSOPHICAL LIFE as a Jesuit has been profoundly shaped by the spirituality of Ignatius of Loyola. When, within weeks of a 1962 high school graduation, I entered the Jesuits, Ignatius was for me an admirable but distant and severe figure, a Knight of the Lord's Kingdom, a soldier of Christ. His appeal was that of inviting me to enlist in a Great Cause. He was the ideal saint for an era of Cold War, ideological frenzy, and widespread militarism. The attractiveness of that military style was obliterated by many forces: the Vatican Council, the Vietnam War, the cultural shifts of the 1960s and 1970s, the evolution of the Society's practice and, I like to think, a growth in personal maturity. Ignatius became a figure in a historical museum until I read his autobiography while I was doing my tertianship (the last stage in Jesuit training) in 1989. Then I met Ignatius not as soldier but as he described himself: a pilgrim who knew that he was on an ever continuing sacred journey. I had developed regard for journeying as fundamental metaphor for life and I appreciated Ignatius anew, especially how his pivotal "Contemplation to Attain the Love of God" reflected the vision of a pilgrim, acutely sensitive to God's presence in the abundance of the world through which we make our ways, graced by rays of light from the sun and by waters flowing from fountains.[1] Quite apart from personal feelings about the man, I had long appreciated that the greatest of Ignatian graces for my life was his spirituality of finding God in all things and it was certainly that vision which motivated the title for my first published book: *Amor Mundi*, Love of the World.[2] Ignatius and his disciples have taught me a love of the world which has had the effect, I now realize, of making me very suspicious of any demonization of people or places.

The New York Province Jesuit Novitiate opened the door for me into one of the most rich and formative experiences of my life. Two vivid interlocutors were among the forces which shaped that initial experience. First, there was the martyrdom embraced by the North American martyrs who were held out as special ideals. Because some of them were thought to have been killed at Auriesville, New York, a site within the Province borders, they had been named the patrons of our Novitiate. Every night on the way to the dormitories we prayed at their shrine and many of us young Novices took them as personal patrons as well. While their saintly manner of living was the model to emulate, it was their devilish way of dying that registered most intensely in our imagination and set the standard for the heroic virtue expected in the religious way of life we were examining. Torture was an inadequate term for the sufferings which were inflicted upon these Jesuits who still, it was said, died joyously.

The second voice articulating the novitiate experience seemed frequently to be opposite to this religious grandeur: the call to obediently fall into what was called the long black line. We took on the disciplines that would determine in the most minute details the schedule and substance of our daily lives. These practices would transform us novices into the marines of the Catholic Church. But intellectual marines who faced a minimum of thirteen years of rigid education ahead of us. Anxieties about a spirit of conformity were often dispelled by recalling the pantheon of formidable thinkers which the Jesuit course of training had produced. And one of the greatest of these, Teilhard de Chardin, was even buried in our own novitiate cemetery. Still there was always a tension between the ambitions of the martyrs and an education which envisioned most of us as future teachers rather than innovative missionaries or researchers. It could be described as the Nietzschean contrast between the Dionysian spirit of excess and passion beyond all borders and the Apollonian determination to order and clarify. That contest was first shown me in the title and argument of William Lynch's study of the literary imagination, *Christ and Apollo*.[3] I read the work in my first year of college studies and I still regard it as one of the books most important for my personal growth as a Christian. Christ was tied to the Dionysiac, to a passionate penetration of the definite and finite. Lynch seemed to say that a Jesuit's intellectual life would have to embody that spirit in some way, that it must run risks, that its goal was far grander than the achievement of academic post and prestige. In the course of my training in philosophy and theology in New York, St. Louis, and Tübingen, Germany, I did encounter some Jesuit and non-Jesuit teachers who possessed that passion. I recall especially William Richardson, the Jesuit philosopher who is a distinguished interpreter of Martin Heidegger's thought as well as a psychoanalyst who writes on Jacques Lacan. He was brilliant and fearless, a wonderful model to encounter while a student.[4]

The practice of combining an immersion in tragic events with an analytic observation of them has helped me deal with my major current project of research, the spiritual culture out of which the Nazi destruction of European Jews exploded. For more years than I am able to remember, my life has been haunted by the Holocaust and I am aware of only some of the reasons why. When I began my academic career at Boston College in 1980, my first presentation at a conference and my first published essay aimed to interpret the evildoing of Adolf Eichmann. He was captured when I was fifteen years old and his trial made a strong impression on me. Even more alive for me are the memories of growing up in Washington Heights in northern Manhattan which at the time had the largest concentration of German Jews in the world. Their neighborhood was known as both the Fourth Reich and Frankfurt on the Hudson; the latter has become the title of a major sociological study of that community.[5] These German Jews created an exotic atmosphere with their European accents, their refined bearing, their own old-world shops, and a heavy sense that something went terribly wrong in their lives. I used to walk by them as they sat on the benches in Fort Tryon Park; I recall animated exchanges but laughter not at all. The great dome of Yeshiva University was the largest structure to be seen through the windows of my family's apartment and Yom Kippur was the only day that competed with Good Friday in spreading a blanket of solemnity over those busy, noisy streets. Growing up in that neighborhood in the 1950s, how could I not have wondered about this intense people?

While I was in the Novitiate, I developed a special esteem and devotion for the Jesuit Alfred Delp, who was executed by the Nazis for alleged involvement in the plot to kill Hitler. His book of prison meditations and essays was published in English in 1963 and every year since then I have returned to his meditations on Advent as spiritual reading during that Season. I was drawn to the witness of his personal courage and to his intellectual boldness in joining a group which was thinking out plans for a post-Nazi just society for Germany. That seemed an exemplary demonstration of a specifically Jesuit style of intellectual engagement. I was encouraged in my vocation when I read what he wrote to his Jesuit brothers shortly before his execution: "The actual reason for my condemnation was that I happened to be, and chose to remain, a Jesuit."[6] In 1973 I studied in Berlin and explored the geography of Nazi cruelty, making a pilgrimage to Plötzensee Prison where Delp was hanged on February 2, 1945. When Santa Clara University invited me in 1995 to lecture on my research, I chose February 2 so that I could commemorate the fiftieth anniversary of his death. I have felt Delp's companionship as I have visited Dachau, Auschwitz, and the numerous archives where I have worked to understand the venomous forces which murdered him and so many others.

As I studied Jewish history, I came to appreciate a special intimacy between Jesuits and Jews and to imagine a unique sense of solidarity in suffering which should have emerged from the historical roles they shared. They were both the most frequent victims for those who sought a total, diabolical explanation for how history operated. They formed, as Lacouture has said, a "tragic couple," both demonized in infamous documents: the *Monita Secreta* for the Jesuits, the *Protocols of the Elders of Zion* for the Jews.[7] Their diabolical character was charted on the axes of space and time. Spatially, they operated outside of any specific territory and aspired for domination over the world; they lurked behind thrones at the same time that we were quite willing to overthrow those very kings and nations. Jews and Jesuits were preeminently people of the city and, thus, were regarded as allied to wealth, loose morality, and a cunning, deracinated intelligence which was contemptuous of the traditions of the rural past. Temporally, they were at home in periods of decadence and collapse and, thus, they were perceived as devotees of modernity: the same spectacles which detected the Jesuits as fathering the French revolution saw the Jews as the creators of the Russian one.

This history echoed in Germany in the years leading to and during the period of the Third Reich. Jesuits and Jews were linked often in the propaganda of the Nazis and other right-wing groups. Identified as international in commitment and urban in attitude, both groups were regarded as disloyal to the German State and as subversive of Aryan culture and morality. And while no group's losses can compare with that of the Jews, the enmity against the Jesuits was also murderous: some eighty-three of them were executed by the Nazis, another forty-three died in concentration camps and twenty-six more died in captivity or of its results.[8]

While the analysis of German Christian culture and its role in the Holocaust was emerging as a major intellectual project for me, the particular philosophical style that has shaped it began to take form during my doctorate studies which I did from 1975 to 1980 at the State University of New York at Stony Brook. Stony Brook provided a very stimulating environment in which to work and its faculty's commitment to contemporary philosophy and interdisciplinary perspectives nicely complemented my earlier studies in ancient and medieval texts at Fordham and St. Louis Universities. While at Stony Brook, I began a dissertation on the thought of the French philosopher Michel Foucault (1926–1984). In addition I was able to study with him in 1979 and 1980 in Paris where I also had the opportunity of several personal discussions. While I have had many gifted teachers both in the course of my studies in the Society and as a graduate student, Foucault had a singular impact upon me. From time to time religious people have expressed surprise that I have such a high regard for his thought and I would point to him, as well as to several other so-called postmoderns, as figures who often are demonized in our intellectual culture. In an age of death camps and gulags, Foucault made his readers aware of other prisons, not those which are imposed upon us but those which we fashion for ourselves in the ways we think, especially about the human person. Although his literary talent created more striking phrases, the most arresting for me when I read it was: "l'âme, prison du corps," "the soul is the prison of the body."[9] This shifts perspectives: how a notion of the soul may protect from the passionate depths of human existence only by locking us into the narrow prison of the self. Its bars are formed from the knowledges through which we think of ourselves: how we construct what is reasonable, normal, healthy in opposition to the domains of the unreasonable, abnormal, sick. For Foucault, the prison of the modern soul has exiled our mystery as human beings, and has locked away our differences and strangeness.

My revised dissertation was published as *Michel Foucault's Force of Flight: Toward an Ethics for Thought*.[10] If anything, Foucault's philosophy was a flight, from contemporary systems of knowledge and power, from current ways of identifying with one's self. Getting free of oneself. As ascetics and religious mystics have recognized through the ages, this getting free of oneself, of leaving the prison of one's soul need not guarantee passage to tranquil seas. If many choose a spirituality which despises the world and provides a shelter from it, Foucault was among those others who seek a spiritual existence which will expose them to the contingent mysteries of themselves and others. Such a spirituality might be thought of as that of the parrhesiast, of the one who speaks truthfully about truths. Foucault's delineation of the parrhesiast in his very last courses is the description of a truth-teller dealing with spiritual discernments rather than the experience of truth attached to the roles of prophet, sage, or teacher. This is one of his formulations: *parrhesia* "is a verbal activity in which a speaker expresses his personal relationship to truth, and risks his life because he recognizes truth-telling as a duty to improve or help other people (as well as himself)." Although his treatment of the practice of "parrhesia" was worked out in relation to Greek culture, careful textual review of his sources shows a definite dependence on Christian understandings of "parrhesia" as well. While the frank-speaking of confessional practice is the most evident of these sources, Foucault appreciated how "parrhesia" took on a unique dimension in Christianity: not the political and moral virtues of the ancient world but the special power of courageous openness to the experiences of mystery. This strength was linked to Jesus of Nazareth's full revelation of God and to the person of prayer's openness to the divine realm. For the religious person, this "parrhesia," this availability for spiritual transformation was a grace and the source of both hope and love.

Foucauldian spirituality exhibits these two forces. Foucault possessed a non-ideological hope, a confidence that effective resistance could take place, even against the most entrenched of political or moral systems. Suspicion was an ally of his hope and its protector from ideological fiction and revolutionary excess. His hope is not built on a sense of sin, but it does reflect a Christian realism about human imperfection. I have tried to develop Foucault's potential for Christian thinkers in a collection of essays which I have co-edited and which appeared in early 2004: *Michel Foucault and Theology: The Politics of Religious Experience.*[11] Here I would like to develop the particular problematic of the Holocaust with which I am dealing and my own approach to it in two steps: first, I want to put my investigation in the context of the Catholic Church's recent penitential moment regarding its conduct during the period of the Holocaust; secondly, I would like to indicate a few of the sources within Catholic culture that supported enthusiasm for or indifference to Nazi hate. In the concluding section of the essay, I wish to briefly identify three practical directions that flow from my scholarly work.

I. Catholicism and Judaism

A major stimulus and support for my work as well as its current context is the changing relationship between Catholicism and Judaism which the Second Vatican Council inaugurated but which Pope John Paul II brought to a decisive moment.[12] If my original inspiration for serious involvement with Holocaust studies was the example of Delp, my persistence with them is owed to a sense of obligation, the need for Christians to confess our faults and ask forgiveness for our share of the responsibility for the Holocaust. Man of theater and seismographer of symbols that he was, John Paul II created a religious drama in which Catholics are performing against a backdrop of overwhelming evil, a stage we would gladly exit. But the Pope's pleas in the year 2000 for forgiveness scripted us who are Catholics into his liturgical play before we were very clear about what it is exactly for which we should feel collective responsibility. Still very early into the performance, we may be already aching for catharsis. But why has it taken so long to seek forgiveness? The Catholic Church did not sleepwalk through the last century. It knew a great deal about what was happening to the Jews of Europe during the actual genocide and, in the decades since, the historical record has cast light into many of the darkest recesses. I believe forgiveness is intimately connected to the need for a new beginning but it was precisely that need which was absent in Catholicism for so long, the desire to begin a new relationship with the Jewish people after the Holocaust.

Without such a desire, why plead for forgiveness? The relationship between Christians and Jews seemed theologically frozen, out of time, stranger to those domains where tragedy and sorrow could transform hearts and minds. There were a few who did prepare for the charismatic role seized by John Paul II: the elderly Jewish scholar Jules Isaac, who pressed to meet with John XXIII in order to talk about the Church's historical contempt for the Jews; John's determination to end that disdain; the bishops' 1965 adoption of the "Declaration on the Relationship of the Church to Non-Christian Religions" at the Second Vatican Council.[13] Still it was John Paul II who effected a new relationship with the Jewish people. How it will develop is for the future to disclose but, if we have an appreciation for how the earlier relationship shaped and malformed Christianity, we can sense the radical reinvention that a loving relationship might entail. I would claim, however, that Catholicism's desire for a new beginning with Judaism is also the desire for a new relationship with itself, for a Christianity beyond Christendom. What I mean by Christendom is not a historical epoch but rather a set of attitudes which generated a fortress Christianity. I shall mention but two of them. The first is that Christianity best interpreted itself through a particular form of European culture that asserted its spiritual surpassing of Judaism. The second maintains that the modern world is a definitive repudiation of Christianity and that the Church is responsible for neither its achievements nor its crimes. These distinctions stand behind the continual argument of Church authorities that there is an absolute border between medieval anti-Judaism and modern anti-Semitism. Taking a cue from the philosopher Charles Taylor, I wish to claim that modernity is frequently an embrace rather than an abandonment of Christianity. Taylor gives the example of modern liberal political culture's proclamation of universal human rights as a "great advance in the practical penetration of the gospel in human life."[14] It was a progress that rested upon exit from an earlier version of Christian practice. While Taylor has stressed the positive side of Christianity's survival in modern culture, the murder of European Jews forces us to regard the sometimes toxic effects of that endurance. Anti-Judaism and anti-Semitism interpenetrate in ways that have not yet been adequately mapped. Christendom's contempt of the Jews is not a place from which some mere new set of ideas allows us egress. Like the Holy Roman Empire, Christendom formed an intoxicating, imaginative piece of theater. Only another drama of more than equal appeal will displace it. We are currently experiencing the opening scenes of that new play.

On the first Sunday of the Church's Lenten Season in the new millennium, the Pope presided at an extraordinary service to confess sin and to request forgiveness. At the heart of the service was the seeking of pardon for sins against the Jewish people. Cardinal Edward Cassidy, president of the Vatican Commission for Religious Relations with Jews, opened the prayer: "Let us pray that, in recalling the sufferings endured by the people of Israel throughout history, Christians will acknowledge the sins committed by not a few of their number against the people of the covenant and the blessings, and in this way purify their hearts." The Pope continued: "God of our fathers, you chose Abraham and his descendants to bring your name to the nations: we are deeply saddened by the behavior of those who in the course of history have caused these children of yours to suffer, and asking your forgiveness, we wish to commit ourselves to genuine brotherhood with the people of the covenant." This confession and plea for forgiveness emerged from the Pope's own journey into ever deeper desire for a totally new relationship between Christians and Jews. His pilgrimages to Auschwitz, the Synagogue of Rome, and Austria's Mauthausen Concentration Camp reached their climax in the Pope's visit to Jerusalem in the year 2000 and especially his speech at Yad Vashem, Israel's memorial to the victims of the Holocaust. He attributed Nazi crimes to a "godless ideology," but then expressed the sorrow that he hoped would be the foundation for a new relationship between Christians and Jews. The Pope declared: "As bishop of Rome and successor of the apostle Peter, I assure the Jewish people that the Catholic Church, motivated by the Gospel law of truth and love and by no political considerations, is deeply saddened by the hatred, acts of persecution, and displays of anti-Semitism directed against the Jews by Christians at any time and in any place." Israeli Prime Ehud Minister Barak's reply captured the historical significance of the Pope's admission. "You have done more than anyone else to bring about the historic change in the attitude of the Church toward the Jewish people initiated by the good Pope John XXIII and to dress the gaping wounds that festered over many bitter centuries. And I think I can say, Your Holiness, that your coming here today to the Tent of Remembrance at Yad Vashem is a climax of this historic journey of healing. Here, right now, time itself has come to a standstill. This very moment holds within it 2,000 years of history. And their weight is almost too much to bear."

Pope John Paul II's ministry stands in sharp contrast with that of Pius XII, who bears responsibility for delaying the Catholic Church's confrontation with the Holocaust. Pius XII's address to the College of Cardinals at the end of the war set the tone for the Vatican's approach to Catholic conduct during the Holocaust for the following thirteen years. He presented the Church as a victim, as a survivor of the "sorrowful passion" which Nazi enmity forced upon it. The effect of Pius XII's strategy was to encourage German Church leaders to stress their own sufferings under the Nazis rather than to examine their failures during that period, even though there were strong German Catholic voices demanding such an examination. After 1959 there was to be an amazing transformation in the German Episcopacy's attitude toward the Holocaust. Various reasons account for the change. Pius XII had passed away the year before; almost all of the bishops who had lived during the Third Reich had either died or been replaced; finally, Germans themselves were conducting trials of fellow Germans who had committed atrocities during the war. On the occasion of the Eichmann trial in 1961, the German bishops requested atonement for the crimes against the Jewish people and composed a prayer for those who had been murdered. This request for atonement was repeated a year later in a pastoral letter released on the eve of the Vatican Council's opening. This period after Pius XII culminated at Vatican Council II when the German Jesuit Cardinal Augustin Bea gave a speech calling for a new relationship with the Jewish people and linked his support for a Conciliar declaration to the Nazi genocide of the Jews. When the declaration was adopted, the German bishops at the Council made a special statement welcoming it and they also pointed to the genocide as part of its context. In the years immediately leading up to the Pope's plea for forgiveness, there were important penitential statements made by European Episcopal Conferences.[15] In its own statement the Vatican did admit guilt: "We deeply regret the errors and failures of those sons and daughters of the Church." The statement deplored racism and anti-semitism, expressed its sorrow for its members' failures and declared itself an "act of repentance" (teshuvah).[16]

The power of Pope John Paul II's seeking of forgiveness is that he brings Catholics with him. As a Jesuit, I feel that his acts and pleas challenge me personally and the Society of Jesus collectively, that we are forced to deal with our history in a new way. The Jesuits too must purify their memory and to do so we need greater understanding of our dealings with the Jewish people. There is work which honors those Jesuits who were killed by the Nazis, those who rescued Jews, and those who have been recognized as righteous gentiles by Israel's Yad Vashem memorial. But the historical experience of Jesuits with Jews is shadowed by shameful conduct as well. The opening moment in the Jewish-Jesuit encounter was both a stance of courage and a leap into cowardice. Ignatius's devotion to the personal figure of Jesus saved him, and initially the Society, from a most common prejudice: the view that Jewish converts to Christianity and their descendants, the so called "New Christians" of Spain, were more Jewish than Christian for they were of impure blood. Such tainted character justified their exclusion from Church posts and religious orders. Ignatius courageously resisted ecclesiastical and political pressures and refused to exclude Jewish converts or their descendants from the Society's ranks and, thus, some of the most distinguished early Jesuits were ethnically Jewish.[17] Unfortunately, the Society was to abandon its founder's courage and in 1593, under pressure from its own members, banned the admission of all with "Hebrew or Saracen stock"; not even the General of the Order could dispense from this impediment of origin. To my knowledge, no systematic effort has been made to trace the effect on Jesuits of this transformation in the attitude toward Jewish heritage from one of honor to that of burden. Only in 1946 did the Twenty-ninth General Congregation abrogate the exclusion but without any explanation of why it was done. The principle of excluding Jews from the Society helps to account for the posture of the single Jesuit institution which evokes the strongest Jewish repulsion: the journal *La Civiltà Cattolica,* which has long been accused of the most vulgar anti-Judaism in many of its articles. Jesuits should not be surprised that for one major Jewish thinker, anti-semitism was indeed the special charism of the Society: "It was the Jesuits who had always best represented, both in the written and spoken word, the antise-mitic school of the Catholic clergy."[18]

There is another institution which needs to be considered in any treatment of Jewish-Jesuit relations, the Papacy. Although Pope Pius XII has become the center of controversy in discussions on the Holocaust, what is really at issue for Jesuits is the special and ongoing relationship which they have had with the Papacy since their restoration as an Order in the nineteenth century. The Vatican's assault upon the modern age's liberalism and democracy, and the Society's service to that polemic as well as to an ultramontane Papacy is a very heavy burden for them. This was the age of the Papal rejection of modernism and of Vatican authorship of the Syllabus of Errors. Sadly, the enemy of the Church was often identified with emancipated Jewry or Jewish influences. Now that Jews had rights in modern society, it was claimed that special pre-cautions were necessary in order to preserve Christian stability. Jews became a convenient target for the denunciation of a culture which was marginalizing the Catholic Church, and attacking them provided a handy vehicle for pro-tecting Catholic identity. Jesuits and Jews are heirs to a history of polemics which made both groups dangerously vulnerable to political assault.

Saul Friedländer, certainly one of the greatest scholars of the Holocaust, has written of "the historian's paralysis" that the Shoah has created: the inability to think the heterogeneous phenomena of Nazism: "messianic fanaticism and bureaucratic structures, pathological impulses and administrative decrees, ar-chaic attitudes within an advanced industrial society." He is not afraid of drawing the possible implication of National Socialism's complexity: We may be led to the "conclusion that the destruction of European Jewry poses a prob-lem which historical analysis and understanding may not be able to over-come." Friedländer has sighted the territory of a modernity that is not beyond Christianity and a Catholicism that is not independent of the modern age. A more critical historical analysis will certainly have its tasks to perform there. But that place is also where the dynamics of confessing fault, seeking forgive-ness and doing penance provide a guide to the operations of sin. But, just as Friedländer has, the Vatican recognizes the limit of mere historical data: The Shoah "cannot be fully measured by the ordinary criteria of historical research alone. It calls for a 'moral and religious memory' and, particularly among

Christians, a very serious reflection on what gave rise to it."[19] John Paul II's pilgrimages are at the center of that memory, a memory which is a reminder that it is we who permit those toxic vapors to determine our feelings and deeds. The Catholic search for forgiveness is a summons to responsibility and to awareness of how dangerous religious faith and spiritual commitment is.

II. On the Nazi Persecution of Jewish and Gay People

As a result of several years of research on National Socialism, I have discovered the strength and, even more, the promise of the project which Foucault originally conceived as a history of sexuality.[20] I am among many who are trying to have Foucault cast some light on German's dark descent into Nazi barbarism. Indeed it could be argued that Foucault's various investigations were invited by Nazism's demolition of the presumed barriers between the social and the personal, the private and the public, the erotic and the political. My own work has studied how a form of Christian eroticism was involved in the Nazi destruction of Jewish and gay people.

Inasmuch as this theme might offend some, I should offer an explanation for my choice. It was at a Holocaust conference several years ago that I was first made aware of the strong negative reactions which could be produced by comments that placed Jews and gays together in their experience under National Socialism. During the final panel discussion in which the conference's major speakers were present, a young man from the audience asked very politely why none of the presentations had dealt with Nazi crimes against homosexuals. In response, one of the panelists erupted in a burning anger and scolded the man for even suggesting that there was something comparable in the destiny of the two groups. The large audience was clearly embarrassed by the outburst and other questioners were immediately recognized. As I have come to discover, the panelist's reaction is not unique. Certainly there are many inappropriate ways to speak about the victimization of these two groups, especially in terms which would fail to do justice to the unique magnitude of Jewish losses and the special place which Jews occupied as objects of Nazi hate. And yet there might be a much deeper issue which we should acknowledge in the resistance to dealing with the two groups together. An analysis of Jewish and gay experience together leads to a direct consideration of the sexual and erotic dimensions of fascism. In my work, I have tried to sketch how a Christian, particularly Catholic, experience of sexuality and a style of moral formation that was its issue might have contributed to the popular appeal of National Socialism, to the identification of two groups of its enemies, as well as to the savagery of its violence.

How was it possible for National Socialism to be so successful in capturing the minds and hearts of so many either as committed believers or as tolerant bystanders? The Nazi period forces us to confront how we fashion ourselves, or are fashioned, intellectually, ethically, spiritually to appreciate or refuse certain types of moral appeal. Such character is the product of what might be called practices of the self, practices which define how an individual comes to feel that a matter warrants moral concern and what steps one is obligated to take in response to that moral signal. Certainly it is the case that National Socialism appropriated a ready-made set of national virtues—honesty, diligence, cleanliness, dependability, obedience to authority, mistrust of excess. Still, if we are to understand why these virtues came to be so characteristic and why people were so prepared to tolerate evil, we must interrogate the dynamics of the spiritual formation which German culture had passed down. To speak of spiritual life at this time might seem to miss the mark when one remembers the brutal reality of Nazi deeds. What has to be faced, though, is that the beginning of the Hitler regime coincided with a passionate desire among the German people for a spiritual renewal, indeed for a politics of spirit which National Socialism attempted to define. Perhaps that crisis's most important element was how one was to relate to one's self, how one might affirm oneself as spiritually worthwhile. But to speak of spirit in the context of a culture which still possessed deep roots in Christianity was also to discuss flesh; cravings for spirit inevitably connect to a discourse of sin, sensuality, and sexuality. If spirit expressed vitality and creative force, flesh possessed many satanic features, assaulting reason and proclaiming human weakness. Here we may have, though, perhaps the source of Christianity's own greatest weakness in its encounter with Nazism, for much pathology seemed to flourish in modern religious culture's charting of sexuality. It is the charting with which I am concerned, not the sexual morality that may be put forward as a response to it. I am not accusing a code of morality as such but rather the ethical-spiritual foundations of the very self who finds suitable a type of morality or its overthrow. Having selected sexuality as the privileged route to moral status, the Churches did not create a very sophisticated palette of insight into it. The broodings of moral theology were isolated from the traditions of Christian spiritual theology and, thus, those interrogations of extreme experiences that might have enabled it to cope better with the psychic forces Nazism was evoking. The Church's determination to exorcise eroticism encouraged such a fierce self-hatred that we can understand why Delp's friend and fellow resister, Helmuth James von Moltke, found one thing to praise in Nazi culture: it taught, he said, a reverence for what is below us—"blood, ancestry, our bodies."

The Church saw in modernity's relaxation of sexual moral codes a decline of faith and, thus, a historical intimacy between Christian existence and the spirit-flesh struggle was reconfirmed and strengthened, now with modern sexuality as its unchallenged center. The pivotal role which Christian moral formation conferred upon disciplining sexuality as a result of this had two major consequences. First, it exposed Christians to a Nazism that could be thought of as either ethically allied with Christianity or as a liberation from religion's inadequacy to the richness of human life. National Socialism found the religious obsessiveness with sexuality in moral formation to be helpful in a variety of ways: it sustained the emphasis on those secondary virtues which made people so compliant; it habituated people to an atmosphere of omnipresent sinfulness which seemed to grow with every step beyond childhood; it educated people into a moral pessimism about themselves and what they might be able to achieve. This was all too often a formation in self-contempt, in a fearfulness which was a paralysis of the inner self. Frequently the sexual dimension of the person was treated as an animal instinct. Such paralysis subverted self-affirmation as a Christian practice. It is this subversion which lies behind the primacy given to obedience as a virtue, and an extraordinary insensitivity to the demands of conscience. Many religious and moral practices established a profound alienation from one's self and one's desires. And this self-alienation was also a mode of alienation from the public space: the model for dealing with moral difficulty was set by sexuality: avoidance of danger and cultivation of an ethereal interiority. Often this trained people into a permanent submissiveness or stimulated an intense yearning to get beyond the sexual guilt of Christianity, a state which Nazism held out as one of its promises and, in case after case, accomplishments.

Nazism in effect put forward the bold project of overcoming the dualisms fostered by religion: body versus soul, flesh versus spirit. The Nazi revolution bound together a celebration of inwardness, of the German spirit, with a profound affirmation of one's historical moment, of one's own German body, social and personal. It was to be praised for its health, its beauty, its utility and, most of all, as the temple for the transmission of biological life. The depth of its sexual morality could be put forward as what is most distinctive of Aryan ethics. In Nazism we have a psycho-politics which is also an erotic politics. Its erotic politics was a strategy of sabotage against alternative relations to sexuality. It made a foe of the sexual libertinism of the Weimar Republic and of the Soviet Union. The sexual laxity which had been identified in the past with that ancient enemy, the French, now was tied to Communism's relaxation of legal restraints. After it had replaced the Weimar Republic, the Third Reich mounted a widespread campaign of sexual purification: denunciations of pornography, homosexuality, and any eroticism not governed by the desire for procreation, for those would eclipse the central status which sexuality had on the "battlefield of life." This crusade against eroticism was terribly attractive for German Christians—and, I might add, made Hitler appear as a force for moral renewal to Christians in the United States as well. Catholic anxiety about Communism included its perceived sexual license and hostility to family values. Thus, on the eve of the Second World War and the Holocaust, Germany was blanketed with a campaign for decency.

The catastrophe of this moral formation had a second face. In that endless searching after the reasons for why the Jews were so victimized by the Nazis, for why so many collaborated in their murder, and especially for why so many stood aside and failed to do what could have been done, I propose that this issue of sexuality gives an essential answer. Before the Jews were murdered, before they were turned away from as not being one's concern, the Jew had already been defined as spiritless, on the one hand, and sexually possessed, erotically charged on the other hand. The Jew was portrayed not only as empty of spirit but as an enemy of it. Deprived of spirit, the Jew was defined in Nazi propaganda as essentially carnal, as excessively sexual, indeed as boundlessly erotic, whose conduct was not under the control of the moral conscience. Lust robbed the Jews of reason and, thus, reduced them to an animal level, a status which would soon come to be reflected in the forms of Nazi torture. And gay people would face similar punishment.

It was in their customary depiction of Jews and gays as an erotic flood that the Nazis spoke to Christian anxieties about the sexual climate of their culture. If we look for the reasons why so few people were troubled about standing on the sidelines, why so many failed to get involved with the victimized Jew, practically or even emotionally, I would claim that this is certainly a major source of that moral indifference. For the Germans who were proud of that spiritual inwardness which was the legacy of their culture and who were humiliated by the sexual war which was waged in their bodies, the carnal Jew represented a contamination, the destruction of the spiritual sense and the eruption of the uncontrollable erotic body. In the light of the predominant Christian style of moral formation, one could have predicted that, even while protests were mounted on behalf of the crippled and the insane, the Jews would be abandoned. Perhaps not since Christianity absorbed pagan religiosity had a radical movement been so successful in absorbing common national virtues, which, at times, were even defended by Christians as particularly appropriate to the religious sensibility. But these so-called secondary virtues were appealing to people and were developed by them because they were eminently suitable for a struggle with one's flesh, that other self which had to be subdued. This campaign's instrumentalization and depersonalization of sexuality was a principal source of that doubling process which some have argued is the key to appreciating how average citizens could function with a good conscience while contributing to mass murder. No less than the homosexual, the Jew, the Nazi, and the Christian possessed sexual identities for a fascist theory and practice which operated in terms of a certain logic of spirit-flesh. National Socialism forged a regime of erotic danger, a manner of relating to sexual life which was less indebted to biology than it was to an inherited sphere of spirituality, the struggle of spirit with flesh. Within that field, Nazism presented itself as overcoming dualisms: a Christian alienation of the soul from the body and a Jewish alienation of the carnal from the spiritual. An Aryan, sexual identity became the refuge from a weak nation-state identity that was joined with the project to destroy all traditional religious identity. My work explores how our most foundational images and concepts for intimate and public lives may contain those seeds of hate and violence which could come to flourish almost automatically in certain cultural crises. The spirit-flesh paradigm was just such a seed. Its operation in the era of National Socialism should lead us to a more comprehensive affirmation of the human being's dignity as sexually embodied and differently so.

III. Conclusion

My academic work has led me to practices that define my relationship as a Jesuit to the Jewish community, to my undergraduate students and to my own grasp of the ongoing character of Jesuit identity. I would like to conclude this essay by several remarks on each of these.

1. The Jewish-Christian Dialogue[21]

A challenging refrain of General Congregation 34 is its call to a pilgrim Society for dialogue with other faiths: the sharing of the joys and sorrows of our common human journey; cooperation in the development and liberation of peoples; the exchange of spiritual experience and theological insight.[22] For me, the most striking of the dialogues to which the Congregation calls is that with the Jewish people:

> Dialogue with the Jewish people holds a unique place. The first covenant, which is theirs and which Jesus the Messiah came to fulfill, "has never been revoked." A shared history both unites us with and divides us from our elder brothers and sisters, the Jewish people, in whom and through whom God continues to act for the salvation of the world. Dialogue with the Jewish people enables us to become more fully aware of our identity as Christians.[23]

There is special importance to this call. It represents a step toward the task of accurately understanding the often difficult history of the Society's relationship to the Jewish community. In addition, this call establishes a supportive relationship with what to my mind was the single most progressive development of John Paul II's Papacy, its effort to establish a new kinship with the Jewish people, which led him to recognize the State of Israel and to visit the Synagogue of Rome. On that occasion he declared that the

> Church of Christ discovers her "bond" with Judaism by "searching into her own mystery." The Jewish religion is not "extrinsic" to us, but in a certain way is "intrinsic" to our own religion. With Judaism, therefore, we have a relationship which we do not have with any other religion.[24]

I was especially pleased by the invitation because I have tried to make Jewish-Christian reconciliation a cornerstone of my own ministry as teacher and scholar. For several years I have taught a course on the Holocaust in which I explore the ethical attitudes of the people who experienced this ruinous event. Although Christianity has not turned its back on the Holocaust, as have most other western institutions, the Churches all too often regard the event with far too innocent an eye, a naiveté that should incite a self-doubt. The Christian faith has sustained, throughout its long history, a clear vision of evil as an ineffaceable, ever-threatening force. Thus Christianity should have been especially alert to the dynamics of Nazism's mass appeal and, later, it should have been particularly empowered to provide insight into the horrors that exploded from the European heart in this century. Whether we are Jews or Christians, believers or nonbelievers, we are in obvious need of new paths on which understanding might advance in its comprehension of the Holocaust and what was done right or wrong within its shadow. Certainly one of the most significant of the current dialogues between Christians and Jews is discussion about the Holocaust.

2. Incarnational Education

As a teacher, I have sought for a more adequate educational integration of the ethical and the intellectual than the average classroom provides. I meet God in the searching and loving lives of my students. For that meeting to pass from the notional to the real required two steps. First, it took me far longer than it should have for me to grasp that I was teaching people and not a field of study. Secondly, I had to find a context where students could learn as full persons. Fortunately, since 1969 Boston College has had a program named "Pulse" which provides that personal situation and, consequently, I have done most of my undergraduate teaching in a course which integrates theology and philosophy with a student's commitment of ten to twelve hours of service to the local communities. They are engaged in carefully supervised service which includes mentoring for troubled adolescents, a visiting program to the elderly and those living with AIDS, tutoring young children, and working at homeless shelters. As I have mentioned, Ignatius the soldier is not a very appealing figure for me but there is one important incident in his military life which my undergraduate students have given me new respect for: the severe wounding which he received fighting at Pamplona in 1521 which slowed him down and forced him to reexamine the direction his life was following.[25] My students have taught me how important a source of education are wounds, those which they confront, through their placements, in society and in the broken personal lives of the people they try to assist. The spiritual growth is visible as the students integrate their experiences through papers and journals with such ancient and contemporary texts as the *Book of Job*, Frankl's *Man's Search for Meaning*, Arendt's *The Human Condition*.[26] Working through the suffering of writers searching to capture the meaning of events and through the pain of people confronting raw experiences today, students are brought to the possibility of a choice: a philosophical way of living which separates neither thought from action nor one's personal journey from service to the human family.

This is an incarnational education and the students become worldly, better able to accomplish something worthwhile in the world and most especially to develop the parrhesia which enables them to speak authentically about experiences which are far too often turned into ghosts by social analysis. GC 34's reaffirmation of the Society's commitment to the ideal of a faith which does justice was very important to me both as Jesuit and philosopher and I see that it was a "particular grace" which GC 32 gave us in that commitment.[27] This faith is the source of the pedagogical conviction of the Congregation: "Profound experience is what changes us. We can break out of our habitual way of living and thinking only through physical and emotional proximity to the way of living and thinking of the poor and marginalized."[28] Encountering those experiences continually through my students, I am brought to the central experience of the *Spiritual Exercises* and of religious conviction: the sublime supremacy of the personal dimension, of our hunger to touch the real, of our passion to make the decision on how to lead our lives only in the presence of God.

3. Jesuit Identity

Finally, my major intellectual projects, and the research to which they led me, force me to question and to refashion two of the major traits which have traditionally defined Jesuit identity: its ideal of obedience and its understanding of chastity. First, I wish to mention obedience. One of the clearest insights we have gained from the terrible events of twentieth-century totalitarianism is the mortal danger of obedience as an ideal. We have vivid memory of that era's many criminals who excused their conduct by appeal to their obligation to obey orders. But beyond them there are the countless others who embraced passivity in the face of evil because of an ordinary respect for hierarchy and authority. The Society's tradition has been an influential force in blessing a conformist mindset and in sanctifying hierarchial structure. Ignatius of Loyola's 1553 letter on obedience and the Society's *Constitutions* forged demonic expressions as a legacy to future history. The letter puts forward an ideal of responding to an order by proceeding "blindly, without inquiry of any kind, to the carrying out of the command, with a kind of passion to obey." The Constitutions adopt an infamous image for this passion: "We ought to act on the principle that everyone who lives under obedience should let himself be carried and directed by Divine Providence through the agency of the superior as if he were a lifeless body, which allows itself to be carried to any place and treated in any way."[29] Rhetorically, Jesuit documents are one of the sources for that cadaver obedience (*Kadavergehorsam*) which became such a prominent idol in the moral pantheon of Nazism. We do know that Jesuit obedience appealed to the Nazi mass murderer Heinrich Himmler and paralleled for him the discipline of his own S.S. organization.[30]

As far as the early Society is concerned, John O'Malley points out that, despite such statements, the actual practice of obedience "correlated poorly with the authoritarian vocabulary the Jesuits used when they spoke of it in theoretical terms."[31] That lack of correlation then was due to the concrete needs of widely dispersed enterprises that were far from central headquarters. In more recent years, the major changes in the Society that came during the 1960s and 1970s most often emerged from contesting the rules that had been established by authority. An important study of the changes in Jesuit formation during that period argues that they were not "an orderly reform initiated by authority" but rather a "revolution coming from below."[32] Perhaps only another revolution from below will be able to adequately criticize the nature and impact of some of our major documents on obedience. It may be a sign of hope that, while producing statements on chastity and poverty, the Thirty-fourth General Congregation of the Society avoided any document on obedience and the term is not even listed in the index of topics for that 1995 meeting. Still, there is need for formal renunciation of a rhetoric, and often a practice, that appealed to some of the most anti-Christian ideologies.

If the Jesuit tradition has spoken of obedience in the ways that it has, perhaps a major source for that has been Christianity's frequent denigration of the sexual and the bodily. With respect to chastity and celibacy, the Society is in the same situation as many organizations influenced by Christian teaching.

We are watching an earlier ecclesiastical approach to the sexual wither away while there is coming to birth a new sexual culture in which the bodily is freshly appreciated. As the result of a more sophisticated historical record regarding the cultural construction of sexuality, we have more adequate knowledge of the price that was exacted by the vision of a spirit-flesh struggle that was interpreted as a dualism between the body and the soul. A portion of that price was a vision of masculinity that identified the male nature with reason and made men superior to women by that fact. Even a theologian of the stature of John Courtney Murray could adopt such a vision: "More importantly, it is woman who offers man the possibility of leadership, of entering into his native inheritance of rule—of realizing himself as head, *Logos*, the priciple of order, which by ordering life rules it. Woman is life, but not *Logos*, not the principle of order." "Man does not know himself aright until he knows he is the head of woman, set above her, having her under his government. This is his part and person; and if he resigns it, he resigns his manhood."[33]

The other side of that masculinity was an ideal of self-control and self-possession that was very distant from a sacrifical life inspired by the Gospel. As Michael Mahon writes: the ascetical practices that were advocated by modern Catholic morality

> have nothing in common with the path of kenosis, of self-emptying, of self-denial; instead the function of such practices of self-control is precisely to constitute the self positively as detached, hardened, impenetrable, impermeable, and distinctively masculine. The self-control they advocate is much closer to the opposite of Christian kenosis. The Judeo-Christian scriptures reveal God as the lover: God actively pursues humanity, desiring to penetrate us with his grace. The human task then is to open oneself, to allow oneself to be penetrated.[34]

Jesuit chastity will increasingly be articulated as a dimension of friendship; as a form of sexuality, his celibacy will be evaluated not just in terms of the service it facilitates but also in terms of the joy and liberation this commitment brings to the Jesuit's life and the lives of his friends. My involvement with Foucault's work has wonderfully enlarged my circle of interlocutors and friends far beyond what I would have anticipated as a priest who teaches philosophy. Many find a powerful, liberating voice in Foucault, especially those who are committed to major social transformation. Among them feminists and gay men and women are particularly numerous. A joy for my life has been the emergence of an openly gay movement in America and in the Catholic Church. It would be premature to state how it will ultimately transform both secular and religious life. Personally I am finding this moment to be a rich spiritual experience and the Jesuit vocation is a blessed way of participating in it. We Jesuits are not ecclesiastical border police and, thus, we may live our lives beyond old mappings, those between Jews and Christians and those which simplify the amazing diversity of erotically graced children of God.

Notes

1. *The Spiritual Exercises of St. Ignatius*, ed. Louis Puhl (Chicago: Loyola University Press, 1951), 101–3.
2. James Bernauer, S.J., ed., *Amor Mundi: Explorations in the Faith and Thought of Hannah Arendt* (Boston: Martinus Nijhoff, 1987). This volume approached Arendt apart from the strictly modern and secular assumptions which ordinarily guide interpretations of her work. My own essay in the volume atttempted to uncover the faith which was operating as a fundamental dimension in her thought. It argued that despite her frequent criticism of religious viewpoints, Arendt was preoccupied by the issue of faith and the necessity for its survival beyond the modern crisis of institutional religion.
3. *Christ and Apollo* (New York: Sheed and Ward, 1960).
4. For a general autobiographical statement, see William Richardson, "An Unpurloined Autobiography," in *Portraits of American Continental Philosophers*, ed. James Watson (Bloomington: Indiana University Press, 1999), 144–52.
5. Steven Lowenstein, *Frankfurt on the Hudson: The German-Jewish Community of Washington Heights, 1933–1983, Its Structure and Culture* (Detroit: Wayne State University Press, 1989).
6. *The Prison Meditations of Alfred Delp* (New York: Macmillan, 1963), 166. I was pleasantly surprised a few years ago to discover that his mother's maiden name was Bernauer.
7. Jean Lacouture, *Jesuits: A Multibiography* (Washington, D.C.: Counterpoint, 1995), 176.
8. These figures are taken from Vincent Lapomarda's *The Jesuits and the Third Reich* (Lewiston, N.Y.: Edwin Mellen Press, 1989).
9. Michel Foucault, *Discipline and Punish: The Birth of the Prison* (New York: Pantheon, 1977), 30.
10. (Atlantic Highlands, N.J.: Humanities Press, 1990). With the disappearance of Humanities Press, it was reissued as a volume of Humanity Books, an imprint of Prometheus Books in Amherst, New York.
11. Coedited with Jeremy Carrette (London: Ashgate Publishing, 2004).
12. Portions of this section appeared in my essay "Catholicism's Emerging Post-Shoah Tradition: The Case of the Jesuits," *Remembering for the Future: The Holocaust in an Age of Genocide*, ed. John K. Roth and Elisabeth Maxwell (Hampshire, U.K.: Palgrave, 2001), 381–95. Full documentation for its claims may be found there.
13. See Jules Isaac, *The Teaching of Contempt: Christian Roots of Anti-Semitism* (New York: McGraw-Hill, 1965).
14. James Heft, ed., *A Catholic Modernity? Charles Taylor's Marianist Award Lecture* (New York: Oxford University Press, 1999), 18.

15. They may be consulted in *Catholics Remember the Holocaust* (Washington, D.C.: National Conference of Catholic Bishops, 1998).

16. "We Remember: A Reflection on the Shoah," *Catholics Remember the Holocaust* (Washington, D.C.: National Conference of Catholic Bishops, 1998), 52–53.

17. See James W. Reites, "St. Ignatius of Loyola and the Jews," *Studies in the Spirituality of the Jesuits* 13, no. 4 (September, 1981). However, Ignatius too was a man of his times and when it came to the matter of Jews who were not and did not wish to become Christians, he could support the oppressive policy of ghettoization imposed by Pope Paul IV in his 1555 "Cum nimis absurdum."

18. Hannah Arendt, *The Origins of Totalitarianism* (New York: Harcourt, Brace and Company, 1976 new edition), 102.

19. "We Remember: A Reflection on the Shoah," *Catholics Remember the Holocaust*, 49.

20. This section is a greatly abbreviated revision of my essay "Sexuality in the Nazi War Against Jewish and Gay People: A Foucauldian Perspective," *Budhi* 2, no. 3 (1998): 149–68. Full documentation for its claims may be found there.

21. This section and the next on incarnational education are revised statements of points which I made in "Meeting God: From Ignatius of Loyola to Michel Foucault," *Promise Renewed: Jesuit Higher Education for a New Millennium* (Chicago: Loyola University Press, 1999), 245–55.

22. Decree 5: "Our Mission and Interreligious Dialogue," no. 131, *Documents of the Thirty-Fourth General Congregation of the Society of Jesus* (St. Louis: The Institute of Jesuit Sources, 1995).

23. "Our Mission and Interreligious Dialogue," no. 149.

24. "Address by the Pope" (April 13, 1986), in Pope John Paul II, *Spiritual Pilgrimage: Texts on Jews and Judaism 1979–1995*, ed. Eugene Fisher and Leon Klenicki (New York: Crossroad, 1995), 63.

25. See *The Autobiography of St. Ignatius Loyola*, ed. John Olin (New York: Harper Torchbooks, 1974), 21–26.

26. Viktor Frankl, *Man's Search for Meaning* (New York: Washington Square Press, 1985); H. Arendt, *The Human Condition* (Chicago: University of Chicago Press, 1958).

27. General Congregation 34, Decree 2: "Servants of Christ's Mission," no. 32.

28. General Congregation 34, Decree 9: "Poverty," no. 287. Also see Decree 13: "Cooperation with the Laity in Mission," no. 338.

29. "Letter to the Members of the Society of Portugal," *Letters of St. Ignatius of Loyola: Selected and Translated by William J. Young, S.J.* (Chicago: Loyola University Press, 1959), 294; *The Constitutions of the Society of Jesus* (St. Louis: Institute of Jesuit Sources, 1966), part 6, ch. 1, [547] 222.

30. Richard Breitman and Shlomo Aronson, "Eine unbekannte Himmler-Rede vom Januar 1943," *Vierteljahrshefte für Zeitgeschichte* 13, no. 2 (April 1990): 342.

31. *The First Jesuits* (Cambridge, Mass.: Harvard University Press, 1993), 354.

32. Joseph Becker, *The Re-Formed Jesuits: A History of Changes in Jesuit Formation During the Decade 1965–1975*, vol. 2 (San Francisco: Ignatius Press, 1992), 69.

33. John Courtney Murray, "The Danger of the Vows," *Woodstock Letters* 96 (February 1967): 423, 424.

34. Michael Mahon, "Catholic Sex," in *Michel Foucault and Theology: The Politics of Religious Experience*, ed. James Bernauer and Jeremy Carrette (London: Ashgate, 2005), 260.

7

Studying Physics and Jesuit Life: Worldliness and Life as an Immigrant

Ronald Anderson, S.J.

Most people are principally aware of one culture, one setting, one home; exiles are aware of at least two, and this plurality of vision gives rise to an awareness of simultaneous dimensions, an awareness that—to borrow a phrase from music—is *contrapuntal*. For an exile, habits of life, expression, or activity in the new environment inevitably occur against the memory of these things in another environment. Thus both the new and the old environment are vivid, actual, occurring together contrapuntally. There is a unique pleasure in this sort of apprehension.

Edward Said[1]

The empirical basis of objective science has thus nothing 'absolute' about it. Science does not rest upon rock-bottom. The bold structure of its theories rises, as it were, above a swamp. It is like a building erected on piles. The piles are driven down from above into the swamp, but not down to any natural or given base; and when we cease our attempts to drive our piles into a deeper layer, it is not because we have reached firm ground. We simply stop when we are satisfied that they are firm enough to carry the structure, at least for the time being.

Karl Popper[2]

I. On the Autobiographic Project

WHEN IN NEW SETTINGS inquiries are made about the origins of my accent and I venture an explanation of how its layers have arisen from the countries woven into my life, I am gently reminded of my immigrant status to the country that's now my home. Having had more than one setting and home in my life, the passage above from Edward Said recently caught my attention and led me further into his writings on the nature of exile in search of a set of resources for weaving together the threads of my life story for this volume. In even a broader sense, to have been reading Said, a literary and cultural theorist, in the first place in the context of one of my present disciplinary homes— that of historian of mathematical physics in Victorian England—was to be reading as an immigrant, in this case across disciplinary boundaries.

The richness of the notion of exile in Said's writings as I was to find lies in how it functions on more than one level; on the actual level of a material home, but also in a wider sense as a metaphor for the attitude of the intellectual:

> The pattern that sets the course for the intellectual as outsider is best exemplified by the condition of exile, the state of never being fully adjusted, always feeling outside the chatty, familiar world inhabited by natives. . . . Exile for the intellectual in this metaphysical sense is restlessness, movement, constantly being unsettled, and unsettling others. You cannot go back to some earlier and perhaps more stable condition of being at home; and, alas, you can never fully arrive, be at one in your new home or situation.[3]

I've usually become at home in the places in which I have lived. Nevertheless, an interpretative stance invoking the condition of exile, of being the outsider, never fully arrived, yielded a perspective that is sufficiently loose and flexible to use for an autobiographic project to embrace and fashion into a unity the diverse elements in my life. It turned out to be a perspective that locates and brings into relief places—disciplines, intellectual projects within disciplines, homes, and Jesuit life—and their interrelatedness, and suggests resources for sketching a spirituality. Moreover, and in a related way, my work as an historian of physics has made me alert to how contexts of all sorts, from direct material ones to larger cultural forces, find their way directly into actual practices of physics and in forming the abstract structures of theories. Exploring that sort of connectedness in my own life is immediately attractive, especially where the dangers of using a particular interpretative stance are muted by the restless and destabilizing reflectivity woven into the perspective of being an immigrant. My resonance with Said probably arises from aspects of life that were formed in my early years. One must have been that I was the youngest by seven years in my family, with two older brothers. Their sporting successes in football and more outgoing personalities added to the age difference to the extent that to me they lived in worlds to which I was an outsider.

As Said well recognizes in the essay from where the opening quotation is drawn, the state of the immigrant and the émigré does not possess the full pathos of the exile, with its involuntary element. And admittedly there's nothing in my life that represents the state of exile that vast numbers at our present time have experienced. Yet much in Said's exposition can carry over. In addition, his celebration of the exile provides a positive way to see the enrichment of a phenomenon that at times can seem like a loss. For Said too the condition of the exile, of homelessness, has an essential link to a worldliness, a notion that represents for Said "a knowing and unafraid attitude towards exploring the world we live in."[4] In several places he quotes Hugo of St. Victor: "The man who finds his homeland sweet is still a tender beginner; he to whom every soil is as his native one is already strong; but he is perfect to whom the entire world is as a foreign land."[5] And quoting Eric Auerbach, Said develops the close connection of such a person in a state of homelessness, paradoxically, to one in love with the world: "the ascetic code of willed homelessness is 'a good way also for one who wishes to earn a proper love for the world'"[6]—a set of qualities and observations with deep resonances to the spirituality of the Jesuit order that forms my home.

For me another theme closely tied to that of homes and immigrating is that of foundations. I have found myself searching for these while always confronting their ever-receding nature. Karl Popper's striking architectural metaphor likening the structure of science to foundations in a swamp captures some of the complex and elusive nature foundations have played in my life. And the spatial imagery inherent in the notion of foundations provides resources from the perspective of the contemporary geographer to map connections and to trace centers and boundaries. As Edward Soja remarks, the historical imagination (which surely dominates autobiography) is "never completely spaceless" and "'life-stories' have a geography too: they have milieux, immediate locales, provocative emplacements which affect thought and action."[7] Here too, like Said's notion of exile, the metaphor can apply in a wider sense than to grounding in a locale: it can point to the nature of knowledge itself, and in my case also to the living of Jesuit life and the forming of a viable spirituality.

As the passages from Said suggest, reflective stances are often brought about by encounters with different cultures and perspectives. One such encounter, whose outcome indirectly gave rise to this exercise of reflective exploration of Jesuit life, arose in the late 1980s in Jesuit planning at Boston College. At issue was the establishment of a research institute with a particular focus on religious matters within the context of academic disciplines that a couple of us had proposed.[8] One key question was what sort of administrative base was most appropriate for such an institute, a related question being the Jesuit role in its running.

A complex series of discussions ensued within the Jesuit Community on these questions, bearing histories of the issues attending the complex creation decades ago of the present Jesuit affiliated Institutions of Higher Education with administration structures separate from those of Jesuit governance. The process also provided me with a new experience of an exercise of power on a matter to do with my Jesuit life, an exercise that was spread over the governance structures of the university, independent of Jesuit life, and those within my Jesuit Order. In addition, both of these issues provided a new recognition for me of the significance of generational differences within my Jesuit life (one that maps to the powerful explanatory role generational differences play in understanding U.S. culture and its vitality). The outcome of the discussions was the location of the institute fully within the administrative context of the university; the Jesuit Institute. For those of us who saw alternative configurations that would have preserved the same values, the outcome focused the issue of Jesuit identity within academic settings in a new and critical way.

The aftermath led to an alternative venture, carrying some of the original hopes of the research Institute as initially conceived, a project we entitled "Jesuit Scholarship in a Postmodern Age." A manifesto type statement by Francis Clooney and myself in 1990 to initiate a new conversation spelled out features of the new worlds we found ourselves in, worlds markedly different from those of previous generations of Jesuits. Two passages in particular sought to capture that reality and spell out an ideal:

> Jesuits today work at institutions which are no longer "ours." Though retaining a strong memory of their Jesuit tradition, they now have constituencies, support systems and goals not identical with those of the Society of Jesus: they intersect with our apostolic work, but do not constitute it. . . .
>
> Our efforts to map out the horizon of a post-modern, post-liberal knowledge will make it possible for us to examine the enormous implications of the new situation for higher education, and in particular for Jesuits in higher education. We will be in a privileged position to contribute to the theory and practice of what Catholic and Jesuit education can be in the twenty-first century.[9]

The venture became an exploration of how our particular fields of study could be resources for exploring matters having to do with Jesuit life.

As the project developed, it raised for me the challenge of locating my present work in the history and philosophy of theoretical physics in relation to the various dimensions of my life as a Jesuit, and in particular to see how it could be a resource for exploring matters having to do with Jesuit identity such as in this essay. At times the project as it was then formulated—to bring the contents and contexts of our scholarly work to bear on understanding issues of our Jesuit life, its practices and identities—gave the impression of being more tailored for disciplines such as the social sciences, theology, and areas of philosophy dealing with human existence. It seemed less related to disciplines associated with the natural sciences. The challenge led me to wonder whether this was simply because the key issues of Jesuit life intrinsically belong in the realm of the personal, religious, and existential. Were they removed from the world of theories of nature and even from nature itself, both local, and in the larger cosmic context? If that was the case, my journey had perhaps led me to being a sort of exile in the project, without the values Said affirms for the exile: the plurality of vision, the contrapuntal presence that gives new insights.

Then, I wondered whether my impression arose from our Jesuit life having lost a grounding in the larger context of nature, given our contemporary Jesuit focus on societal issues such as justice. Or the impression could have related but broader, deeper roots: the influence in our theologies and philosophies of an intellectual culture forged in mid- to late-twentieth-century Europe, where existentialist and personalist philosophies of human existence dominated over philosophies of nature and science. Such philosophies flower in societies ravaged by wars of the sort that were fought in Europe in the last century—wars having many of the debilitating effects that go with civil wars. If something like this flowering had occurred, then perhaps the project provided the opportunity to unearth the mechanisms and structures of contemporary Jesuit life that have made the natural world invisible as a result. As Said points out, home and language come taken for granted: "their underlying assumptions recede into dogma and orthodoxy."[10] Then a role for the immigrant consists in revealing the orthodoxies that in this case point to a "worldliness" crucially absent from my Jesuit home.

Along this line, I discovered the original intuitions and energy informing the project that is the Jesuit Scholarship in the Postmodern Age remain in force. They confirm and reflect how my original discipline of physics, and subsequent engagement with disciplines that study physics, together with a long fascination with nature, have been the context in which the personal and religious are lived out for me, even if at times that context has formed a merely distant horizon. I have remained haunted by the project of making the significance of that horizon more articulate and visible in my life.

Said's perspectives on a plurality of vision and contrapuntal relationship of worlds also provide encouragement for persistence in such a project, the autobiographic being a key way the immigrant can bring together scattered homes and cultures. And the quality in Said's writing of weaving features of his life (as an immigrant to the U.S.) into his intellectual stance, weaving the personal and intellectual, further captivated me about his work. The following sections then undertake an exploration of my various studies in physics and the disciplines that relate to physics, and their connectedness to the other realms in my life.

II. On Early Foundations

As part of the steady process of interpreting and re-interpreting my past I've increasingly become aware of how early concerns in my life—Said's "old environment" and "memory of these things in another environment"—lie not far from the surface and retain the vividness that Said writes about. I grew up in a rural coastal area in the south island of New Zealand with farms, forests, rivers, and lakes. It was a setting of natural beauty. Mountains running down the center of the island formed a backdrop on one side, with the sea on the other. From early times I've always felt captivated by nature, something I inherited from my father. And as nature has always held for me a sense of mystery, my sense of God has blurred with that mystery. It was in an experience of nature that I locate my first religious experiences, set in the context of my low-key Presbyterian-Anglican upbringing. I've since come to recognize another aspect of that experience. In its cool beauty there's something unsettling about nature—its strange beauty has both fire and ice. This is a feature I've never been able to work out completely, but one which I put down to the capacity of nature to invite but distance at the same time, to be home but also foreign. It was only a few years ago that I relaxed in this experience, accepting that it may remain forever as a given in my life, without resolution: a hint to me of the basis of a spirituality of the immigrant or exile, for one who has never fully arrived and is always unsettled, yet bound to the context of the experience. Edith Cobb's study of autobiographic reflections of childhood has recently provided me with another context to view this experience. For Cobb there's a time in childhood where nature can play a special role:

> There is a special period . . . approximately from five or six to eleven or twelve . . . when the natural world is experienced in some highly evocative way, producing in the child a sense of some profound continuity with natural processes.

Thinkers often return to this part of their life to "renew the power and impulse to create" with the twin experience of dislocation from yet connection with nature:

> In these memories the child appears to experience a sense of discontinuity, an awareness of his own unique separateness and identity, and also a continuity, a renewal of relationship with nature as process.[11]

Without city lights where I grew up the stars at night filled the sky down to the horizon. I developed a fascination with the night sky and by the time I was in high school I'd become familiar with the constellations and had an interest in astronomy.

I trace my later immersion in physics to my father, who started me playing with wires, batteries, switches, and lights in my pre-teen years, an interest that led to building radios, amplifiers, and working after school in a radio/TV repair shop. It also led to an interest in amateur radio, and by the time I was sixteen I had studied for and obtained an Amateur Radio operator's license. Around that time, school studies took a distant second place to these interests for a year or so, but I tuned back into studies for my last two years at school. Radio waves fascinated me: something invisible was spread everywhere throughout space, something that could be tapped into anywhere. That even now, so much later in my life, I am exploring as a philosopher of physics the nature of the reality to be ascribed to such electromagnetic energy and to parts of the mathematical formalism of the theories of electromagnetism that form radio waves, is something I find an attractive unifying feature of my life as well as something that intrigues me. During these years I developed another of the abiding passions and interests in my life: mathematics—a discipline with cool austere completeness and certainty. Perhaps the attraction for me (other than doing well in it) was the hint of foundations it possessed.

There also occurred what I would have seen as a minor event then, but a major one in terms of influence on my life until my later studies in philosophy. During my last year in high school I discovered and became absorbed in Bertrand Russell's *History of Western Philosophy*. Russell's book provided my first introduction to the world of philosophical analysis, to a style of argument where critique dominated. In a journal I'd kept in those years, I wrote down a quote from Russell's history that had impressed me: "The search for something permanent is one of the deepest of the instincts leading men to philosophy. It is derived, no doubt, from love of home and desire for a refuge from danger. . . . Philosophers have sought with great persistence, for something not subject to the empire of time." The quote I now see as charged with the issue of home and foundations.

I later discovered Russell's work in the foundations of mathematical logic and felt a natural resonance with his way of writing about the beauty and power of mathematical form. Russell has remained a philosophical hero for me, not so much because of any philosophical position he took, but because of the areas of thought he worked in, the style of his work, and the passionate quality of his life. Then too I've often returned to his vivid statement about his life as a quest for certitude and foundations, a quest with resonances to Popper's statements of foundations in science:

I wanted certainty in the kind of way in which people want religious faith. I thought that certainty is more likely to be found in mathematics than elsewhere. But I discovered that many mathematical demonstrations, which my teachers expected me to accept, were full of fallacies, and that, if certainty were indeed discoverable in mathematics, it would be in a new field of mathematics, with more solid foundations than those that had hitherto been thought secure. But as the work proceeded, I was continually reminded of the fable about the elephant and the tortoise. Having constructed an elephant upon which the mathematical world could rest, I found the elephant tottering, and proceeded to construct a tortoise to keep the elephant from falling. But the tortoise was no more secure than the elephant, and after some twenty years of very arduous toil, I came to the conclusion that there was nothing more that I could do in the way of making mathematical knowledge indubitable."[12]

At eighteen, I entered a new world, going to the University of Canterbury in Christchurch, a small city a hundred miles from my home. I reflect occasionally that I could easily have taken a path other than going to university had I followed the practical world my passion for amateur radio had opened up to me. It was the return to school studies, and becoming part of another peer group that also went on to university, that made the difference. Going to university made me an émigré from the country area where I grew up, and became the first significant migration of my life.

At university I majored in physics and mathematics. During my last year we were required to do a research project for the year. We had a general choice of areas, whether theoretical or experimental, one of the key divides in physics. I chose the theoretical, and was assigned an appropriate supervisor, Geoffrey Stedman, who provided a topic referred to then as the "conventionality of the one-way speed of light" or the "conventionality of simultaneity." While my topic had a mathematical and physical dimension, I subsequently discovered that it also had a long history within twentieth-century philosophy of science.

The starting point was a phrase by Einstein in his famous paper on relativity in 1905. He says that when using light signals as a method for synchronizing clocks, one needs to define the speed of light to be the same in both directions. The point is a moderately accessible one and worth spelling out. The spirit of what is at issue was to emerge as a central feature of my later work, and it powerfully raises the issue of where the foundations of our knowledge of nature lie. The issue arises from the need to have clocks at separated points to measure the speed of an object, in this case light. The speed of light between two points is the distance between those points divided by the length of time taken for the light to travel that distance. To know the length of time, however, requires the two clocks to be synchronized with each other. This sets up a problem of circularity, since to synchronize clocks at distant places requires sending a signal between them the speed of which is already known. Einstein expressed it as following in his 1905 paper:

If there is a clock at the point A of space, then an observer located at A can evaluate the time of the events in the immediate vicinity of A by finding the clock-
hand positions that are simultaneous with these events. If there is also a clock at
point B—we should add, "a clock of exactly the same constitution as that at A"—
then the time of the events in the immediate vicinity of B can likewise be evaluated by an observer located at B. But it is not possible to compare the time of an
event at A with one at B without a further stipulation: thus far we have only defined an "A-time" and a "B-time" but not a "time" common to A and B. The latter can now be determined by establishing *by definition* that the "time" needed
for the light to travel from A to B is equal to the "time" it needs to travel from B
to A.[13]

The speed out and back of the light beam is known without the need to
synchronize clocks at distant places, since its value depends on measuring the
time of travel made with a single clock. The issue emerged as a topic in the
philosophy of science in the 1920s. The unknown speed of light in a particular direction is equivalent to the need for a convention or definition of what
is to count as simultaneous through a region, that is, the spreading of a "now"
throughout a region.

The conventionality thesis maintained that nature is such that there is no
way around the need for a convention, a definition. The element of convention can be built into a formalism by introducing a parameter that allows for
different one-way speeds, but which keeps the round-trip speed the same (a
speed that is able to be measured without a convention). Whether there is a
way to measure the speed of light in a given direction and thereby determine
in a natural way simultaneity throughout a region, was for decades a contested
issue. When I later returned to the topic, the philosophical issues came more
to the foreground. At this stage, when I was twenty-one, it was posed as a
mathematical problem of providing a generalization of the formalism that
had been used in the debate until then. The world of the university opened up
new horizons for me. I studied hard, and the energy expended made physics
forever the prime discipline of my life.

Starting in my last year in high school and during my undergraduate studies I had been reading Teilhard de Chardin, a Jesuit paleontologist. This introduced me to the Jesuits. I had been on a religious pilgrimage of sorts as well
during these years. Through reading Thomas Merton's *The Seven Storey
Mountain* and through the influence of a friend from high school, Peter Nor-
ris, who was then in the diocesan seminary, I joined the Catholic Church during my third year of university. These were the heady years just after Vatican
II. I sensed an engaging energy and vitality in Catholicism, in the ritual of the
Mass, and in the sense of community and tradition. It was not on the level of
doctrine or particular beliefs that Catholicism drew me, and my Catholicism

knew little of a pre-Vatican II Church. My formal introduction to Catholicism came by working through the *Dutch Catechism* with a priest at the diocesan seminary, Vincent Hunt. Its nuanced treatment of the tradition, in the spirit of the expansive and cultural accommodating mood of Vatican II, confirmed my attraction to Catholicism.

Karl Rahner's *Encounters with Silence*, with its God of horizon, always present yet ever receding into mystery and silence, and Teilhard de Chardin's *The Divine Milieu* and *The Phenomenon of Man*, with their God woven into the evolutionary unfolding of the universe, joined the *Dutch Catechism* in laying the foundations for my intellectual sense of Catholicism. I see now as guiding themes in my spirituality Teilhard's invitation in *The Divine Milieu*—"Those who spread their sails in the right way to the winds of the earth will always find themselves borne by a current towards the open seas"[14]—and Rahner's play of home and restlessness:

> "I'm constantly tempted to creep away from You . . . to things where my heart feels so much more at home . . . yet, where shall I go? If the narrow hut of this early life . . . were my real home . . . wouldn't it still be surrounded by Your distant Endlessness?"[15]

Both explore the question of being at home in being on a journey. Reinforcing these Jesuit writers, the existentialist themes of authenticity, of search for depth in life in Kierkegaard's *Journals* and Viktor Frankl's *Man's Search for Meaning* introduced further worlds that entailed a journey, ones that were both intellectual and personal. I've thus been an immigrant to Catholicism. It became my religious home, yet home in a sense different from that experienced by a native and in particular from those generations who had experience pre-Vatican II Catholicism.

III. Leaving New Zealand

Various influences—which would take a lot to uncover and relate—came together in a way that led me to join the Jesuits rather than to pursue doctoral studies in physics. Due to the canonical need for a few years to pass after my joining the Church before joining the Society, it was arranged for me to spend a year as a "pre-novice" in theology studies at the Jesuit Theologate in Melbourne, Australia. This year provided a remarkable immersion into Jesuit life. I was welcomed into one of the small communities and made to feel very much at home. I dived, with little preparation, into graduate level courses in scripture, church history, and some philosophy. During the year, however, I started to wonder again whether to do a doctorate in physics with the long-

term view of joining the Society after finishing the degree, or to join the following year. There was an opportunity to do a thirty-day retreat with the first-
year novices during the year. Discerning what to do next was a theme of the
retreat. However, it was only at the end of the year that I decided to join the
Society the following year and to give up the idea of doing a doctorate. An important factor, which I recognized later as crucial, was the feeling I had discovered a new home.

I'd kept up my reading in Teilhard; and as I now look back to my early
twenties I can see that I had been developing a vision built on Teilhard's work,
one where ideas themselves fired me up. It could be described as an intellec-
tualist vision whose texture unraveled in the later reconfiguration of the intellectual and emotional that took place in my Jesuit formation. From a
later—reconfigured—perspective, it is hard to recapture fully the nature of
the earlier vision and its role in my life at that time.

The novitiate was located on attractive grounds in a northern suburb of
North Sydney, in a building that had originally been the house of theology
studies for the Australian Jesuit Province. The novitiate was an immersion
into a more intense community life, with a routine of novitiate-type activities
such as looking after the grounds, classes on Jesuit life and spirituality, and
Biblical Greek. Some of the routine had me wondering if I was expending time
in activities that were not leading anywhere. In a vague way, I think, I came to
the conclusion that while the formation structure (novitiate, a time to follow
of teaching in a school . . .) of the older pre-1960s Society of Jesus was still in
place, a rationale for it was no longer fully worked out in the new Society of
Jesus that I had joined. This led me instinctively to sense that unless I took a
lead in proposing courses of action, I could drift from stage to stage in Jesuit
formation without a larger vision in place. The journey needed taking in
hand. Another of Said's observations on the life of the exile provides an insight into the pattern of my life. He says that, at bottom "the exile is a jealous
state. With very little to possess, you hold onto what you have with aggressive
defensiveness."[16] Taking the initiative here, and later in my Jesuit life, was the
move of an immigrant cautious not to lose what he had achieved.

The Society I experienced in the early 1970s was the New Society of Jesus,
in an age of discernment and rethinking. Without any prior experience of Jesuit life to contextualize the spirit that those in charge of formation of
younger Jesuits possessed, the message I picked up was that to be a Jesuit was
to be always in discernment about the fundamentals of Jesuit life. Said's spirit
of restlessness, of "constantly being unsettled," was woven into my understanding of the life. This was not an understanding, as I later discovered, that
was shared as deeply by those who had entered the Society either earlier or
later than this period. Matters to do with physics receded into the background,

although I did spend a valuable six weeks or so in Canberra during my first novitiate year. The purpose of this was to provide an opportunity to keep in touch with physics while at the same time helping in various social service agencies. At some stage during the novitiate, about the beginning of my second year, I proposed starting a Ph.D. in physics, and in the middle of that year moved from the novitiate back to Melbourne to start a program at the University of Melbourne.

I was going to choose either an area of physics that came from an earlier interest of mine, astronomy (possibly radio astronomy, as that figured large in various places in Australia), or something at the other extreme (in terms of objects of study), elementary particle physics. The latter won out and in August of 1975 I started a doctorate in theoretical physics working with Girish Joshi as my supervisor. The degree did not have the preliminary course work that figures in American graduate programs. The dynamic of the degree, which began on the day I turned up in my supervisor's office, involved working on papers for publication in the field. At the end of four years, seven of these were gathered together and woven into a thesis and unified with the title "Studies in Multiquark States." The degree gave a good and valuable experience of working on a topic for a paper, but, looking back now, was probably not the best foundation for later research in physics. The area of physics in which I specialized sought models to describe the properties of new hypothetical particles in terms of their composite quark, and had a style of drawing on aspects of various quite different models in a somewhat opportunistic manner to explain particular properties of particles. The new proposed particles were taken to be composed of four and five quarks, more than the number of quarks that formed the well-known elementary particles such as protons, neutrons, and mesons.[17] At that stage there existed no fundamental theory to describe how quarks formed the standard elementary particles. Afterwards such an approach to doing physics did not seem so attractive to me, as it lacked a unified mathematical framework, grateful though I remain for Girish Joshi's friendly and encouraging way of shepherding me through the degree with a focus on publications. Trying to find my way into another style of doing physics preoccupied me in the years following the degree.

While a prominent focus in Jesuit life in the Australian Province in the 1970s, as elsewhere in the Society, was on social ministries, I don't recall feeling out of place in doing a Ph.D. in physics. I was following a standard academic path, commonly accepted in the older generation as part of Jesuit life. During the time I also did a number of philosophy courses at the Jesuit Theological College.

One, on the thought of Bernard Lonergan by Thomas Daly, was of particular influence. The enticing meta-epistemological vision of Lonergan's *Insight* had a captivating effect on me. Its foundational promise was stated in the preface: "Thoroughly understand what it is to understand, and not only will you understand the broad lines of all there is to be understood but also you will possess a fixed base, and invariant pattern, opening upon all further developments of understanding."[18] This, and its examples of insights involving mathematics and physics in the introductory chapters, appealed to my quest for foundations.

My interest continued through to the late 1980s during which time I attended various conference workshops on Lonergan's thought at Boston College, but faded for a cluster of reasons. One was the emergence of ontological issues associated with contemporary physics as an interesting field for me, rather than the project of inferring cognitive structures of the mind from personal introspection. The first was the exciting realm where any foundations were to be explored and from the perspective of this realm the tendency to infer ontological features of the world from epistemological issues by those within Lonergan studies appeared puzzling. Another was the absence of intersection of those working in Lonergan studies with mainstream currents within philosophy of science. My admiration for Lonergan's achievement in the 1950s in *Insight*, however, remains. At that time *Insight* proposed a radical new way of doing philosophy compared to the older scholastic philosophy of early to mid-twentieth-century Catholicism—in Foucault's terms, a text of resistance (a reading I owe to James Bernauer). But by now the projects of the Lonergan movement have been largely supplanted with others, such as those of the cognitive sciences. The displacement of relevance and interest in the epistemological focus of the Lonergan movement, is not unlike the displacement of an analogous project in mid-twentieth century philosophy of science—the attempt to map the structure of knowledge—by a rich range of other disciplinary projects on the nature of science. And as well there has been a more general displacement of traditional epistemology from the philosophical landscape. One awaits contextual and historical studies which might locate the epistemological focus in Lonergan's work in relation to twentieth-century Catholic thought[19] and 1950s philosophy of science.

IV. Leaving Australia

The degree was followed by two years of postdoctoral work in Oxford, 1979–1981. The years in Oxford remain in my memory as an uncertain space in my life; I was marking time without much progress in research. In trying to find another style of doing physics, I aimed for a topic in the foundations of mathematical physics. As seen from my present perspective, I was then in captivity to the spirit of mathematics as completeness and certainty, the spirit that looks for foundations. However, attainment of the realm of creative research of the sort I was looking for in the foundations of mathematical physics required a longer and more extensive preparation than I already had. Moreover, creative developments on this level are rare. It was a quest, then, that misled me.

Following Oxford, I started theology at the Weston Jesuit School of Theology in Cambridge, Massachusetts. This choice was motivated by my association with the physics department at MIT and seen as a way to keep in touch with physics during theology. Little did I anticipate that the United States was to become my home. Life at Weston and theology studies absorbed my time and energy and I did not get into a new research project in physics that captivated my interest and reached a productive stage. This led to my rethinking the question of whether to continue in physics. By this time I had also nearly finished the master's of divinity, since my prior coursework meant I could finish the degree in two years. After a period of uncertainty I proposed doing a Ph.D. in the philosophy of physics (a plan that also covered my need for further philosophy courses for ordination to the priesthood).

In the fall of 1983 I started a post-master's Ph.D. at Boston University. Abner Shimony, a philosopher of physics, was one of the main attractions there for me. There was also the advantage of being in Boston, and I stayed at Weston as a special student. I was ordained deacon that year, with the class I had started with at Weston. The initial topic for the Boston University thesis was exploring the role of symmetry or invariance principles in physics, high-level principles that describe general properties of objects. This soon became narrowed to the role of such principles in describing the nature of electromagnetism, one of the basic forces of nature.

Invariance properties have had a long association with the investigation of what exists and the manner in which it exists. For example, ordinary space possesses an invariance property such as translation invariance: as Leibniz famously expressed it, if the whole universe were moved (uniformly) in a particular direction there would be no observable difference, a feature that says something about the nature of space. In this case such a property has been taken to support a position that space is nothing but a set of relations between objects, without any substantial reality itself.

It turns out that the central mathematical structures that describe electromagnetism have the same sort of invariance properties, called gauge invariance. This raises analogous issues about the reality to be associated with the mathematical terms that describe the electromagnetic field. Here follows a short mathematical interlude required to spell this out. This can be skipped, or read for the surface sense.

Three equations illustrate a point underlying a good bit of my research since first formulating the topic. The force between two fixed charges, with amounts represented by q_1 and q_2, and distance r apart, is given by the formula:

$$F = k\,\frac{q_1 q_2}{r^2}$$

The symbol, k, represents a constant that characterizes the strength of the force. The expression has the same form as Newton's law of gravitation between masses. Something at the heart of the description of nature by physics takes place in a formula such as this. Mathematical symbols represent entities and their properties or, in more philosophical language, applying a mathematical formula to a physical situation can be viewed as providing either a referent (denotation) or a physical meaning (connotation) for the mathematical terms in a formula expressing the law. That is, it may be taken as giving an interpretation to the mathematical symbols of the formula. The metaphor at work in this way of expressing the application of a formula in a physical theory treats mathematics as the language of nature. It is an old metaphor, going back at least to Galileo. Of the "two books" of our Early Modern culture of the sixteenth and seventeenth centuries, the book of God and the book of nature, the language of the latter is that of mathematics.

Usually there are no real problems associated with the meanings of the mathematical terms and the ways in which nature is described by mathematical formulae. Sometimes, however, in the case of complex formulae, interpreting parts of the mathematical formalism is an intricate and contested issue. Often the question is not to do with using the formulae to predict and explain results, but rather what sort of physical reality should be ascribed to some of the properties or entities to which a term appears to refer. In the case of the above formula, the forces, charges, and distances that are referred to by parts of the formalism are pretty much real entities and properties in the world. An alternative mathematical expression of the above law, however, can be given in terms of a mathematical structure called a potential. Here the referent of the term becomes more complicated. A potential associated with one of the charges q_1 is defined by:

$$V = \frac{k q_1}{r}$$

and the force on another, q_2, has the form,

$$F = q_2 \nabla V$$

This expression is mathematically equivalent to the earlier one for force, but there is a special mathematical operation in the last formula known as a derivative, represented by ∇. It is this term that raises the issue of the meaning of the potential.

The derivative of a constant term (such as a pure number, 1, 2, or 3 . . .) is zero, so one can add a constant amount to the potential V and still get the same force (analogous to the property of space where moving uniformly in space still gives rise to the same physical situation). So a range of different numerical values of the potential still gives the same force between the two charges. For this reason the potential is often taken to have no direct "physical significance." It is often referred to as a "pure mathematical term" in the mathematical structure, with a different physical significance from the other terms such as force and distance which have a more direct association with empirical features of the world. That this term represents a central property of electromagnetic interactions, yet has such an "invariance property," raises questions about its interpretation within physics. There also arises a project in the philosophy of physics that seeks to use physical theories to provide a comprehensive and basic understanding of the ontological status of fields that mediate interactions such as electromagnetism.

The other forces of nature (such as gravity) have similar laws describing the force between entities. For them too, potentials can be introduced; there arises the same question about their physical significance and meaning.

Similar issues arise in the cases of mathematical structures in physical theories. Sometimes it is clear that parts of the mathematics that form the "superstructure" of a theory are used merely for mathematical calculations and as such do not refer directly to actual entities in the world, or to their properties. In such cases they have no direct physical significance.

For me, thesis work on this topic started another initially unintended disciplinary migration. It began with the application of the above issues to some contemporary situations in physics that touched directly on the issue of interpreting the significance of potentials. However, the pursuit of the origins of various contemporary interpretations of potentials started me on a historical project that ultimately led me to nineteenth-century Victorian England where most of the theory of electromagnetism had been developed. There had been in nineteenth-century British physics a long dispute among physicists related to the meaning of potentials, one involving detailed physical as well as conceptual issues. Potentials were of central importance to the Scottish physicist James Clerk Maxwell (d. 1879), one of the founders of modern electromagnetic theory. But by the time the century had closed the consensus was that they had little physical significance, although for one or two key physicists the issue was by no means settled. There's a twentieth-century twist to this story: discovery of physical situations (in the microscopic realm) where potentials can be shown to have direct physical significance.

When following this story I found it encouraging to note that some of the standard histories had overlooked the full significance of the features that my physicist and philosopher worlds had drawn to my attention. This started my entry into the history of science, a discipline characteristically suspicious of scientists, with their tendency to trace success stories in the development of science, and suspicious too of philosophers, with prior systematic agendas in search of verification in the history of scientific theories.

This path as the immigrant into the history of science made me conscious of the historiography of science—the theory of how to do the history of science—with questions such as how best to represent past scientific practices and texts and the type of knowledge embodied in them. Of its very nature science generates questions about proper approaches to its history, different from historical questions relevant to other disciplines.

The final result of my doctoral studies at Boston University, "The Ontological Status of Potentials in Classical Electromagnetism," was a somewhat unstable combination of philosophical analysis and historical research. But it unearthed a history of disputes on the interpretation of the physical significance of a formalism. In addition, Abner Shimony's powerful and attractive vision of building a naturalized metaphysics in close accord with the natural sciences become a vision that inspired my own projects, one building on my own intuitions.

V. Transferring Homes

In 1984 I spent a semester in Melbourne, Australia, prior to ordination to priesthood in September of that year. Since my leaving Australia, Melbourne had remained my home base in Jesuit life, one built on a familiarity with Melbourne and on Jesuit and non-Jesuit friends. Then in 1985, shortly after starting my degree at Boston University, I started teaching part-time at Boston College; in 1986 I moved there, across Boston's Charles River, starting in 1987 a full time tenured position—premature, in that my thesis work was only just starting.

I joined a small community setting, Barat Jesuit Community on the Newton Campus of Boston College. This situation provided an extraordinary immersion in a community of those involved in university work, able to reflect directly on its significance for Jesuit life. It was also a time of energy in the whole community, which was reflecting on its purpose and ministry in a university setting, perhaps a time that has not since been matched in energy.

Since my completion of the doctorate, my work has been contextualized largely by research in history of science. A year at the Dibner Institute for the History of Science and Technology at MIT during 1993–1994 helped settle such a context. One result has been to refine a sense that all ideas are embedded in and share features of particular social, institutional, linguistic, and cultural contexts (how else?). Also, focusing on the nineteenth century, rather than the twentieth where contemporary systematic issues overlap more with historical projects than the nineteenth, has solidified my identity as an historian of science.

Two features stand out from my work in the 1990s. The first arises from the topic of gauge invariance in physics. It entails confronting the issue of how certain properties in a theoretical formalism are under-determined in crucial ways by an empirical situation, and how this leads to a contesting of their interpretation. The lesson here, the larger significance of which I've gradually recognized, is that at the heart of a foundational enterprise such as physics one confronts what is, in precise formal terms, a form of under-determination. This lesson has formed a backdrop in my intellectual life—the unsettling yet enticing issue of foundations.

It has seemed to me that if foundations in knowledge are to be found anywhere, they are to be found in the natural sciences, in mathematical physics in particular. Even here, there are situations where anticipated determination of empirical features fail. Foundations then have an open-ended quality: to use Popper's metaphor, they are sufficient for the building of knowledge at a given stage, but they are not set in bedrock. In less secure forms of knowledge, foundational projects could only be more open-ended. It may be, too, that because I am an immigrant to a post–Vatican II Catholicism, I resist the residue of the earlier neo-Thomist thought that often lives on subtly in those generations formed by it, a system of thought that saw itself as stable and settled with secure and complete foundations.

The other feature stems the aggressively ahistorical character of science. As Whitehead has expressed it: "A science which hesitates to forget its founders is lost."[20] Given my grounding in science I've wondered how I got into the history of science. Looking back now, however, I can see at work that which led me into foundational areas in science, mathematical physics of elementary particle physics. Hunting through archives is itself a foundational project, one that aims to discover the actual events from which scientific theories arose, to find connections previously overlooked. My increasing involvement in the history of physics also made me aware of resources for understanding the present practice of science; this has also given me a sense of the power of history for assessing theories about science.

During 1994 I took the step of transferring to the New England Jesuit Province from the Australian Province. It was not an easy move to leave the Australian Province. It was one of my Jesuit homes. However, the move reflected the reality that another place had steadily found its way into my heart and mind as home. The two quite different Jesuit cultures formed my Jesuit life, perhaps made me slight strangers to both. I still occasionally reflect on never being able fully to translate between these worlds. But that reality of now not being able, in Said's words, "to go back to some earlier and perhaps more stable condition of being at home" in either Australia or New Zealand, has gently settled as a given in my life; my native and my home countries are discontinuous. When writing on the state of the exile, Said again touches on an experience I've occasionally dwelt on: looking at the non-immigrants the exile asks—"What is it to be born in a place and to live there more or less forever, to know that you are of it?"[21] I'm a slight stranger as well to what various of my Jesuit brethren at Boston College must feel like to be teaching at a university which they attended as undergraduates or to be living now no more than ten miles away from where they were born.

VI. Returning to Former Topics

During the 1990s, I returned to work with my former undergraduate thesis supervisor Geoffrey Stedman on the topic of the conventionality of simultaneity. He had reworked my original study into an article which formed a joint publication—my first—and I'd kept an eye on the field. It had been proposed that there were ways around the conventional or definitional quality of simultaneity, and in a couple of articles we argued that such arguments were flawed. That work nicely led to developing a major review of the area, touching on the historical, philosophical, and physical issues.[22] Our collaboration on this topic still continues. This provided me with another context to doing the history of physics in a way that was complete and detailed, yet at the same time had the intent of pursuing foundational and philosophical issues. At this stage the philosophical issues came more to the foreground for me. Like the under-determination that is part of the property of gauge invariance that I had explored in another context, the issue of the conventionality of simultaneity now provided a further example of the world not delivering an anticipated foundational quantity. Our natural sense is that we should be able to determine simultaneity throughout space: we instinctively extend a "now" throughout our lived space. The absence of such a simultaneity specification could be given an ontological reading: it is not simply a matter of lack of knowledge of something that actually has a value but rather that nature has failed to determine such a value.

Yet another unifying theme in my life during this time was a project with my former physics supervisor at Melbourne University, on the role of a particular form of mathematics (quaternions) in the development of physics. This again was an endeavor that mixed systematic philosophical issues with the history of physics and the actual practice of physics. The relationship between mathematics and physical descriptions of nature has been a matter of long speculation: why is nature such that abstract mathematics is needed to describe it? Further, of the wide variety of possible mathematical structures and forms, why are some relevant for describing nature and others not? In these questions lie remnants of the old Pythagorean vision that the essence of nature is number and that mathematics is the language of nature. The book of nature is written in a language, which like all languages stands in need of interpretation.

VII. New Settings

In recent years, the area of science studies has increasingly played a role in structuring my historical projects and this has been another form of disciplinary migration. Science studies bring a range of disciplinary projects to bear on the study of science. The sociological predominate, although all the features that go into the construction of scientific knowledge are at issue. The spirit of these studies has been attractive to me in the sense of providing further resources for digging into the foundations of scientific knowledge. Another resource in line with this has been various post-structuralist writings, those of Jacques Derrida in particular, that explore new ways in which texts and symbolic structures represent and constitute meaning. It was during a year on sabbatical at the Office for History of Science and Technology at the University of California, Berkeley in 2002–2003 that these new resources solidified within my research. Bringing these to bear on my nineteenth-century project has generated new perspectives on the ways mathematics—viewed as a language—is written about and given physical significance and meaning in physical theories. The focus here is on theoretical practices that constitute meaning, a concern at the heart of poststructuralism: it's not *what* a text means, but *how* it means: how do the forces of signification in a text, often at war with each other, generate meaning?

Since my concern has been with the interpretation of mathematical structures which have had a long tradition of dispute over their meaning, the resources of poststructuralism have appeared as natural ones to draw on for new readings of this history. In such studies language comes to the foreground, as one text on literary theory, drawing on the Bakhtin school of literary studies, has framed it:

... languages had to be considered in a social context. Every utterance is potentially the site of a struggle: every word that is launched into social space implies a dialogue and therefore a contested interpretation—Language cannot be neatly dissociated from social living; it is always contaminated, interleaved, opaquely colored by layers of semantic deposits resulting from the endless processes of human struggle and interaction.[23]

This perspective carries over in an endlessly rich manner to suggest ways to attend to the functioning of mathematics (as a text) in physical theories in the period I've been working on. Also, the questions of literary theorists such as Said, as to how texts adhere and "fix" to the world, translate naturally to the question of how mathematics describes the world. And in the words of two recent commentators on Said's work, the personal and autobiographic dimensions of his life that drive the theorizing on exile also touch his literary practice:

> This tension between personal desolation and cultural empowerment is the tension of exile in Said's own work, a tension which helps explain his own deep investment in the link between the text and the world. For that very worldliness is the guarantee of the invalidity of the text's *ownership* by nation or community, or religion, however powerful those filiative connections might be.[24]

Their interpretation of Said suggests to me a way to see my journey in various disciplinary contexts as migratory on different levels; that experience provides the energy, the basis, and resources for my focus on links between the text of mathematics and the world. Following this path has also brought to the foreground ways of exploring how the history I was tracing in a physical theory has resonances in other disciplinary contexts. In early Victorian thought, for example, concern with the meaning and interpretation of symbolic and abstract structures occurred in mathematics, logic, the study of language, and to a lesser extent even the interpretation of scripture, which had arisen as a contested issue mid-century. The elusive and rich historical nature of this project lies in focusing the influences of such areas on a development in mathematical physics. However, this complexity is common to all contextual studies of systems of knowledge.

VIII. Resonances from the Worlds of Scholarship in Larger Contexts, Jesuit and Spiritual

As I have only recently realized, one of the threads featuring persistently in the trajectory of my various studies, and forming the energy behind them, has been that of excavation of foundations of knowledge. This captivating quest has taken various forms, in deep resonance with the spirit of Russell's quest for foundations. In the beginning it was formed by the ideals of physics to understand the nature of physical reality. It was also influenced by the foundational nature of mathematics, the study of precise relationships between mathematical objects that appear true at all times and places. That ideal took me into a foundational part of theoretical physics—elementary particle physics—and from there to the philosophy and history of physics. My work within philosophy of physics has concerned itself with the basic interactions that hold all matter together, and thus with a feature of that which structures the foundational aspects of our material existence.

When out in nature, I've dwelt at times on how to blur this intellectual project with the captivating aesthetic experience of nature. Certainly part of the energy that has kept me with the project comes from a sense of the mystery and beauty of nature. I've wondered whether this is a way in which I have sought to obtain a connectedness with nature that overcomes that unsettling experience indicated earlier of the distance of nature, the ice of that strange beauty.

The foundational quest has been a journey through various disciplinary contexts: from a science, to the study of its nature as a systematic undertaking, from there to a historical and sociological study locating what has gone into its formation, and thereafter to basic questions about various theoretical practices as to how meaning is constituted in such a science. The foundational quest, though, has revealed that features of indeterminacy are inherently woven into the nature of the world.

The spirit of post-structuralism and the projects of Derrida have been a natural continuation of a quest for foundational issues. Deconstruction in a broad sense is such a quest in the way it explores the manner in which the systems of our philosophical tradition are assembled. My reading of these projects therefore differs from the common perception that post-structuralism is relativist. This last stage has brought home to me the necessary yet exiling nature of all interpretation: reality is mediated through representation and only accessible through the giving of meaning to such forms of representation. Said's celebration of the exile brings one to appreciate the condition of all human knowing.

A further discipline that has been part of my life has been twentieth-century symbolic and mathematical logic, largely through teaching it for fifteen years. This is surely a discipline that claims to be foundational, yet within it Gödel's Theorems reveal the haunting issues of undecidability and incompleteness in logical form. That too has confirmed the lessons I have taken from post-structuralism.[25] Together then, from various starting points—scientific, mathematical, and philosophical—a position of a type of "foundational post-foundationalism" emerges, one that naturally weaves into my personal journey. The seeming paradoxical element in such a position has been identified perceptively by a recent commentator on postmodernism, hermeneutics, and foundationalism as the "paradox of *centralizing the decentering of foundations,* a paradox which lies at the heart of the postmodern crises of criticism."[26]

As to the part of my spiritual life that has been a quest for a vision that blurs the intellectual and aesthetic: for me that quest bears the marks of incompleteness and open endedness and therefore resists full articulation. Again I take this as an invitation to form a spirituality of the immigrant or exile appropriate for a poststructuralist age, able to live with a complex question of foundations.[27] Buddhism has been a major influence in my spiritual life for the past decade, an influence that has seamlessly formed part of my spiritual quest. The Buddhist themes of impermanence and the absence of a stable enduring self resonate with central concerns in my life. Since contemporary sciences suggest an evolutionary, dynamic, unfolding universe even to the foundational levels and marked by the emergence of complexity and order, even perhaps on the level of the laws themselves, a theme of impermanence naturally is in accord with such a universe. Moreover, the cognitive sciences suggest that consciousness is an emergent property of biochemical neurological networks that shares in the fragile and temporary nature of those networks. The self that arises from these studies again resonates nicely with Buddhist themes. God can be the ontological guarantor of permanence amidst the universe's impermanence. Along with these developments and perhaps in accord with them, the music of the contemporary composer, Philip Glass, with its fluid, haunting, and open rhythms has gradually replaced most of the traditional classical music canon that used to be part of my life.

Also, in the context of teaching in the area of science and religion in recent years, the project of rethinking a credible and interesting God in the light of contemporary science has provided me with ways to focus the quest. This area has also helped provide me with tools for a more refined theological reflection on nature, and enhanced the project of forming a unified worldview that combines my world of science studies with my religious intuitions, thus picking up on my early absorption with Teilhard. The spirit of these studies too has provided a sense of ways to make God an alive and relevant presence in the world of the academy, in contrast to the safe and at times seemingly distant way higher educational institutions with a religious affiliation blend mention of God into their public statements of religious identity. Another outcome has been to convince me that God will share some of the features of the God of the process theologians. God's role as the ontological guarantor of the universe's creative emergent unfolding brings a temporal dimension into God. Such projects of natural theology, though, will always bear the marks of the fragile inference—the necessity of interpretation—from human knowledge to a realm of a God who is always the horizon beyond that knowledge.

Here, Jesus is a companion traveler who enables the religious space of that gap to be lived and given new meaning. He has been the steady presence from the early Bible lessons of my Protestant past through my years as a Jesuit and priest. Jesus is the warmth in the midst of the ice of nature's beauty. Reading the life of Jesus in the Gospels through Said's categories of the outsider I see Jesus as the exile in-between two worlds. Restlessly working for God's Kingdom in the worldliness of creation, often in conflict with his religious home, Jesus touches all levels of my life, and in particular my life as an immigrant.

Our long tradition of engagement as Jesuits with the disciplines that study nature, both directly by working within scientific fields and indirectly through our associations with academic institutions, has provided a confidence that I'm within a tradition inspired by the religious significance of the study of nature. In terms of the resources they draw on, and through giving rise to the technologies that shape our culture, the natural sciences constitute the dominant and most influential forms of knowledge in our contemporary world. This too provides a motive to persist in engaging the projects of science as a Jesuit. The thread in Jesuit spirituality of a God who can be found in all things is another motive for exploring the ways nature and the study of nature can be sites for finding the trace of God.

There is a link then between the spirit I sketched in the past few pages with that of a Jesuit always being in discernment as to what it is to be a Jesuit, the spirit that I picked up in my early years in the Society. To be wondering about the nature of Jesuit life is to worry about its meaning and foundations; this resonates with the sort of unsettled foundationalism I've identified in post-structuralism. It's a spirit that always looks under and beyond particular claims as to the nature of Jesuit life. Moreover, such a spirit informs my Catholicism which has been mediated almost entirely by my Jesuit life.

I have to acknowledge, however, that the open-ended, always mobile spirit of the foundationalist dimension of my intellectual projects is grounded in an intuitive sense that God, nature, and disciplines such as mathematics have an objectivity and the security of a type of foundation that comes from their being forever beyond me. Again, to use a passage from Russell that has long appealed to me: "Mathematics, rightly viewed, possesses not only truth, but supreme beauty—a beauty cold and austere, like that of sculpture, without appeal to any part of our weaker nature, without the gorgeous trappings of painting or music, yet sublimely pure, and capable of a stern perfection such as only the greatest art can show."[28]

God, nature, and mathematics are steadily present to me as that which I can grasp only by respecting their independence from me. I find here another sort of resonance, an at-homeness with this sort of "recalcitrant fixity" which characterizes nature and mathematics that is not unlike that inevitability of the unfolding of a Bach Fugue. Thus, in being an immigrant to the world of post-structuralism and post-foundationalism I find a contrapuntal presence of the sense, even if distant, of a foundational home on the horizon; this is not the former home Said speaks of perhaps but one that rides alongside. It is home that perhaps makes possible my ease with the spirit of radical deconstruction found in parts of post-structuralism.

Related to this contrapuntal sense is a resonance with the "iconoclastic" spirit that permeates the practice of science: a spirit (at least in the ideal) that rigorously resists any forces that prevent one getting closer to understanding nature, a spirit that values originality deeply. Science is a continually changing enterprise, built on the husks and shells of previous scientific theories. It has a spirit that forms my intellectual life, one that often places me at odds with practices of philosophy that appear traditionalist and retrievalist, in search of a return to origins.[29] And also often places me at odds with a philosophy conducted in the ambiance of theology. Rorty's expression of the "rogue philosopher" pointing out that the foundations are not as secure as imagined provides an appealing image for the philosophical life.[30]

It's a spirit that I hope is at work in analogous realms in my immigrant Jesuit life. When working on new approaches, from my areas of scholarship to forming a spirituality, the ideal for me is to be cautious and critical of past approaches (a spirit that is instinctive in the practice of science) but in a way that's balanced by a horizon of foundations, even if ever receding: a spirit of "critical complicity" where one belongs and becomes at home but remains unsettled, hoping in Said's words that "'seeing the entire world as a foreign land' makes possible originality of vision."[31]

Notes

1. Edward Said, "The Mind of Winter: Reflections on Life in Exile," *Harper's Magazine*, issue 269 (September 1984): 35, 49–55.

2. Karl Popper, *The Logic of Scientific Discovery* (London: Hutchinson, 1959), 111.

3. Edward Said, *Representations of the Intellectual: The 1993 Reith Lectures* (New York: Pantheon Books, 1994), 39.

4. Edward Said, "Between Worlds," *London Review of Books* 20, no. 9 (May 7, 1998), http://www.lrb.co.uk/v20/n09/said01_.html.

5. For example, Said, "The Mind of Winter," 55.

6. Edward Said, *The World, the Text, and the Critic* (Cambridge, Mass.: Harvard University Press, 1983), 7. For a review of this text of Said's sensitive to these themes see Bruce Robbins, "Homelessness and Worldliness," *Diacritics* 13, no. 3 (Fall 1983): 69–77.

7. Edward W. Soja, *The Reassertion of Space in Critical Social Theory* (London and New York, Verso, 1989), 14.

8. The proposal, drawn up by Arthur Madigan and myself, may be found at the website for the Jesuit Scholarship in a Postmodern Age project: http://fmwww.bc.edu/jspma (in particular at http://fmwww.bc.edu/JSPMA/institute.1987.html).

9. The document is at http://fmwww.bc.edu/JSPMA/proposal90.html on the same website.

10. Said, "The Mind of Winter," 54.

11. Both quotations occur in a consideration of Cobb's work in David Sobel's *Children's Special Places: Exploring the Role of Forts, Dens, and Bush Houses in Middle Childhood* (Tucson, Ariz.: Zephyr, 1993), in particular 77–88. The basic experience at issue here too occurs steadily in our aesthetic tradition. For example, Vanessa Rumble notes the power of Norwegian painter Edvard Munch to express moments of human existence where we are confronted with "an indifferent, if ravishing nature." See "The Scandinavian Conscience: Kierkegaard, Ibsen, and Munch," in *Edvard Munch: Psyche, Symbol, and Expression*, ed. Jeffery Howe (Boston: McMullen Museum of Art, 2001), 29.

12. Bertrand Russell, *Portraits from Memory and Other Essays* (New York: Simon and Schuster, 1956), 54–55.

13. Albert Einstein, "On the Electrodynamics of Moving Bodies" (1905), in *The Collected Papers of Albert Einstein*, trans. Anna Beck, vol. 2 (Princeton: Princeton University Press, 1989), 140–71, especially page 142.

14. Teilhard de Chardin, *The Divine Milieu* (New York: Harper and Row, 1968).

15. Karl Rahner, *Encounters with Silence* (Port Talbot, Glamorgan: Newman Press, 1960), 6.

16. Said, "The Mind of Winter," 51.

17. During the past year such particles appear to have been discovered, most likely the five-quark state. For a review, see Michael Ostrick, "Pentaquarks: Experimental Overview," *Progress in Particle and Nuclear Physics* 55 (2005): 337–49.

18. Bernard Lonergan, *Insight* (New York: Philosophical Library; London: Longmans, 1958), xxviii.

19. The same focus occurs in the writings of the Spanish Catholic philosopher Xavier Zubiri, of earlier in the century, whose writings contain some remarkable anticipations of the thematic concerns of Lonergan's work.

20. Alfred North Whitehead, *The Aims of Education* (New York: The Macmillan Co., 1929), 111.

21. Said, "The Mind of Winter," 52.

22. "Conventionality of Synchronisation, Gauge Dependence and Test Theories of Relativity," with I. Vetharaniam and G. E. Stedman, *Physics Reports* 295 (1998): 93–180.

23. Raman Selden, Peter Widdowson, and Peter Brooker, *A Reader's Guild to Contemporary Literary Theory*, 4th ed. (New York: Prentice Hall, 1997), 152.

24. Bill Ashcroft and Bill Ahluwalia, *Edward Said: Routledge Critical Thinkers* (London, New York: Routledge, 2001), 43.

25. Bringing together the realms of science and logic, Freeman Dyson has recently taken Gödel's Theorem to imply that physics has an inexhaustible nature: "The theorem implies that even within the domain of the basic equations of physics, our knowledge will always be incomplete." "The World on a String: A Review of Brian Greene's

The Fabric of the Cosmos: Space, Time, and the Texture of Reality," *The New York Review of Books* 51 (2004): 16–19. (For further on this point see letters in response to Dyson's review, ibid., July 15, 2004).

26. Horace L. Fairlamb, *Critical Conditions: Postmodernity and the Question of Foundations* (New York: Cambridge University Press, 1994), 10.

27. For an impressive exploration of a spirituality based on rethinking and deconstructing the notion of "home" in a Christian context, see John Martis, "Living Away from Home—and Loving It: Tweaking a Christian Metaphor," *Pacifica* 15 (2002): 123–37. The article ends with a striking quote from Malebranche with echoes to Said's reference to an ascetic code of a willing homelessness given earlier: "I will not take you into a strange country, but I will perhaps teach you that you are a stranger in your own country." For other resources for rethinking God along these lines, see Richard Kearney, *The God Who May Be: A New Hermeneutics of Religion* (Bloomington: Indiana University Press, 2001); John Caputo, *On Religion* (New York: Routledge, 2001).

28. Bertrand Russell, *The Study of Mathematics Philosophical Essays* (London: Longmans Green, 1910), 73.

29. Such a spirit can be traced in the thought of Hans-Georg Gadamer, for example. Richard Wolin, in a review of Jean Grondin's biography of Gadamer remarks on Gadamer: "It is of little wonder that his doctrines have enjoyed such an enthusiastic reception among neoconservatives as well as educators who are concerned that the Western canon is losing its sanctity." *Book Forum* (Summer 2003), http://www.bookforum.com/archive/sum_03/wolin.html.

30. Richard Rorty, "Philosophical Convictions: Review of Richard Wolin's 'The Seduction of Unreason,'" *The Nation* (June 14, 2004).

31. Said, "The Mind of Winter," 55.

8

Francis Xavier, and the World/s We (Don't Quite) Share

Francis X. Clooney, S.J.

T HE FOLLOWING ESSAY is at first hard to read, since the eye is puzzled by its two columns and cannot decide where to settle or how to take in a whole paragraph or page at once. Moreover, it is partly composed of excerpts from other essays, both about the Jesuit missionary tradition and about my own experience as a scholar of Hinduism and for twenty-one years a professor at a Jesuit university—and then suddenly, during the last revisions of the essay, as the Parkman Professor of Divinity at Harvard University.

To explain: I have written elsewhere on everything contained in this essay, about Jesuit tradition and about myself. Such writings could be further multiplied, but what needs to be composed now is not something new and unpublished, but rather a new way of locating what we have already said—about dialogue, Jesuits, ourselves—in the template of a postmodern world where there are numerous "pieces" to intellectual discourse, pieces that do not necessarily fit together, pieces such as the larger Jesuit story and my own journey as an individual Jesuit scholar.

There are real parallels between the rise and fall of traditional Jesuit language about other religions and strategies for learning about others on the one hand, and the rise and fall of traditional ways of imagining the life and work of a Jesuit scholar on campus. But such parallels are not instances exemplifying a general theory, for there is no general theory today that might successfully cover all the examples: insights about the Jesuit tradition and about myself as just one particular Jesuit are rather true parallels—insights and sentiments that do belong together, that do stand in tension, and that never finally converge. The reader cannot read all the larger and smaller Jesuit stories all at once, but must make choices about where to read—which column, which narrative—and how to make connections. Only by such choices can a reader construct a sense of the Jesuit story/stories. The whole is indeed larger and more fully instructive than the parts, but the parts resist, and are never smoothly blended into a unified whole that tells just one story. This essay seeks to exemplify the tensions involved, as does *Jesuit Postmodern* as a whole: chapters, lives, works, insights, all near one another, yet never a single line.

So here is a suggestion on how to find your way through the following pages: each column reads fairly coherently beginning to end, and you might first want to read each by itself, only thereafter studying the columns back and forth in order to discern the echoes and similitudes that exist across the intervening spaces. Even if traditional and modern Jesuit discourses about self and other lack the force they had in the past, isn't it also true that we do in fact still think, write, read as Jesuit—and Christian, and religious—intellectuals in a series of personal narratives that belong together as the narratives of our tradition? Since to read our lives writ large and small is a remedy for the fragmentation of our communities, can we not practice reading back and forth across boundaries, making sense of the parallel but stubbornly individual accounts of who we are? The essay to follow is, I hope, practice in the work we must do on our own, and together.

I. Roberto de Nobili Wrote

I Wrote

"My contention stops at suggesting that it would prove very suitable and would serve the cause of converting souls to the Faith if some of the usages in vogue among the heathen with superstitious implications were purged of these implications and invested with some other overtones of a truly religious and sacred nature. It is very hard and extremely difficult, at least at the start, for our neophytes to leave off and reject at a moment's notice the habit of performing absolutely all human actions to the accompaniment of special rites or prayers. [The Fathers] were unanimous in deciding that great indulgence was to be shown to recent con-

"As a Christian believer—who also happens to be trying to be a theologian—I willingly profess my faith in the God of our Lord Jesus Christ, who was born as the child of Mary, who died on the cross for our sins, rose into glory, and sent forth the Spirit upon us. By direct implication this faith claim, which is not intended to be true just for some people, excludes other such faith claims.

"But this admission, in itself rather obvious, leaves us exactly where we started. If I wish to speak of my faith as a theologian and make considered and intelligible judgments as a theologian, then I still have to make a case that is plausible and persuasive

verts to Christ, that many practices which were gradually and in course of time to be eliminated should at first be tolerated, and that for the sake of suavity a good many could be transformed from superstitious ritual into sacred rites of a Christian tenor and complexion.

"In truth, one cannot understand why India should be dealt with more strictly than the other countries where the Church was in its infancy and where men of a saintly character governed their Christian communities with such suavity and tolerance."[1]

in an interreligious theological conversation. As I have stated previously more than once, truth is not exempt from the interreligious, comparative, and dialogical process. I still need to be able to explain why the Christian and Roman Catholic theology that follows from my faith is more convincing than that which follows from the faith of a Salika Natha Misra or the faith of a Sripati Pandita Acarya. Otherwise, my faith claim, uninformed, vague, and unpersuasive at least in the public and interreligious conversation will, though admirable as faith, fail to win over anyone who might be listening in. So the requirements of an interreligious, comparative, and dialogical practice still pertain."[2]

II. Early Jesuits Learn to Encounter People of Other Religions

Roberto de Nobili's Society of Jesus was twice born, right at the beginning. First, there is the birth of the Society according to the charism of Ignatius and his first companions, its approval by the Pope in 1540, etc. This Society was a new and vital force in the Europe of early modernity and the Protestant and Catholic Reformations. Jesuits quickly became a known force, excelling in preaching and teaching, and soon thereafter known for the establishment of colleges of great quality according to an educational rationale of great inventiveness.

I Learn to Study Another Religion

My identity in the Society of Jesus took form in stages. Like most Jesuits who entered the Society right from high school, I was twice born: I became a Jesuit in response to a calling, and much later I figured out what God wanted me to do as a Jesuit. First, there was the matter of being educated, shaped, tested—and testing—during the years of formation, and becoming a priest in the Roman Catholic Church. This was for me a basically positive process, rich in practice and theory, spiritual and intellectual learning. By the time I was ordained in 1978 this process was largely complete; I was formed.

At the same time, the global Society experienced a second birth. No sooner had the Society been born than did Francis Xavier permanently leave Europe, to travel to India in 1542 and thereafter to East Asia. By 1600 there were Jesuits also in the Americas, embassies to the Moghul emperor's court in India, and plans for outreach to Thailand, Vietnam, and still other parts of the newly opened world.

Xavier's brief and intense mission already contained the seeds for a characteristic way of being Jesuit: an erudite and intellectual encounter with people of other religions and cultures, an encounter driven by intense curiosity, optimism about the possibility of communication with people of every cultural background. To preach the Gospel of Jesus Christ in a way that could be understood, the early Jesuit missionaries had to be scholars of a new kind, learning languages and customs hitherto unrelated to the Christian tradition, and even as they were learning, they were also quickly entering into argument and conversation with learned members of the new cultures. In Europe, the arguments were with Protestants and Renaissance intellectuals, about issues as old as the Church and the Greek heritage of Christianity. In the wider world, the Jesuits extended those arguments but recreated them for new audiences. All along, Francis Xavier and his successors seemed never to wonder whether what they said made sense, nor about what to say next.

But at the same time, in the late 1970s, my second birth as a Jesuit took place—when I became a priest and Jesuit who was also a scholar—in my own way, but also in the Jesuit tradition, modeled upon some fine Jesuit scholars I had encountered during my early years as a Jesuit. My particular "vocation within a vocation" was to be a theologian dedicated to the study of the Hindu religious traditions. This second choosing in part had to do with using my inclination to language learning and theological reflection as the stuff of a career in academics. In part it also had to do with wanting to chart a course not previously taken: instead of Latin and Greek, Sanskrit and Tamil; instead of the great Christian tradition, the great traditions of Hindu India.

Much of my life as a Jesuit has been energized by a sense of these two trajectories: to be a Jesuit priest, but also to be a Jesuit priest who spends his time studying India and who claims that studying Hindu traditions makes a difference for Christians and Jesuits. To find words for one's encounter with Jesus Christ is in a way a traditional task, still a matter of being a scholar of a particular kind, learning new languages and customs and so very quickly entering into argument and conversation with learned members of new cultural frames. Over thirty-seven years a Jesuit, over twenty-seven years a priest, and over twenty-one years out of graduate school, this Francis Xavier still wonders whether what he has already said makes sense religiously, and whether he still has something useful to say next.

III. How They Thought

In a 2002 essay for *Studies in the Spirituality of Jesuits*[3] I reflected on the Jesuit charism for interreligious encounter as a matter of scholarship, a way of living, and a matter of faith: "As we seek balance in the present situation, we do well to pay renewed attention to Jesuit origins, in search of what I will be calling the Jesuit charism for dialogue as revealed to us in the work and writings of the early Jesuit missionary scholars, that is, those missionaries from the sixteenth to the eighteenth centuries who left for us extensive writings as records of their cross-cultural learning and interpretation of it. My guess is that just as the Society has profited greatly by a retrieval of the basic Ignatian charism in the *Exercises* and *Constitutions*, today we can also profitably reflect on the insights, experiments, opinions, and hopes of the missionary scholars, reading the signs of our times in light of theirs."[5] In the essay and in related research, I pondered the early Jesuit missionary

How I Think

Much of my reflection on my own study of India is rooted in an awareness of how scholarship is a way of living, and a matter of faith. At stake is whether I have a charism for interreligious thinking. Over the years, I have found the exploration of different religious traditions to be enriching and satisfying, but also a challenge to my Christian identity. Early in my Jesuit life, I decided to travel beyond the boundaries of my familiar Christian upbringing by going to St. Xavier's High School in Kathmandu, Nepal, for two years of teaching known in Jesuit lore as "regency." Because I was teaching in a traditional Buddhist and Hindu culture, and because I realized I had to understand before I could be understood, I learned more than I was able to enable my students to learn.[4] Asia was as monumental for me as it was for the early Jesuits, and I shall never be done with the challenge and the learning. After ordination back in the United States, I followed up on the experience by working for a Ph.D. in South Asian Studies at the University of Chicago, and committing myself to serious research on Hindu religious traditions. Since then, I have had occasion to travel to India a number of times for longer and shorter periods of study and exploration.

For several decades, my major projects have included Hindu liturgical theology, nondualist Vedanta, vernacular devotionalism, Hindu systematic theology, and the theology of Hindu goddesses. Presently I am immersed in a comparative spiritual theology, as I read the fourteenth-century Hindu theologian Vedanta Desika, particularly his *Srimad Rahasya Traya Sara* ("Auspicious Essence of the Three Mantras"). By studying this classic, I am hoping to learn what Hindus have meant by tradition, scripture and its meanings, and the encounters with other cultures and religions. My study was intended largely as an appreciative glance at those amazing pioneers who traveled such a long way in order to teach and persuade. They form a lineage to which we are very much indebted. But I also wanted to draw a line, marking where we can and can't imitate those missionaries today. Thus, "some features of the early views of Jesuits stand out prominently. First, cultures and traditions, no matter how distant, are never entirely alien or unintelligible. All traditions and cultures share a common origin in God's creative plan and continue to be touched by divine providence. Second, most of what one encounters in Asia and the Americas and throughout the world is good because it is from God. Third, reason functions and communicates successfully across all linguistic and cultural divides. Fourth, the Trinitarian God is present and at work in the texts, symbols, and actions of various cultures and reli-

ideal and practice of surrender to God. The text begins with the verse, "We speak in reverence for our gurus and likewise for their gurus . . . ," words that could well begin yet a third column to the right of this one—what is my lineage, whence my connection to the beginnings?—but even by itself a verse that can also be taken as explaining why the whole left column of this essay is dedicated to thinking about my Jesuit ancestors—my teachers and their teachers—from Francis Xavier to Pierre Johanns (early twentieth century), Richard DeSmet, and Ignatius Hirudayam (both mid- and late twentieth century).

Personally, I have found this intellectual labor to be very demanding, but also enriching and immensely pleasurable. Learning takes a long time, we know, and I have had to keep paying attention. The more I have learned, the more interesting I have found the Hindu traditions to be, and the more I have benefited from contact with Hindu people, their ideas and images, texts and practices. I have learned much, and spiritually I have been helped much. Intellectually I have found very little of significance that I disagree with in some specific way. In the end, as at the beginning, I still seek to dedicate my life to Jesus Christ, but every factor is now seen in a different light; unrestricted intellectual respect, accompanied by a deepening religious respect, is not diminished by the gift of continuing to be a companion of Jesus.

Ten years ago, in an essay entitled "In Ten Thousand Places, In Every Blade of Grass," I wrote about how I went from being a person who spent two years abroad after college, to becoming a life-long scholar of Hindu traditions:[6] "I realized that if my scholarly career was to last longer than my time in graduate school, I would have to fashion a way of life

gions, and can (by grace) be recognized in them. Fifth, the actual religions of the world are deficient, distortions of the true and the good, and possess only fragments of the truths and values fully possessed by the Roman Church. Sixth, while sin and demonic influence are possible, the major root of false religion is ignorance. This can be overcome by an education that includes reasoned argument and the correction of errors; seventh, it is possible and worthwhile to argue about religious matters, since the triumph of truth is to the intellectual and spiritual benefit of those corrected in debate."[8] As the early Jesuits educated Europe, in the same way they intended to educate all nations, ever confident in their ability to persuade.

Their knowledge was seamless and generated a flow of confident words. Much of what they said has not been read in a long time, so in 2000, with Anand Amaladass, S.J., I published a translation of two of Roberto de Nobili's Tamil writings which fostered intellectual commitments. What I personally liked to do, I also had to cherish and protect. Particularly because I wanted to be a theologian in a way that would cross so many intellectual and cultural and spiritual boundaries, I needed to fashion a life in which I could continue to bring together and reflect for a long time on religions, my own experiences and study of Hinduism, within this specific American religious context, here, today."[7]

This 1996 essay, useful background for this essay, was a rather straightforward intellectual autobiographical piece. In it I combined attention to the Jesuit intellectual tradition with a sense of my own choices on how to be a scholar; the purpose was to investigate my calling to be a companion of Jesus. Now, almost a decade later, the questions are still complex, the situation rather different, and answers elusive, but such tensions continue to give me life and energy as well.

I still confess that everyone, everywhere, will do well to hear the Good News and enter into a free relationship with Jesus Christ. I could not but keep admitting that preaching the Gospel is intrinsic to my Christian and Jesuit identity. Nor do I believe that obedience to this Gospel mandate can be indefinitely postponed, simply because I appreciate the positive values of interreligious learning and dialogue, or because I want to gather more information first. It cannot be so, for Christ is always now. Yet how I, the Jesuit who is a scholar, speak of Christ, and walk as his disciple, remains an event of faith that for me can never be merely a matter of placing Christian answers before people who seem not to share the questions such answers presuppose. I have had to keep refashioning my place in the Christian intellectual tradition, so that a

and a revised translation of a key Latin treatise.[9] The aim of *Preaching Wisdom to the Wise* was primarily to show how one early Jesuit thought—like us, yet in many ways a figure from a different world.

De Nobili's writings are erudite, argumentative, and imbued with an eagerness to win over those with whom he is arguing. De Nobili wanted to enter as deeply as possible into the Indian world, embracing all that was good and reasonable, while rejecting as superstition all that differed from the Christian faith. De Nobili had great confidence in the cross-cultural power of reasoning, and he confidently charted the way in which reasonable people were supposed to conclude to the truths of Christianity. His writings do not speak of his personal experience, however, nor readily yield hints that other religions could teach him something he did not already know.

In his view, the Indians were not truly other. They were like himself, even if bereft of the advantages

thinking that serves faith is first of all true thinking. Knowledge of other traditions has entailed respect, a respect seemingly in harmony with the most simple foundation—Christ alone—but also rather bereft of reasons why being a Christian is *intellectually* preferable to being a Hindu or Buddhist.

Knowledge opens a gap and interrupts the flow of confident words. I have often found myself possessed of insights and experiences—ordinary ones, nothing overwhelming, but still strong and enduring—that unsettle and complexify how I think about particular instances of what people in other religions believe, think, and practice. I have had to travel a path the Jesuit missionary scholars did not travel. They spoke of Hindu idolatry in horror and fascination, but I put it this way in a plenary address at the Catholic Theological Society of America annual meeting in June 2003:

"The Vedanta Desika Koil is a rather old Hindu temple in the Mylapore section of Chennai, India. During 1992–1993, I used to visit it several times a month. Inside, to the right, and at the side of the main shrine for Lord Visnu, there is a smaller but nonetheless imposing shrine for the goddess Laksmi, Visnu's eternal consort. The shrine is dark, quiet, and attractive. It has a kind of aura to it. I also knew from my reading that in the Srivaisnava tradition Laksmi is presented as the perfect spouse who gives life to Her husband, Visnu. She is a maternal figure, gracious and compassionate, welcoming strangers and outsiders, a friend to the poor. I felt oddly, entirely at home at her shrine. I used to stop in and stand there for a few minutes when visiting the temple, as long I might stay—without attracting too much attention.

"To visit this temple and stand before the goddess Laksmi opened for me new possibili-

of Roman Catholicism, and they could be talked to, and could be instructed and corrected, so as to become even more like himself, not on the surface, but rather at the deeper levels of knowing and faith. The Jesuit was always in control, as the one who could understand both his own and the other religion, and who could, by using his erudition, persuade others to act in new and more appropriate ways, though apparently without being changed himself.

ties of vision beyond what I had seen or thought before. I was face to face with a reality—a kind of real presence—from within a living religious tradition other than my own. I knew that according to the Hindu tradition, I was also being seen by Her.

"I did not have, nor do I have now, some easy words by which to explain this concrete and in some ways very foreign moment of encounter. There is no room for Laksmi in Christian theology, no easy theory that makes sense of Her presence. Seeing and reflection ought to lead to an appropriate response. I suppose I might even have worshipped Her, because I was already there, as it were seeing and being seen. But Christians do not worship goddesses, so I did not. I just stood there, looking."[10] Standing there at the edge of the temple precinct, I'd managed to lose control. In a way I had been won over to what I had seen, in the way I had seen it. I was persuaded. I was erudite, and I was learning something I did not already know.

In that plenary address, my hope was to sketch that wider theological world—not just the comparativist's world—that opens like a lotus for those who seriously bring their own religion into living encounter with another. But the price of venturing into that world is to encounter so many people who are unlike myself but who tell me something of who I am. I keep learning things that seem not to fit into any single, coherent view of reality, and I have had to dwell patiently with that unsettling newness. Accordingly, I've also learned not to control the implications of my learning, nor to imagine that I am in control, able to persuade others to act in new and more appropriate ways without at the same time being likewise changed myself.

IV. Recreating the Brahmin in the Mirror of the Jesuit

In 2003, in preparation for the Bellarmine Lecture at Fairfield University, and since then in additional reading, I have been learning more about the Jesuit missionary tradition as a lineage of interreligious practice. In particular, I have been examining the Jesuit-Brahmin encounter in sixteenth- to eighteenth-century India, and I have worked at deciphering "Brahmin" and "Jesuit" as a mutually dependent pair of terms. I found that "Brahmin" was explained and assessed in both positive and negative ways by Jesuits. Brahmins were often imagined to be frauds, superstitious priests, arrogant in their resistance to the Gospel or as essentially religious, but in a way that was open to correction and improvement by Christian values and culture. But other Jesuits, and sometimes the same missionary scholars, saw Brahmins also as the most civilized and essential guardians of a culture that with a little correction would flourish as a Christian culture. Despite numerous differences, those Brahmins were like Jesuits. This ambiguity—"the Brahmins are the worst, they are the best"—was never to be resolved.

We cannot say much about what the Brahmins thought of the Jesuits—Brahmin texts from the period do not mention the missionaries—but from the Jesuit reports we know that the Jesuits and other foreigners were lumped in the category

Recreating Myself in the Mirror of the Brahmin

More than twenty-five years into my study of Hinduism, I am still a Jesuit—indeed, more a Jesuit than I was at the beginning of my studies—and in a way I have cultivated my own place in the lineage that reaches back to St. Francis Xavier—like my Jesuit ancestors, I am a Jesuit thinking about Brahmins. Even today, the writings of the Brahmins still offer the easiest access to the Hindu religious traditions. They wrote books that have endured over time and traveled around the world, documents that even now remain the most readily available sources for study. So it is hard to avoid encountering Brahmins and thinking along with them. Brahmins are at the top of the social and religious hierarchy; they tend to benefit from and make peace with, justify, and tolerate unequal and unjust social structures. And yet they are also great intellectuals, and their world is a wonderfully rich intellectual realm. Brahmins are in a real sense, even if not exactly, like the educated class in the West. Despite numerous differences, they are like Jesuits—like me. I can in part at least understand them, and if I do, I begin also to appreciate them, and to become their partners in explaining them to a wider audience. All of this is true even if I also condemn pernicious hierarchies, exclusions, radical divisions between rich and poor—such as occurs in my America, such as

of the "prangui"—barbarians, the Francs, foreigners, perhaps even the crusaders. They were judged to be inferior, indulging in practices and relationships offensive to Brahminical ways of living.

Xavier and de Nobili are well-known figures, but I have also been gathering a wider company of Jesuit scholars to ponder, lesser known but important eighteenth-century figures. In a lengthy 1701 letter—from among the famous *Lettres Édifiantes et Curieuses*[12]—a Fr. Mauduit affords us a vivid sense of the standard Jesuit way of negotiating Brahmin life, practice, and expectations; he is in a way as attentive and alert as any of us could hope to be, yet at the same time—as when he destroys the home shrine of a family hosting him—appallingly crude. Brahmins remain the competition to be defeated and yet for him too, as for Xavier and de Nobili, they were also his most learned conversation partners.

Fr. Jean V. Bouchet, S.J. (1655–1732) vividly and with great erudition describes Brahmin thinking and practices—regarding the gods, spiritual and ritual practice, reincarnation—and also draws them into elaborate comparisons with Biblical and Graeco-Roman beliefs and practices. He also places his experience in the south Indian missions in the service of a specific European debate, on whether it was the Resurrection or Christian political power that defeated paganism and ended the famous oracles of the Greek and

is present in India, among these Hindu religious elites, and among elites such as that of my Church and Society. This ambiguity is one I am unlikely to resolve.

I study Brahmin writings today not so much with a fear of idolatry or demons, but a fear of compromise on justice issues. In a recent reflection for *Conversations*,[11] I described the difficulties that arise in my own thinking about Jesuits and Brahmins, by way of recounting a dilemma arising with respect to a particular text, the famous and infamous *Laws of Manu*, which I was teaching at the same time I was writing the piece for *Conversations*: "Composed about 2,000 years ago, *The Laws of Manu* is a vastly influential legal classic, a synthesis of major law codes and central to the Hindu intellectual tradition. It is a thoughtful synthesis and organization of the rules and regulations of orthodoxy arranged as an ideal portrait of the life of the Brahmin from youth to old age and death, and (less amply) of members of other castes as well. As jurisprudence, *Manu* also undergirds norm and practice by a theory of the origins and nature of the world as such, and a moral analysis of human nature and action. . . .

"There is, however, a problem with this academic exercise in the study of a religious classic. *Manu* is also a controversial and hated book. Numerous Indians, some Hindu, many Dalits (including outcaste, untouchable, some tribal communities) and some Christian intellectuals, despise *Manu*

Roman worlds. As has happened many times since then, India was useful in providing information for a largely European and Christian debate.[13]

G. L. Coeurdoux, S.J. (c. 1760) was a pioneering anthropologist, and his *Les Moeurs et Coutumes des Indiens*—brilliantly even if hypothetically reconstructed by Sylvia Murr from the two versions attributed to other authors[14]—was a full length study of the Brahmins that explored every available aspect of Brahmin history and culture, the most religious or idolatrous or mundane, for the sake of understanding who they were. In a series of sober and unhesitating analyses, Coeurdoux characterized them also according to their moral flaws. Like Jesuits before him, but more thoroughly and in more depth, Coeurdoux studied the Brahmins from every available angle, knowing in advance that they would be useful interlocutors through whom he could peer into Indian society, without their ever being his religious peers. In doing so, he remained primarily in dialogue with his European interlocutors—those intent on using reliable knowledge in order to convert Indians, and also those who were merely interested in filling out their knowledge of the human race.

Reading *Les Lettres* and *Les Moeurs* demonstrates how early Jesuits sorted out cultures other than their own, understanding them in familiar terms, and in ways that made adaptation possible. The array of philo-

as a dangerous and oppressive book. It appears the very icon of Brahminical oppression, a skillfully composed and forceful legitimation of elitism and oppression, of values offensive to the Christian way of living.

"It is true that *Manu* sanctions hierarchy and privilege, though binding Brahmins by more rules than anyone else. Its author appeals to rulers to enforce humiliation and deprivation on unruly inferiors, for the sake of right religious order. *Manu* can easily offend us as egalitarians, Christians, allies of the oppressed. But *Manu* is also a complex text more easily vilified by those who have either never read it or read only its most villainous verses. Of course, I do point out the infamy of *Manu* to my students, and I do highlight some of the more unpleasant parts of the text. To know it well brings out its problematic features, but also its admirable ones, and the complex over context in which both the good and the bad occur. In teaching *Manu*, I have gained for it more fans than enemies, since it is harder to despise absolutely something one understands."[15]

As I keep reading in the Brahmin tradition and learning what their classic texts say and mean, this reading becomes more than a matter of a sober and efficient analysis; it is a rather more complex and interactive enterprise that does not easily lead to any single conclusion. Scholarly discipline now teaches me that any single, fixed view of the religious person

sophical, literary, and ethnographic strategies is impressive. Understanding was at stake for the sake of disciplined and focused knowing, and this discipline was at the service of salvation. We see here the missionaries' earnestness to understand and also their determination to make sense of cultures, reading them both with and against indigenous self-understandings. But key, perhaps, is their de facto strategy of shaping Brahmins into the kind of religious competitors whom they could challenge and defeat, because they were infused with a passion that seemed always to be very certain as well.

of another tradition is improbable. If I teach *Manu* properly, I am teaching students both to admire and dislike the text, but first of all to take it seriously and listen to what its author has to say, for he is a religious peer who shares with me the problem of scholarship as promise and compromise.

Research and teaching have dynamics of their own; scholarship can be intensely religious in its roots, and still not have the expected results; my writing on India has a life of its own. Like any responsible teacher, I try to teach and enter deeply, even with excitement, into the materials I teach, even if now I cannot be in the position to stipulate the meaning or fruit of what I teach. Gone today is the expectation and perhaps even the possibility of a knowledge that programs a single disciplined mode of action; the discipline remains, but it is not easily marshaled to rationalize and guarantee a particular religious end, even the highest of ends. Jesuit passions thus remain high, but the goal is a bit uncertain, for my others are no longer competitors whom I can challenge and defeat. For my passion, though real, does not become certain in that way.

V. Disconnecting Scholarship and Apologetics

I recently wrote an essay entitled "Understanding in Order to Be Understood, Refusing to Understand in Order to Preach."[16] It was deliberately meant to be provocative. In it I argued that the Jesuit missionary scholars, in

Reconnecting Scholarship and Mission

As a Jesuit scholar I am on mission. This is supposed to be apparent; everything I do is part of my mission. But today it

part distinguished by their extraordinary effort to understand other traditions, wrote in a way also distinguished by an inevitable negativity; and that when scholarship and apologetics had sufficiently diverged, perhaps beginning in the nineteenth century (in India, at least), the age of such missionary scholarship was over, even if scholars and missionaries were still be to be seen.

Missionary scholars strove to be meticulously honest, but always with the expectation that errors, gaps, and deficiencies would in the end be demonstrated and thereafter refuted, corrected, and healed, after what the natives had meant to say was stated clearly. However much good is discovered in the other, there must also be something wanting. The breadth and energy of Jesuit scholarship could afford to be mostly laudatory or neutral, as long as somewhere a fatal flaw, requiring a Christian remedy, was discovered. This proclivity to find fault seems to have been built into missionary scholarship as a defining feature; such scholarship thus differs from what we must mean by scholarship today: "We must be impressed with de Nobili's careful and intelligent appropriation of Indian culture, even as we notice how deliberately and systematically he identified an irreducible surd, a small set of beliefs and practices which could not be assimilated into a Christian worldview and which had to be rejected as superstition, idolatry in theory and practice. He was as stubborn in refusing to comprehend such features as he was steadfast in his generally broad understanding. What was distinctively religious and indigenous to India—what we might popularly call 'Hinduism'—had to be found defective in some way or another. Deities like Rama had to be labeled false insofar as they indicated anything more than reasonable inklings of God. De Nobili's diligent scholar-

becomes more difficult to discern the particular nature of the mission, and what kind of scholarly work might conceivably not be part of my mission as a Jesuit.

I spent most of the time between 1984 and 2005 at Boston College, but I also was fortunate to have studied and worked with Hindu scholars in India. During 2002–2004, I had the opportunity to work more closely with Hindu scholars at the Oxford Centre for Hindu Studies where I served as academic director. Life in Oxford's venerable university setting turned out to be both pleasant and complex; one had to be neutral, involved, and sensitive to differences, all at once. Yet it is in places like Oxford that the traditions of learning from different parts of the world meet. Old and decentralized, Oxford seems no longer the uncontested property of a ruling class. In our post-imperial age, Oxford seems potentially at least a place for scholarship that crosses cultural and religious boundaries in every direction.

ship had to support his belief that the error of idolatry is traceable in theory (in the *Inquiry*) and in worship (in his *Refutation of Calumnies*), to particular epistemological origins (in the *Dialogue on Eternal Life*), and as a harmful overlay spoiling generally sound social structures (in the *Report on Indian Customs*). . . . His lack of understanding occurs when (consciously or not) he no longer wishes to improvise; it is a correlative and necessary feature of his project of understanding, since total sympathy and understanding would not serve his project well." Propaganda can be both a promotion of the Good News and a way of contrasting our good news with their bad news.

I concluded, "While one could easily introduce data from the Indian context that would challenge de Nobili's critique, we would miss the point of his project by trying merely to correct it. . . . Whatever he might have learned, the logic of his missionary scholarship would still not allow him to embrace wholeheartedly the traditions he found in south India, nor even to sympathize with their imperfections as he would with the imperfections others found in his own Catholicism. Generous approval on most fronts required some remnant deserving fierce condemnation. The realm of the unintelligible and the unacceptable had to exist, had to be discovered and conceptualized, if the work of conversion was to remain clear and urgent even among missionaries inclined to scholarly work. . . .

"The construction of an intelligible realm of contact is not sufficient to define the missionary enterprise; rather, there is a double movement of understanding and refusing to understand, a dialectic, which superimposes onto the object culture a bifurcation between its intelligible and non-intelligible elements. Neither 'understanding in order to be understood,' nor 'a refusing to understand in order to convert,'

Returning to Boston College from Oxford, at home I noticed how the notion of real cooperation among institutions and scholars—such as would facilitate easy communication may become all the more elusive. Universities employ scholars; scholars need a salary, so they work for universities even if their conversations largely occur elsewhere. To keep the distance that allows thinking to occur and be taken seriously, I have had to question somewhat intensely my own Jesuit tradition of interreligious scholarship on Hindu traditions, a tradition reaching from Francis Xavier to the present. I have had to ask whether that tradition was based on presuppositions no longer entirely adequate today. If conversion is not the goal for which discovering the deficiencies of Hinduism is a necessary step, why should I study the religion at all? Or, if preaching the Gospel does remain the goal, then what happens if the necessary justifications for this can no longer be expressed in conventional

would on its own have sufficed to constitute missionary scholarship."[17] It is in the pairing of the acceptable and unacceptable—enormous praise for the culture, accompanied by smaller but intensely focused areas of rejection—that the distinctive Jesuit missionary achievement lay.

terms? Perhaps it is in these ambiguities, at the edge where rationales fail and break down, that the distinctive Jesuit missionary achievement now lies.

VI. Scholarship and Apologetics Diverge

Scholarship and Public Relations Diverge

As far as I can see based on my even more preliminary study, the nineteenth century makes clear the divergence of erudition and apologetics: strong opinions on Christian uniqueness without solid knowledge about people of other faiths, alongside solid knowledge unaccompanied by vocal opinions about salvation and related issues. Here are just two examples. Leo Meurin, S.J., Vicar Apostolic of Bombay (1867–1887), wrote a long essay entitled "God and Brahm," (1865) in which he demonstrated that the Hindu notion of Brahman as ultimate reality is only a poor substitute for the Christian understanding of God; he did not, however, also demonstrate much knowledge of Hindu thought.[18] In 1876, Augustus Thebaud, S.J., first president of Fordham University, published *Gentilism: Religion Previous to Christianity*,[19] a book rather impressive in its sweeping survey of the world religions. The whole book, however, is an argument with Western scholars about the origins and development of religion; his main thesis was that God gave the

I taught at Boston College for twenty-one years. I was generally very happy, and when I shifted to Harvard University in the summer of 2005, it was with gratitude for Boston College as a place where scholars can work. But in retrospect I can see that I never "bonded" with the institution to the point of imagining that my interests and those of the institution coincided in a full and complete fashion. Though amicable, the administrators and I always seemed to be going our own way, meeting on occasion. Much of the rhetoric about Boston College as Jesuit always appeared to me peculiar, written about Jesuits by writers who would only rarely consult me, and who wrote for an audience that did not include me. The intellectual life of Jesuits was appropriately lauded, but there seemed to be no need to consult the Jesuits like myself who were primarily scholars. Rather, what needs to be known about the Jesuit intellectual life is sufficiently known in advance. The good publicist often enough turns out to be less than subtle, a promoter of

truth to the world in the beginning. The original humans had a real knowledge of God their creator, and did not begin with primitive beliefs about self and world, life and death, God and heaven, and then progress toward beliefs more like those of nineteenth-century Europeans. The religions were thus fuel for an argument that did not directly include the people of those religions nor even anticipate conversations with them. What needs to be known about the natives was always already known. The good apologist often enough turns out to be a poor scholar.

The critique of religions and the actual study of them were gradually diverging, even if the difference was not immediately noticeable. Even if those who studied the religions and the others who judged them tended to be in agreement, the fruits of scholarship and the project of apologetics no longer cohered.

To show where this led, however, we can also turn our attention to twentieth-century Western Jesuits in India who studied Hinduism during the waning moments of the long colonial missionary period. Early in the century, we find Pierre Johanns (1882–1955), the Belgian Jesuit, working in Calcutta, whose "To Christ through the Vedanta" constituted one of the last great works of Jesuit missionary scholarship. In 1912, the British Jesuit C. C. Martindale (1879–1963) edited five volumes dedicated to the study of religions, of which the first volume was on world

good news only. Some of us were the scholars, and our work is always ambivalent, while others among us ran the university and determined what scholarship would mean for the university community.

There is no point in blaming anyone, for everyone worked with good intentions. Quite probably, I myself did not play my role skillfully enough. While scholarly reflection on religious traditions can help shape a Jesuit institution, my study of Hinduism was not likely to be easily integrated into any particular institutionalization of Jesuit religious and interreligious ideals. There may be no easily charted path from the study of religions and the scholarly life to comforts of a sure, evident, and reliable religious identity. Unlike the missionary scholar, I have never succeeded in dramatizing the Catholic and Jesuit ways as intellectually preferable, and consequently could not play a useful role in Boston College's self-presentation. As a scholar with a reserve of difficult questions, I could not be relied upon to shore up the settled view of what a Jesuit university—as institution, as ministry—is supposed to be. Institution and scholarly practice, administrators and professors, now seem at odds, on friendly terms but vaguely disappointing to one another.

Perhaps we are still witnessing the waning moments of the twentieth-century model of the "modern" Jesuit intellectual life. What now remains has to be inconveniently postmod-

religions. Camil Bulcke (1909–1982) lived in India for many years, and was a respected scholar of the Hindi language and literature. He sought out the historical roots of the story of the important deity Rama, perhaps seeking to highlight the historical core of the epic over its theological developments. Richard DeSmet (1916–1997), also a Belgian and scholar of classical Hindu theology, wrote on a range of Indological topics and contributed a pioneering dissertation on the theological method of Sankara, the great Hindu theologian. DeSmet was a respected scholar and had come to India as a missionary; and yet his work, primarily a contribution to the study of Vedanta and no longer deeply connected to an apologetic enterprise, arguably stands at the very end of missionary scholarship. For it is with these twentieth-century figures that "modern scholarship" comes to the fore, just as the idea of a specifically missionary learning declines. The expectation that close study will reveal the inherent inadequacy of non-Christian thought becomes vague, ever receding into some future moment when differences will finally become clear and credible; it can hardly be said to have a vital role any more. The tension has slackened, while the label "Jesuit" is still applied to the missions, the institutions, and the scholarship. There were still scholars and still apologists, but most often they went their separate ways, perhaps to meet up at the journey's end.

ern, as insights, images, emotions, and deeds remain near to one another, contiguous yet always distinct, on their own. Not that the shift is immediately noticeable. Even a Jesuit university without Jesuits who are scholars will still call itself "a university in the Jesuit scholarly tradition." Even a Jesuit scholar like myself, working outside the Jesuit university, will still think of himself as sharing the lineage of Jesuit scholarship. What has slackened is the unique tension between the Society as an institution and the Society as a company of men—scholars included— on an identifiable mission. We all remain in contact, we all go our separate ways, planning to meet up at the journey's end.

At the beginning of the twenty-first century Jesuit scholars such as myself must redefine ourselves as missionaries again—apart again, no longer working with large numbers of my Jesuit brothers, yet meeting all kinds of new sisters and brothers, all in the light of Christ. Harvard professor or not, I will be a better Jesuit scholar if I can reclaim the pilgrim status of Francis Xavier, who left Ignatius behind and went off to the East on his own. When learning and the duties of a campus intellectual are brought back into tension, this may catalyze a more intense core for Jesuit identity, even as explicit institutional Jesuit identity ceases to be the issue. Now that I am the Parkman Professor of Divinity at the Harvard Divinity School, I can only hope that my Jesuit

By the end of the twentieth century, there were very few Western Jesuit missionary scholars left working in India, and these seem to have put aside the missionary determination to find fault in the other. As missionaries, and then as apologists and theologians of religions, the Jesuits were as earnest and sincere as ever, and as scholars, perhaps more erudite than ever; but the creative tension embodied by missionary scholars had dissipated, as learning and zeal go their separate ways. But this need not be the story's ending; there should be another chapter for us to write.

story has not reached its ending; there should be another chapter for me to write.

VII. The People of Other Religious Traditions Become Truly Other to Jesuits

Even if the deep integration of scholarship and the mission to convert is largely dissipated and impossible to revive, why then might Jesuits engage other religious traditions in this century? As the older missionary scholarship has waned and largely disappeared, today the Jesuit encounter with other religions, distinguished by the emphasis placed on this at the 1995 Thirty-fourth General Congregation, serves rather the goal of creating real dialogical possibilities that cross the boundaries among traditions. At issue, beyond an interest in Jesuit history and the quandaries of personal experience, is the nature of scholarship about religions in the

I Become Other unto Myself

Even if I insist that being a Jesuit and being a scholar of Hinduism can be deeply integrated, the effects of this Jesuit's study of another religion cannot be integrated as in past centuries. Or so I have found. Hindus, Jews, and people in also the various traditions are truly other to me, never quite what I want them to be, and I am the better for this. The path of learning is then inherently open and even multiple. However deeply I comprehend my identity and however intensely I hope to live by faith, when I begin to learn I will always be in conversation with others whom I only partially understand, who are never reducible to what I say about them, and who will also keep re-assessing me, adjusting their responses, and thus affect-

United States academic setting today—pluralist, postmodern, and postcolonial, newly autobiographical—and the price of entrance to the scholarly world for a Jesuit scholar today. The situation remains unresolved in the postmodern world, as not only disciplines but also persons shift identities; "confessional" and "autobiographical" are increasingly prominent dimensions of work of many younger scholars today, as the interplay of zeal and inquiry is all the more intensified.

This scholarship, insofar as it is distinctively Christian scholarship, will be distinguished by a concern to create and preserve a common space for dialogue, premised on an honest discovery of an enduring even if not impermeable otherness. The challenge today is to lay foundations for a dialogical scholarship in which there is always an expectation of meeting God in meeting religious others who are never simply or finally who we think they are. The new dynamic is not only being-sent to bring others the good news, but to witness to the good news by learning what has never fit into our view of the world and Christ, but rather remains nearby, on a parallel path.

How we experience our nearby others—diverse Catholic theologians, for instance—affects how we enter into dialogue with Brahmins and other religious intellectuals of diverse traditions. Again limiting myself to Western scholars—for

ing how I think of myself. To decide to study Hindu traditions for a lifetime is also to enter into encounters (personal, textual) that are never fully explained by a theory or finished off in an act of conversion. I live in conversation with religious others who will never become merely "us," as if their otherness might evaporate. In conversation, the dynamic between settled and changing identities becomes all the more intense.

Accordingly, what I had thought might be a vice is now shown to be a virtue: I have learned to be other—friend, companion, but on my own path—in relation to the universities in which I have worked, to the Society itself as a Catholic institution, and even to other Jesuits who are scholars. Being a scholar cannot be adequately institutionalized or homogenized; the scholar can always move elsewhere. That I should feel privatized or isolated in scholarship is not a misperception, but rather a key feature of my situation. Perhaps the old missionaries were not more alone than I am today. A scholar must keep looking for intellectual soul-mates when venturing to say anything that would be both self-revelatory and also worth saying. As I present myself in interreligious dialogue, so I will live alongside others who are much more like me; nearby, but always on parallel paths.

By dialogue with Hindus, I am also learning to enter into an informed dialogue with my nearby others, the

nowhere in this essay am I reflecting on how Jesuits native to the various world cultures relate to the religions of those cultures—I think of examples such as the most recent books of Jacques Dupuis, S.J., perhaps the last great Jesuit theorist of religions who could still hope for a universal explanatory theory, and Michael Barnes, S.J., whose work inaugurates a newer, postmodern venture. Here is what I said about them in a recent review essay in *Religious Studies Review*[21]: "In *Christianity and the Religions* [Dupuis] returns for a third time (after his earlier *Jesus Christ at the Encounter of World Religions* [1991] and *Toward a Christian Theology of Religious Pluralism* [1997]) to the task of explaining how fidelity to Jesus Christ, God and savior, can be shown compatible with a more inclusive conversation with people of other faiths and with an openness to learning religious truth from those religions. Dupuis suggests an inclusive pluralism based in an understanding of the Christ in light of the full mystery of the Trinity. The three divine persons do not work apart or separately, and so there is still no salvation 'outside' Christ; but neither is the work of God reduced to the work of Christ, the Son. We thus move beyond theories contending that the world religions are fulfilled, but also superseded and made largely superfluous, by Christianity. But since Christ and the Spirit are to be distinguished yet remain inseparable, so

institutions and communities that are and have been part of my life: the Society, the Church, for many years Boston College, and just now Harvard University. Here too, there is no single, harmonious relation among traditions and no smooth presentation that shows how this relation is to be understood.

All this is what I had in mind in a 1990 essay[20] in which I suggested the need to move beyond "collaboration" as a model. I suggested that a university wishing to remain Jesuit would have to develop a more nuanced vocabulary by which to hear and affirm the qualitatively different natures of Jesuit and non-Jesuit participation. As a Jesuit, I have to learn to see my university as one of my others, with whom I have a dialogical relationship. University administrators, Jesuit included, need to keep remembering just how "other" their own scholars can be and should be. Once this is accomplished, more constructive developments can occur. I can take a position at Harvard, yet remain a good neighbor to Boston College where I continue to live and still work with advanced graduate students; I can live at BC, but make Harvard a central site for my intellectual practice.

To capture a sense of this new dynamic, in that same essay I indicated that instead of "collaboration" I would use the term "counterpoint," a musical term, as capturing more adequately the irreducible distinction between the Jesuit and non-Jesuit

too this inclusive pluralism is presented as entirely orthodox: all is in Christ, yet generously inclusive within the unlimited play of Christ's Spirit."[22] Yet more can happen.

"In *Theology and the Dialogue of Religions* Barnes works from an explicitly theological perspective in order to reject casual conceptual pluralism as ineffective in fostering real dialogue, and to highlight instead the experience of dialogue and the obligations inherent in a dialogue genuinely open to new, other voices in a continuing counterpoint. He explores the dynamics of encounter in which the other is real, and otherness transgressed but not denied. To understand this, Barnes explores the demands and tensions of a 'heterology,' alert to strictures inherent in a discourse where both self and other are truly present, and accordingly draws on the thought of Michel de Certeau, S.J., in order to find ways of appreciating the other that allow it still to remain other. Useful theological reflection therefore moves beyond a consideration of the religions in abstract form to reflection on the dynamic and implications of actual encounters, and for this there is necessary a second level of theorizing on one's 'others' in light of encounter with the other. At issue is not simply the maintenance of self-integrity, but also the fashioning of a way to encounter the other as a true other who is neither too alien nor falsely similar, and from whom one can thus actually learn."[23]

voices, and the dynamic, historical process by which Jesuits and their universities relate to one another in lively negotiations that cannot be hushed to a monotone nor reduced to the replaying of an already available score.

In suggesting that I would speak of "counterpoint" instead of "collaboration," I did not imagine any immediate or dramatic change in myself or my university, precisely because the shift to a language of counterpoint was all about catching up with what had already been taking place. In fact, I had never been able to make my own that eventful and remedial post–Vatican II period in which clergy and theologians of an older generation had to learn to put aside standard and received practices of hierarchy in order to work with lay people in either ecclesial or university settings. Jesuits like me were busily acquiring newly refined sets of goals that might or might not harmonize with those of any particular institution. I decided I would be better off when I myself could no longer control the dialogue into which I enter, when I could no longer predict that the fruits of my scholarship are useful on campus. I was learning to be free to chart out new positions—and, as it turned out at the very end of the shared project that is *Jesuit Postmodern*, in a new location, Harvard University.

In studying for so long one religious other—Hinduism, Hindus whose writings I have studied, Hin-

Barnes clears a new path into a world where we keep moving to different places and where we learn to honor people who are very nearby but still other to us. Such is the Jesuit mission, even if the price is the loss of a single and predictable worldview. If Barnes is right, then the future of Jesuit scholarship of religions, fragile as it is, opens into an uncharted space where we no longer control the dialogue. Uncertainty, but not a lessening of passion, comes to characterize the situation in which Jesuits find themselves having to start thinking all over again. In this way we can still be a missionary Order, distinguished by encounters with people of other faith traditions whose mysteries we never finish with, and who remind us that we too are mysteries unto ourselves. We thus find ourselves yet again mysteriously in God's presence, called and sent, now.

dus who are friends—I came to acknowledge another series of others, closer to home, composed of Christians, Jesuits my colleagues and friends at Boston College, and now new friends and colleagues at Harvard—as neighbors who must keep being encountered, freshly and not in an entirely familiar space. And so, I cannot map conclusively the future of the Jesuit intellectual tradition, or of my contribution to it. It is into this uncharted space, marked by uncertainty because its truth requires me to think all over again, that I must travel if I am to figure out how to be a Jesuit intellectual in the twenty-first century. Such is my Jesuit mission.

Now, on the farther shore of the Charles River, I still have to keep writing with passion if I am to be a scholar and religious thinker in the Society of Jesus, writing in light of new encounters that never exhaust the mystery of the people I read and meet, nor of myself. I thus find myself yet again mysteriously in God's presence, called and sent, now.

Notes

1. Roberto de Nobili, "Report on Indian Customs," in *Preaching Wisdom to the Wise: Three Treatises by Roberto de Nobili in Dialogue with the Learned Hindus of South India*, introduced, annotated, and trans. Anand Amaladass, S.J., and Francis X. Clooney, S.J. (St. Louis: Institute of Jesuit Sources, 2000), 214.

2. *Hindu God, Christian God: How Reason Helps Break Down the Boundaries between Religions* (New York: Oxford University Press, 2001), 180.

3. "A Charism for Dialogue: Advice from the Early Jesuit Missionaries in our World of Religious Pluralism," *Studies in the Spirituality of Jesuits* (March 2002).

4. For an account of this learning, see "In Ten Thousand Places, In Every Blade of Grass: Uneventful but True Confessions about Finding God in India, and Here Too," *Studies in the Spirituality of Jesuits* 28, no. 3 (May 1996).

5. "A Charism for Dialogue," 4.

6. "In Ten Thousand Places."

7. "In Ten Thousand Places," 15.

8. "A Charism for Dialogue," 6–7.

9. Anand Amaladass, S.J., and Francis X. Clooney, S.J., *Preaching Wisdom to the Wise* (St. Louis: Institute of Jesuit Sources, 2000).

10. "Learning to See: Comparative Practice and the Widening of Theological Vision," *Proceedings of the Catholic Theological Society of America* 58 (2003): 1 (plenary address).

11. "When Researching and Teaching, Where and with Whom Is My Heart?" *Conversations in Jesuit Higher Education* 24 (Fall 2003): 46–48.

12. A useful English translation of Fr. Mauduit's report on his journey, originally in the famous *Lettres Édifiantes et Curieuses, écrites des Missions Étrangères, par quelques Missionaires de la Compagnie de Jésus*, can be found in John Lockwood, *Travels of the Jesuits*, vol. 1 (New Delhi: Asian Educational Services, 1995 [1743]), 423–46.

13. Pere Bouchet à Pere Baltus, "Sur les oracles que les démons rendent aux Indes et sur le silence de ces mêmes oracles dans les pays où la religion s'établit," in *Lettres Édifiantes et Curieuses, Écrites des Missions Etrangères, par quelques Missionaires de la Compagnie de Jésus*, vol. 9 (Paris: 1781), 42–79. See also Francis X. Clooney, S.J., *Fr. Pouchet's India: An 18th-century Jesuit's Encounter with Hinduism* (Chennai: Satya Nilayam Publications, 2006).

14. *L'Inde philosophique entre Bossuet et Voltaire* (Paris: École Française d'Extrême-Orient, 1987).

15. "When Researching and Teaching," 46–47.

16. In Karin Preisendanz, ed., *Contributions to Indian and Cross-Cultural Studies: Volume in Commemoration of Wilhelm Halbfass* (Vienna: Austrian Academy of Sciences Press, forthcoming).

17. From the manuscript version of the forthcoming essay.

18. Leo Meurin, S.J., "God and Brahm" (a lecture delivered in the Bombay Catholic Debating Club, 1865), in *Select Writings of the Most Reverend Dr. Leo Meurin, S.J.*, ed. P. A. Colaco (Bombay: C. M. Braganca and Company, 1909), 1–37.

19. Augustus Thebaud, S.J., *Gentilism: Religion Previous to Christianity* (New York: D. & J. Sadlier and Company, 1876).

20. "From Collaboration to Counterpoint: A Different Way to Talk about the Jesuit University," *Presence* (Spring 1990): 8–11.

21. "Theology, Dialogue, and Religious Others: Some Recent Books in the Theology of Religions and Related Fields," *Religious Studies Review* 29, no. 4 (2003): 319–27.

22. Page 321.

23. Page 323.

9

A Tale of Two Comings Out: Priest and Gay on a Catholic Campus

Thomas J. Brennan, S.J.

If your heart always did
What a normal heart would do
If you always play a part instead of being who
You really are,
Then you might just miss the wonder of it all . . .

"Love Don't Need a Reason"

I HEARD THESE LINES on a compact disc produced by the New York Gay Men's Chorus. At the time (2000 or 2001) I was writing my dissertation: a deconstruction of the mourning subject as it applies to Wordsworth, Tennyson, and Eliot. Awash in critiques questioning the possibility of the individual or subject, I found the essentialism of the song appealing. Not only does it assert identity— "who/You really are"—but it embraces that identity in "wonder." In addition, the lines contain an assurance: "your heart," the song tells its listeners, is distinct from "a normal heart" but that difference may uphold its authenticity. At the same time, "normality" becomes the derived characteristic or the "part" to be played.

Much of this interpretation depends on some large assumptions. The homogenized voice of the chorus—for this performance contains no individual parts— advises its listeners that falling in love represents the surest route to discovering "who/ You really are." The song then moves on to its celebratory refrain:

Love don't need a reason
Love don't always rhyme
And love is all we have for now
What we don't have is time.

The chorus presumably blends many male-sounding voices, and even if not all of them are gay, or even men, they nonetheless have furnished me and other listeners with a product that allows us to access or perhaps invent the identity that the song articulates. Michel Foucault's question—"What difference does it make who is speaking?"—might simply be answered with "nothing" (Foucault 120). No difference exists in this song among the singers as I hear them. For that reason, I can easily make the jump to imagining that this collective voice is addressing me as a potential player in their allegory of love.

On the other hand, we might say that everything depends on who is speaking in this song. In particular, if it were a solo piece, it would lose much of its anthem-like quality. The solitary singer might remind us that the community— I envision it as the chorus—may not be present for comfort if the envisioned love affair fails. Additionally, following Judith Butler's logic, what would my experience of this song be if I were to project my rather peculiar performance of gay identity onto this singer? In other words what if that solo singer is a celibate gay priest (Butler 317)? Same sex identification—seemingly reinforced at the level of the group and perhaps seeking sexual involvement as its terminus—may suddenly look less attractive when the possibility of sexual contact no longer forms part of the anticipation.

The odd staying power of gay identity and the need to interrogate this concept on a college campus is the focus of this essay. In the first section, I review recent arguments in favor of coming out and of not coming out in various campus venues. Carefully planned "comings out," I propose, remain politically necessary on many campuses as a kind of strategic or radical essentialism. I then argue in the next two sections that such essentialism thwarts two kinds of discourse that have victimized gay people. The first and most visible of these discourses, prevalent at Catholic schools like my own, invents the homosexual as a "deviant" or "aberrant" threat to the community's safety. The incoherence of this discourse becomes apparent, however, when one of its supposed defenders—the priest—also identifies as gay. The second discourse, more subtle but very prevalent among students, characterizes coming out as a passage from bondage to freedom. As the now visible gay reader, I take up the notion that coming out brings freedom but deploy against this idea James Baldwin's *Giovanni's Room*. In the process I hope that all of my students begin to see that the freedom they do have, instead of being reducible to particular choices that an individual makes, really inheres in its negotiation.

I. To Come Out or Not to Come Out?

In the debate about the efficacy of coming out on campus, the visibility of gay and lesbian faculty remains an important issue. On the one hand, lesbian and gay scholars who have been at work since the 1960s and the 1970s often argue for a mixture of activism and assimilation in advancing the rights of increasingly "out" members of a university community. According to Toni A. H. McNaron, this model has fairly tangible measures of success: obtaining funding for studies of lesbian and gay issues, getting appointed to university committees to study lesbian and gay issues, and formulating new questions related to sexual orientation for further research (McNaron 122). Additionally, McNaron stresses the need for alliances with other groups in order for lesbians and gays to achieve progress. For example, because lesbian and gay studies programs often prove difficult to establish, faculty members frequently teach these courses "under the rubric of women's or cultural studies, English, history, psychology, and anthropology" (182).

Theorizing in this model assumes the existence of a gay or lesbian subject—both in and outside the classroom—who stands to benefit from lesbian and gay academics' increasing freedom. Most importantly, narrative that stresses the precariousness of these gains and the obligation for younger critics to continue the tradition of coming out sums up the task of the activist scholar: "Those of us who have been in the academy the longest will have to tell our war stories to younger colleagues all too ready to believe 'that was then and this is now'" (212–13). Conspicuous here is the assumption that younger scholars—and, by extension, students—are properly implicated in the stories of their precursors and the ongoing struggle for freedom that these narratives instantiate.

Queer critics, on the other hand, envision a mode of theorizing that does not assume the gay or lesbian subject with a story to tell as its starting point. Susan Talburt raises this question directly: "What if 'lesbian' is not a 'personal identity'?" (55) By refusing to take a subject position such as "lesbian" or "gay," Talburt suggests that a teacher may actually resist an institutional "incitement to discourse" that may only encourage the identification of "token" minorities in the interest of a shallow "diversity" (57). For this reason, an activist rhetoric of "diversity" may subvert the teachers' and students' freedom rather than enhance it.

To illustrate how resistance to a prevailing discourse might work, Talburt presents "Olivia," a composite of three lesbian faculty members she interviewed (75). Instead of thinking of an identity as something that remains the same through time, Olivia characterizes "identification" as a process or "performance" that could begin with positioning oneself as "lesbian" or "gay" but refuses any attempt to remain fixed there, an approach that colors Olivia's view of power. Although she does use the authority her institution has granted her to speak on lesbian issues, she regularly challenges the idea of the category itself and its expectations (61). In particular, these expectations are most visible in terms of the discipline of lesbian and gay studies she is sometimes called upon to represent.

Olivia's "antidisciplinarity" is most suggestive in her pedagogy. Refusing to make herself the subject of inquiry in class by "coming out" to the students, she lays claim to a "norm of objectivity in order to engage students with the subject matter instead of with herself as a subject who matters." In particular, she encourages students "to create questions whose effects cannot be known in advance" (70). By doing so, she hopes to have them challenge the assumption that the professor can represent a "lesbian identity." Underlying this approach is a theoretical commitment that resists personal authenticity as the foundation for how teachers address students:

> Although intuitively appealing in their basis in "personal authenticity," calls for teachers to name their sexuality ignore the contextualized circumstances under which it might be more efficacious to rethink the intentional mediation of subjects through "personal positioning" as an inherently valid pedagogical strategy. (71)

Thus, for the queer theorist, McNaron's "war stories" yield to Olivia's "questions"—questions with unforeseen consequences and questions that supposedly evacuate the classroom of the distracting spectacle linked to coming out.

Between these two positions, however, other critics recognize that the divide between those who advocate an identity-based politics and those who advocate a queer one may not be final (Kopelson 26). My project shares this theoretical commitment, particularly with regard to the ideas put forward by Brenda Carr and Jonathan Dollimore. Arguing that an identity may be deconstructed by identities, Carr stresses "that while we might need the 'enabling fiction' of identity for agency, we can immediately interrogate the idea of identity as a 'stable home'" (Kopelson 27). Dollimore takes a similar "both/and" position, claiming a "radical essentialism" with regard to personal identity, but demanding "an equally radical and anti-essentialist critique" of the systems of belief that have perpetuated oppression (Kopelson 27). On the one hand, Carr's stress on an "enabling fiction" linked to identity allows a place for the coming-out narrative as a way of articulating the struggle lesbians and gays still face both inside and outside of academia. Especially at religious institutions where lesbians and gays remain on the margin, this stress may demand a "radical essentialism" about identity that can resist the still powerful homophobic discourses that characterize these institutions. On the other hand, the critique of such discourses must situate the coming-out narrative not as the foundational story in the person's view of her or his identity but as an account of one identity that is probably in tension with many others. Only by recognizing this ongoing play of identities—and the need to negotiate among them—can we then experience freedom ourselves and empower others to take on the same work.

II. Playing with Identity: Priest and Gay

Two years ago, in the fall of 2001, I started teaching at St. Joseph's University, a Catholic school sponsored by the Society of Jesus (Jesuits). In October of that year, I attended a panel discussion sponsored by the school's Gay Straight Alliance. Titled "Gay and Catholic," it consisted of representatives from a Roman Catholic parish in Philadelphia with many gay members, a representative from Dignity (the Catholic group that supports sexual relationships between members of the same sex), a representative from PFLAG, and a Catholic moral theologian who teaches at St. Joseph's.

In the question and answer period, I asked a question to the panel and to the audience as a whole about whether or not the situation of gay and lesbian persons, and especially gay and lesbian students, had improved in the twenty years since I was an undergraduate at a Catholic college myself. I don't recall the exact wording of the question nor the answer given. I did preface my question, however, by identifying myself: by name, as a priest, as a professor in the English department, and as gay. Three years later, I notice how secondary the question I asked and the answer I received were to my making this public statement. In Talburt's idiom, I made myself the "text" to be considered even though my question was ostensibly about past and present conditions for lesbian and gay students. By disclosing that I was both a "priest" and "gay," I ensured, at least in the context of St. Joseph's, that as "text," I would capture some attention. What surprised me, however, was the kind of attention I did receive. From prior "comings out" in Church environments, I expected some people would express appreciation—and they did. From my studies of Church teaching on homosexuality, I thought I also might be attacked—in fact that did not occur.

The surprise came the following week. In the student paper, an editorial criticized the lack of emphasis by the panel on chastity as an expectation for gay persons. The writer lauded my disclosure as a "valiant attempt" to address "this deficiency in the discussion" because I proposed myself "as an example of such chastity" (Bernacki). Yet, I had said nothing in my comment and question about chastity. For this student, therefore, the weight fell equally on my disclosures that I am not only gay but also a priest. In the Roman Catholic Church priests make a promise of celibacy at the time of ordination. Since the Church teaches that sexual relations should never take place outside of marriage, priests are obliged to live a life without sexual relations. In addition, as a member of a religious community, I also promised perpetual chastity, poverty, and obedience when I took my first vows ten years before ordination. Without my saying anything about chastity, and in spite of my asking whether the situation for gay persons had improved in the twenty years since I attended college, I was still associated with the position that the chastity I attempt to live is also to be expected of all gay persons. That I made no such claim was beside the point.

I stress this interpretation of my coming out because it illustrates that at least two identities informed my comment that evening: being gay and being a Catholic priest. Of course, I anticipated that link in the way I introduced myself. What I did not expect, however, was the way in which I was read as a sexual person. My refraining from engaging in sexual relations with others was translated into an expectation that all other unmarried persons—and perhaps especially homosexuals—should have the same goal. That I do not, in fact, have this expectation of others, like my not making any explicit claim about chastity, also proved to be beside the point. The lesson I have taken from this incident is that coming out becomes problematic when aligned with another element of identity—that of priest, for example.

In part this anxiety about gay priests is connected to the larger anxiety about the decreased number of men coming into the priesthood over the last forty years and the increased proportion of gay men now in its ranks. As Donald B. Cozzens points out, it has become a commonplace among superiors of seminaries to speak of the disproportionate number of gay men preparing to be priests relative to the population as a whole. This recognition parallels the result of various surveys that estimate the number of gay priests to be anywhere from 20 to 60 percent of the total. Additionally, the percentages among those under forty and those within religious orders—such as the Society of Jesus—may be even higher (Cozzens 99).

Yet even as these trends are generally acknowledged, it is still fairly easy to find gay priests targeted as scapegoats. Most recently, this was true as the clerical sexual abuse scandal became known across the country. Since the majority of victims speaking up were male, one argument that received serious attention in the media was that by not accepting gay people into the seminary, the problem would be solved in the future. The issue was particularly pressing in Philadelphia. Discussing the policy of "zero tolerance" for priests who have abused minors, Cardinal Anthony Bevilacqua, then Archbishop of Philadelphia, also claimed that the American cardinals were in agreement about how to deal with gay seminarians:

> We feel that a person who is homosexually oriented is not a suitable candidate for the priesthood, even if he has never committed any homosexual act. . . . There's an obligation of celibacy in every priest. There's a difference between a heterosexual candidate, what his choice of celibacy is, and that of a homosexual celibate. When a heterosexual celibate chooses to become a celibate in the priesthood, he's taking on a good—that is his own desire to become a priest—and he's giving up a very good thing, and that is a family and children that could follow. That would not be true of a homosexually oriented candidate. He may be choos-

ing the good, but . . . he's giving up what the Church considers an aberration, a moral evil. ("Cardinal")

Later that year, when asked how the Archdiocese of Philadelphia would deal with a gay candidate for the priesthood, Auxiliary Bishop Michael Burbidge, the seminary's superior, responded by saying "'then he would not be a candidate.'" He then clarified that this restriction applies regardless of whether a candidate acts on his sexual desire or not. Burbidge also emphasized that his view is consistent with Cardinal Bevilacqua's. Each year, when Bevilacqua speaks to the seminarians, he reminds them, as Burbidge characterizes it, about homosexuality: "'If that is their orientation, they have an obligation to the church to come forward and say they are no longer a candidate'" (Simpson).

What we need to stress is that Burbidge's and Bevilaqua's views are consistent with the Church's general statements on homosexual behavior. *De Persona Humana*, issued by the Vatican's Congregation for the Doctrine of the Faith in 1975, refers to homosexual acts as an "anomaly" and a "depravity" resulting from a rejection of God (*De Persona Humana* 747). The Congregation's subsequent "Letter to the Bishops on the Pastoral Care of Homosexual Persons" marks a development in doctrine because it recognizes, for the first time in Roman Catholic teaching, the reality of a homosexual "orientation." Nevertheless, it still equates "the abandonment of homosexual activity" with a "conversion from evil" (*Letter* 757). Particularly significant about the latter document is its terminology. Written in 1986, it uses the term "homosexual" rather than "gay" or "lesbian. Thus, it bypasses both the history of gay and lesbian liberation and the possibility that such persons play an active political role in contemporary society. Such a refusal of a political role to lesbian and gay persons in general is consistent with the abjection of gay candidates for the priesthood we have already noted. Not trusted to be chaste, and therefore to live out a potential call to priesthood, we are nonetheless subject to the regime of chastity put forward in these two documents and in the bishops' statements.

The most important feature of this negative discourse is that for all its attacks on the gay priest, it nonetheless needs this figure. As the attempt to blame the abuse crisis on gay priests illustrates, he can easily serve as a scapegoat. Yet, even when this project fails, the moral obligation placed on a gay seminarian is clear—recognize your orientation and then leave the seminary. Oddly, coming out seems to be required by the teaching that homosexuality is a moral evil—at least in the case of priests and seminarians. Most importantly, the requirement has force not because it assumes that homosexuals can be eradicated from the seminary but because it assumes that the homosexual's danger is always present. The same logic applies to the Church and to society

as a whole. If the gay seminarian is such a pervasive threat to chastity—his and
everyone else's—that he must always be removed from the seminary, the same
threat multiplies when such a person is ordained and begins to work. Discourse preoccupied with "aberrant" and "morally evil" sexual behavior—
whether homosexual or predatory—does not allow for distinctions or nuance.

Statistics, however, only glimpse at the extent to which priestly identity and
gay identity have become intertwined. For more personal evidence of this
linkage, we should consider this statement from a thirty-six-year-old gay man
in the final stages of his training to become a Jesuit priest:

> Many of my friends in the Society are also gay—and that has been a mixed bag.
> The positive end is that I have had the opportunity to be pretty honest about my
> affective self with many more people than I would have outside the Society. The
> challenge is that some of our communities can have a gay subtext which borders
> on the stereotypes of that subculture in general: a generally upscale life and a
> heightened sense of sensuality tends to only add to my horniness. (McDonough
> and Bianchi 104)

This disclosure is striking for its directness. Homosexuality—whether expressed genitally or not—is, according to this man, a fact of community life in
the Society of Jesus. Above all, the speaker finds that his ability to be "honest"
about his "affective self" derives from his being a member of a religious order.
The implication seems clear. This man's coming out, where we might have expected it to be thwarted by joining the Jesuits, has actually been enhanced by
this choice.

Formed in a milieu similar to the one this man describes, I find that two
identities have subsisted with each other throughout my career as a Jesuit and
now as a priest. On the one hand, most of the time I have been out to myself
has also been spent in a religious community among men who have consistently supported and helped me to understand my identity as gay. On the
other hand, because the freedom I have enjoyed has been broad, the harshness
of the Church's overall position toward gays has paradoxically made my identification as a priest and as a Catholic a matter of constant negotiation. In such
an environment, I find that a radical kind of essentialism becomes necessary.
The Church's official teaching, as I have shown, is far from dismissing the existence of the "homosexual." Rather, it appeals to an essentialist notion of this
person and her or his behaviors as a way of rationalizing bigger institutional
failures such as the abuse crisis. Not taking up the role of "gay priest"—and
the activist and assimilationist strategies that McNaron describes—would be
to walk away from the tradition and the history in which I have been nurtured
over the past twenty years.

Yet the challenge of the setting in which I first "came out" at St. Joseph's is
not adequately addressed by anyone's coming out and being out. In particu-

lar, as I think about the student's response to my disclosure at the "Gay and Catholic" meeting nearly three years ago, I note how easily "coming out" actually could be put at the service of the official teaching on "homosexuality." That is because the possession of a stable and secure "identity"—gay or straight—is an assumption from which both the Church and many gays—including me—begin. Yet, my experience increasingly suggests that such an identity is not a guarantee of greater freedom either for an individual gay person or for the group. Are there sites where competing identities—provisional as they are—may be allowed effective play? One possibility is the classroom.

III. Teaching the Text

Since coming to St. Joseph's, one of the books that I have taught regularly is James Baldwin's *Giovanni's Room*. Written in the mid-1950s, it is the narrative of David, a young American expatriate in Paris. Evicted from his hotel, he moves in with Giovanni, a handsome young bartender from Italy. Simultaneously, David is also conducting an affair with a young American woman named Hella, who has gone off to Spain to decide whether she wishes to accept his proposal of marriage. This love triangle, given to us by David through flashbacks, eventually comes to a crisis when Hella returns from Spain, and David attempts to cast off Giovanni.

In the fall of 2002, I used this novel as part of an elective course for second, third, and fourth year students in Lesbian and Gay Narrative. However, I would like to focus on teaching it as part of a course titled "Texts and Contexts," a literary survey that our school requires for all of the first year students. I discuss the first year course for two reasons. First, the students in "Texts and Contexts" generally are not English majors. Typically, they choose this course not on the basis of the texts to be covered but on what section of "Texts and Contexts" will fit into their schedule around various other humanities requirements that compose the bulk of each first year student's schedule. Second, when I have asked these students to write anonymous statements to me about what the experience of reading this book was like, some report that it was the first time a class had addressed the issue of homosexuality in a work of literature. Perhaps, therefore, I encounter a less "edited" kind of student in "Texts and Contexts" than I would in "Lesbian and Gay Studies." While certainly aware of homosexuality as an element of human experience—and sometimes their experience—these students are generally quite new to the work of interpreting it in literature.

Prior to our first meeting on *Giovanni's Room*, I introduce the book by emphasizing that the discourse connected to homosexuality has a history that, at least in the last century or so, can be linked to the words used to describe it.

In particular, we consider the invention of the term "homosexual" and how other words—such as "gay" and "lesbian"—have subsequently come to describe persons attracted to members of the same sex. At this point, I also emphasize that homosexuality is a topic that some people find difficult to discuss publicly and stress that nobody will be required to speak or write about this text if she or he is not comfortable doing so. We then move to a discussion of homophobia as connected with fear and shame about sexual orientation and the relevance of language in intensifying or alleviating these feelings. Generally, students can easily recognize that the harsh epithets directed at persons who "are" or "are thought to be" homosexual cause pain and should be avoided.

Developing their ideas of how words can hurt, I then come out to the students myself. As an example of my discomfort with being gay as an adolescent, I describe how the mere mention of the term "homosexual" often made me blush in both high school and college English classes. We then discuss how this sort of uneasiness illustrates the visual field's power: I feared that other people could read off my body that I was gay. At the same time, I try to demonstrate that words like "homosexual" and then "gay" also proved quite liberating. Their use helped me to recognize that I was not alone in being attracted to members of the same sex.

This discussion about terms for homosexuality then provides a useful segue into *Giovanni's Room* itself. I start by asking the students to notice the words various characters use to describe homosexuals and deviance in general. The most noted term—"fairy"—is used by the narrator David and by Giovanni to describe their older homosexual patrons. Other terms—such as *chéri* ("dear"), *les folles* (the silly ones or fools), and *le milieu* (the environment or atmosphere)—evoke the bars, cafés, and pensions of Paris's Left Bank where much of the narrative is set. How different characters react to terms like fairy, *folle*, or *chéri* is an important element of class discussion at this point. The students generally can recognize when these words are being used derogatorily. In a counter-intuitive move, I try to stress that some of the people using these terms derive a pleasure from them that is not ultimately homophobic. Rather, their use may represent one member of the group's attempt to register recognition of another. In this way I try to get the students to see that such coded language has an important role in identity formation. Whether one describes this formation as straight or gay, black or white, male or female, American or European—and Baldwin has much to say about each of these binaries—it does not take place in isolation.

Identity formation also focuses discussion on David. Fascinated and frightened by his past, he resists affiliation with what today we might term a "gay subculture." One of the common student critiques of David centers on his supposed failure to "come out" as "gay." Such a move would have enabled him to express his "true feelings" and allowed him to be honest with his girlfriend Hella as well as with Giovanni. As a counterargument to this type of interpretation, I point out that neither the word "homosexual" nor the word "gay" appears in the text. Though David acts on his sexual attraction to men, he does not show any recognition of "the homosexual" as a politicized category with which he might affiliate. In this way I try to show the students that identity is something negotiated between the self and others.

This negotiation, however, does not guarantee a stable identity through time. Rather, at both the beginning of the narrative and at its end, David stands looking at himself—first in a windowpane and later naked before the bedroom mirror. As he contemplates his "troubling sex" at the novel's close, he seems anything but clear about what it may signify:

> I look at my sex, my troubling sex, and wonder how it can be redeemed, how I can save it from the knife. The journey to the grave is already begun, the journey to corruption is always, already, half over. Yet the key to my salvation, which cannot save my body, is hidden in my flesh. (Baldwin 168)

The reference to castration suggests that David's masculinity, as much as the nature of his sexual attraction, is uncertain. At the same time, he also speaks of a "salvation" that depends on his "sex" but ultimately does not save his body.

I like to conclude the discussion of *Giovanni's Room* with this quotation because it remains so open-ended. "What does David understand by salvation?" A positive answer to this question still eludes me even after several readings of the book. What I can offer to my students is only a negative answer. Salvation is not simply a matter of an individual's "coming out" with the allegedly essential "truth" of one's identity. David would have been more honest with the people in his life if, in contemporary parlance, he had been "out" to them. Or at least he might have been able to accept love when it came his way if he had been "out" to himself. This embrace of an identity in the act of "coming out," however, does not guarantee a happy ending that I, as well as some of my first year students, would like. Rather, David's closeted questions about identity persist. Most importantly, these questions may not stop even after repeated "comings out." Though "coming out" as gay has its pleasures, the identity itself never completely fits.

It is this failure to find a "fit" in identifying as gay that I ask the class to dwell on as we finish the book. Whatever individual freedom we might imagine to be gained by "coming out" is never absolute or complete. That may be because one's identity as "gay" or "lesbian" inevitably stands in relation to her or his other identities. David's case has particular significance because, unlike many of the other homosexuals in the narrative, he does not appear particularly effeminate. Indeed, his ability to escape the most negative consequences of sexual relationships with more effeminate males—his boyhood friend Joey, the "fairy" he met in the army, and even Giovanni—suggests that an important component of what imprisons him centers on his conception of masculinity and femininity.

His identification as male—indeed as an *American* male—is anxious because inside it is his refusal of a homosexual identification. Discussing Hella's impending return with Giovanni, David stresses the dirtiness and criminality of homosexuality:

> "It's just that she'll be terribly hurt if she does find out, that's all. People have very dirty words for—for this situation." I stopped. His face suggested that my reasoning was flimsy. I added, defensively, "Besides, it is a crime—in my country and, after all, I didn't grow up here, I grew up there." (81)

In the face of a heterosexual relationship (with another American) that is to be resumed, the homosexual one (with a foreigner who is also dark) becomes a matter of shame. Thus we see the struggle between identities that Baldwin plays out in David. Coming out, as I emphasize to my students, would not necessarily take away David's fears, but it might help him to recognize same-sex attraction as one of the competing and unnamed identities that he refuses.

This refusal to live in a tension between identities is closely linked with David's sense of being already on "the journey to the grave" and to "corruption." His tragedy is not that he has failed to come out and thus become free from heterosexist tyranny—a claim that many of my students accept uncritically—but that he fails to recognize the distinction between "freedom from" a broad and vaguely defined heterosexual oppression and "freedom for" responsible living and loving in the world as he finds it. Richard Gula explains the latter idea as the recognition of identity in the process of growth. No one action can show "that anyone has embodied the full meaning and commitment of the self" (78). Rather, Gula calls attention to the process by which humans discover the overall direction to their lives:

> What seems more likely is that we come to actualize who we are through a whole series of actions which, when taken together, express the basic character or dominant direction of our lives. The basic direction of our lives, which manifests a rather consistent personal identity, is our fundamental stance. Those significant moments of choice in our lives, which establish or affirm more strongly than others the character or direction of our lives, are fundamental options. (Gula 78)

David, in Gula's terms, apprehends that he did have significant choices to make in his life—especially with regard to Giovanni and Hella. *Giovanni's Room* may simply be the record of coming to this understanding too late.

While Gula is astute in emphasizing the process involved in coming to this recognition, narratives like *Giovanni's Room* and my own process of coming out suggest that it is "identitie*s*" or "basic direction*s*" that lesbian and gay persons may be trying to negotiate. Most importantly, the sometimes volatile collision of these identities should make us question whether a complete and final reconciliation between them is possible. In this framework the "coming out" narrative may help students to recognize what they are freed up to do in the future—their "freedom for" love. This anticipation of the future, however, provides no guarantee that the fact of competing identities will ever be finally solved. Coming out, while perhaps enabling a person to embrace a lesbian or gay identity, also is a moment of dissonance because identities are constructed by competing discourses that do not necessarily coalesce themselves.

I characterize this unit on *Giovanni's Room*, therefore, as a queering of the process of coming out. By "coming out" as gay to my students in the course of introducing the novel, I perform the role of a gay teacher and hopefully trouble some of the students' preconceived ideas about gay or lesbian identity as mediated to them by the Church's discourse. By then moving the discourse from my "coming out" to David's remaining closeted, I try to demonstrate that the two moments may not be as distinct as one might initially think. David's inability to recognize the connection between his life and the people around him would not be reversed by the act of "coming out." Indeed, David's remaining in the closet not only points to the complexity of an authentic act of coming out but challenges those contemplating such a move not to let their story be reduced to an easily described spectacle.

* * * * *

What I have tried to sketch out here is not so much a plan for how one might integrate one's gayness or lesbianism with one's work as an academic; still less do I offer my intervention in the panel discussion or my reading of *Giovanni's Room* as in any way definitive of how the practice of one's sexual identity should express itself concretely in an academic setting. Rather, my desire has been to stress that the need to make lesbians and gays visible on university campuses remains an important and, at places like St. Joseph's, still incomplete work. For this reason, "coming out" as "lesbian" or "gay" remains a vital faculty contribution. At the same time, since "coming out" narratives are easily stereotyped as a passage to freedom, I believe that lesbian and gay faculty should not become trapped in the essentialism to which such narratives are so easily prone. Only in this way will the freedom of lesbian and gay visibility be preserved from the imprisoning specularity of popular culture. Indeed, such a culture, by so stereotyping gays and lesbians, may prove more inimical to our freedom than outright condemnation.

Note

This chapter was previously published in *Modern Language Studies* 34, nos. 1–2 (Spring/Fall 2004). Reprinted with permission.

References

Baldwin, James. *Giovanni's Room*. New York: Delta, 1956.

Bernacki, Matthew. "Important Issues Left Out of Gay and Lesbian Panel." Editorial, *The Hawk*, November 2, 2001: 9.

Butler, Judith. "Imitation and Gender Insubordination." In *The Lesbian and Gay Studies Reader*, ed. Henry Abelove, Michèle Aina Barale, and David M. Halperin. New York: Routledge, 1993: 307–20.

"Cardinal Bevilacqua on 'Zero Tolerance,' Gays in Priesthood." *Philadelphia Inquirer*, April 27, 2002: A5.

Cozzens, Donald R. *The Changing Face of the Priesthood*. Collegeville, Minn.: The Liturgical Press, 2000.

Foucault, Michel. "What Is an Author?" In *The Foucault Reader*, ed. Paul Rabinow. New York: Penguin, 1986: 101–20.

Gula, Richard M., S.S. *Reason Informed by Faith: Foundations of Catholic Morality*. New York: Paulist Press, 1989.

Kopelson, Karen. "Dis/Integrating the Gay/Queer Binary: 'Reconstructed Identity Politics' for a Performative Pedagogy." *College English* 65, no. 1 (September 2002): 17–35.

McDonough, Peter, and Eugene C. Bianchi. *Passionate Uncertainty: Inside the American Jesuits*. Berkeley: University of California Press, 2002.

McNaron, Toni A. H. *Poisoned Ivy: Lesbian and Gay Academics Confronting Homophobia*. Philadelphia: Temple University Press, 1997.

New York Gay Men's Chorus. "Love Don't Need a Reason." *Love Lives On*. Virgin Recordings, Ltd., 1991.

Sacred Congregation for the Doctrine of the Faith. *De Persona Humana*. In *The Christian Faith: Doctrinal Elements of the Christian Church*, ed. J. Neuner, S.J., and J. Dupuis, S.J. New York: Alba, 1990: 745–53.

———. "Letter on the Pastoral Care of Homosexual Persons." In Neuner and Dupuis: 753–60.

Simpson, Victor L. "Vatican Nears Decision on Banning Gay Priests." *Philadelphia Inquirer*, November 6, 2002: A2.

Talburt, Susan. "On Not Coming Out; Or, Reimagining Limits." In *Lesbian and Gay Studies and the Teaching of English: Positions, Pedagogies, and Cultural Politics*, ed. William J. Spurlin. Urbana, Ill.: NCTE, 2000: 54–78.

Epilogue

Do Jesuit Scholarly Endeavors Cohere? Self-Reckoning and the Postmodern Challenge

William Rehg, S.J.

HOW DO JESUIT SCHOLARS connect their scholarly endeavors, their teaching and research, with being Christian and Jesuit? The question at the heart of this anthology might, in view of its surface grammar, seem to call for a descriptive reply. But for Jesuit scholars themselves—certainly for me and, I submit, for the other contributors—a merely descriptive reply does not suffice. The question ultimately calls us to a self-reckoning, something like an *apologia pro vita nostra*, in which we gratefully account for the tremendous gifts, support, and opportunities we have received as part of the Jesuit vocation. Writing as a Jesuit scholar not involved in the discussions leading to the anthology, in this epilogue I pinpoint more precisely what this self-reckoning involves and how it emerges in the essays. Above all I want to address the postmodern fragmentation that threatens the collection as a whole, that is, the resistance to articulating a common vision, a normative account, of Jesuit scholarly commitment. If there is no shared rationale or unity among Jesuit scholars, then scholarship lacks any living connection to the Jesuit religious vocation and might even conceal a kind of self-indulgence.

As I hope to show, the essays themselves do not warrant resistance to a shared account—provided we understand what such accounts involve in relation to lived practice. To provide readers with some background, I draw on past Jesuit practice and official documents to sketch the idea of the Jesuit vocation as a "charism" with distinctive features (section I). After describing the postmodern challenge as it emerges in Clooney's introduction (section II), I examine the different senses of "postmodern" operative in the contributions themselves; this analysis suggests that the contributions belie the challenge as

Clooney describes it (section III). In fact, we can discern an important Jesuit scholarly commonality at work, centered on commitment to dialogue (section IV). I close with some general reflections on Jesuit scholarly solidarity in practice (section V). My hope is that the approach I take here not only illuminates the vocation of Jesuit scholarship but also speaks to other vocational and professional callings that require those who are called to live up to exemplary ideals and standards in postmodern times.

I. Jesuit Charism as a Problem: History and Documents

From its beginnings, the Society of Jesus has been associated with a commitment to the intellectual life and scholarly expertise. Among the original founders of the order, three (Diego Laynez, Alonso Salmerón, and Claude Jay) served as theological experts at the Council of Trent. In subsequent decades, Jesuits made scholarly contributions not only in theology and philosophy but also in the sciences and mathematics, political theory and law, theater and art. This commitment has remained unbroken over the centuries, as evidenced by such outstanding Jesuits as Karl Rahner, Bernard Lonergan, Teilhard de Chardin, Walter Ong—to name just a few.

In light of this history, a life of scholarship appears as a stable possibility for living out a Jesuit vocation: although most Jesuits do not engage in scholarly research as their life work, there always seem to be some who do, with the Society's blessing. So it may appear counterintuitive to approach Jesuit commitment to scholarship as a problem. But the Jesuit charism requires just such an approach, both for the Society of Jesus as a whole and for the individual Jesuit scholar. In fact, the problem is multi-layered. To explain, I must say something about that charism, as I understand it. This term will help clarify the kind of self-reckoning to which I alluded above. I claim no scholarly expertise on the matter of the Jesuit charism beyond my quarter century in the Society.

The term stems directly from the Greek word "charisma": "a grace, a favour; a free gift, grace."[1] Saint Paul uses it to describe the diverse gifts and powers of ministry distributed differently among members of the early Christian community (for example, 1 Cor 12: 4, 31). Writers on the spirituality of religious life typically use "charism" as a covering term for the features that constitute a more specific way of living out the Christian life. Thus the "charism" of a religious order or other mode of Christian living (Benedictine, Jesuit, Catholic Worker, married life, etc.) encompasses the ways of living and working that together make that order or way of life distinctive within the Christian community.[2] Closely related to the ideas of vocation and spirituality, the word "charism" underscores the belief that the vocation is a free gift, a favor of God.

The foregoing suggests we think of the Jesuit vocation as a call to live out a *distinctive* set of personal and communal gifts and talents. If Jesuit life has distinctive features, however, then we should expect certain ways of living and working to be typical, others rare or nonexistent, still others excluded as violations of the core commitments (that is, the three vows, to non-ownership of goods, celibacy, and obedience to superiors). The possibility of violation brings out the normative dimension of a vocation, its association with mutual expectations about how members ought to live and work. But the term "normative," if associated with rules and the possibility of rule-violation, captures only the barest minimum of the vocational charism. As a call to live out a set of gifts, the vocation invites and challenges the Jesuit to realize the distinctive gifts of the vocation as best he can, energized by gratitude. Both the vows and other aspects of the charism are above all positive in character.

Thus the Jesuit vocation itself poses something like a problem for the individual Jesuit—not in the negative sense of something amiss, but rather in the sense of a question, challenge, or task that calls for a response. In this positive sense, the "problem" of the Jesuit vocation is not a burden but a gift that requires active acceptance and ongoing self-reflection. This is one reason why Jesuit scholars can perceive the leading question—how do I connect scholarship and a Jesuit vocation?—as a question calling for self-reckoning that goes beyond mere description. The character of religious vocation as both gift and challenge has the power to lead any Jesuit, and not just Jesuit scholars, to the question of self-reckoning: how have I responded to the call, employed the gifts, realized the opportunities? Although these are given, to accept them one cannot remain passive. If a life of scholarship is a life in which one strives to realize one of the possible gifts of the Jesuit charism, then the leading question of the book simply represents a more specific version of the question facing each Jesuit, and inscribed in the ideal of the *magis*, the "greater good" that beckons the Jesuit beyond complacency at any point in life.

As described above, the individual's problem of self-reckoning, or self-evaluation, assumes the scholarly life indeed fits with the Jesuit charism in general—that the Society of Jesus, in its history and institutional commitments, has affirmed this fit. As background for our reflection on the individual's issue of vocation, it helps to recall this general commitment, as found in the history and documents of the Society.

The issue of scholarly commitment for the Society as a whole concerns its understanding of the charism it has received from God. Society documents provide the official articulation of this self-understanding: the papal bulls first approving the Society and its Constitutions, the General Congregations, official letters from the General, and so on. I do not want to add to the lengthy commentary on such documents. What deserves mention is the ease with which one can construct rationales that link scholarship and the Jesuit charism. Already in the Formula of the Society, the founders connect the chief purpose of their Society with advancing the faith "by means of public preaching, lectures, and any other ministration whatsoever of the word of God."[3] At least some forms of scholarship would seem to fit here, namely those connected with theology. Although this formulation still appears rather limited—how would this include the teaching of mathematics or the sciences?—the *Constitutions* broadens the possibilities considerably when Ignatius, its chief architect, gives pride of place to the "more universal good" as the overarching criterion for accepting institutional and apostolic commitments and assigning Jesuits.[4] And judging from Ignatius's fondness for "helping souls," "good" presumably includes whatever helps people live morally upright, religiously faithful lives.[5]

In other words, prefer initiatives and works that have the greater multiplier effect. This criterion works in favor of educational endeavors. Indeed, Ignatius had already committed the Society to higher education before he completed the *Constitutions*, and he explicitly linked Jesuit university education with Jesuits engaged in teaching the arts and sciences (although he excluded members from teaching law or medicine).[6] The norm of the more universal good and the acceptance of universities opens the door to scholarly writing, whether as a means of reaching a larger audience, as a means of influencing currents of thought that can have a long-term effect on culture, or as an important component of credible university work. Subsequent developments and documents have broadened the range of rationales on which one can draw to justify a particular scholarly commitment as consistent with the Jesuit charism.[7]

Society documents and the long tradition of Jesuit scholars, then, firmly establish scholarship as a valid work flowing from the Jesuit charism. Looking to these sources, the Jesuit scholar can draw upon a number of official reasons—the importance of credible Jesuit universities and colleges, the dialogue between the Church and culture, the dialogue with atheism, and so on—that could justify research and writing for many areas of scholarly concern. Nonetheless, a top-down approach starting with official documents does not resolve the personal issue for the individual scholar, namely the self-reckoning that discerns a call to the scholarly life as one's *individual* vocation within the Society of Jesus.

II. The Postmodern Challenge

As the contributions reveal, answering the problem of one's individual vocation as a Jesuit scholar involves on the one hand a uniquely personal act of self-appropriation, an integration of one's life history, role models and formative influences, desires, and particular scholarly interests. On the other hand, integration cannot succeed without the recognition, assistance, and confirmation of others (at the very least, superiors must allow the Jesuit to pursue higher studies). And such recognition and confirmation requires some shared vocabulary, values, and norms.

The Jesuit scholarly vocation, then, requires one to reconcile individual uniqueness and shared purpose. This perennial challenge of religious life has intensified today under the pressures of professionalism and pluralism. As the old disciplines gradually disappear into increasingly fine-grained specializations, and as sensitivity for the diversity of perspectives heightens, it becomes increasingly difficult to articulate a credible shared purpose that goes beyond abstract platitude. As a matter of training and history, Jesuits indeed have a shared stock of stories, vocabulary, and official documents. The question is whether these resources suffice for a substantive, normative account of what the scholarly vocation requires and allows of Jesuits. Beneath the shared jargon ("faith and justice," "dialogue," etc.), are Jesuit scholars pulling in the same direction?

The contributors to this volume are keenly aware of the above challenge. Indeed, they appear to view it as currently insurmountable. According to Francis Clooney's introduction, the authors resist general statements of Jesuit scholarly identity based on traditional formulas. Instead, they strive to work from the ground up, to speak "stubbornly from within our actual scholarship, rather than about it" (7). The traditional Jesuit rhetoric fails to capture "the particular energies that make our scholarship possible, urgent, exciting" (7). While not ruling out a common account as a priori impossible, Clooney maintains that "right now there is no agreed upon set of words that succeeds in expressing our Jesuit way of acting and thinking, nor any singular, shared memory nor set of images that might translate the Jesuit scholarly enterprise or our particular essays into a discourse that would serenely float above the particulars" (4).

On one interpretation, Clooney's caution about commonalities among Jesuit scholars is hardly controversial: why should we expect general formulations to translate without remainder into the particularities of actual practice? Moreover, Clooney remains open to the possibility that a general pattern might emerge. The collection, after all, rests on the hope of retrieving and resuscitating the Jesuit intellectual tradition, presumably via a kind of induction: Clooney proposes the collection as "a series of experiments" that might allow "careful inferences" regarding the actual practice and ideals of Jesuits (18). Thus he attests that the contributors' "lives and work do succeed in forming a web of partial correspondences and connections, overlapping stories and practices in which the Christian and Jesuit practices and worldviews imperfectly but nonetheless brightly continue to show forth" (20).

Other formulations in the introduction, however, undermine this inductive approach by linking it with a distinctively postmodern sensibility signaled by the title *Jesuit Postmodern.* Clooney has the sense that the essays "do not cohere," that they are "near one another, but written in parallel lines that never meet" (17, 21). This sense of working in parallel universes of discourse informs the two-column style of Clooney's own contribution to the collection. In choosing this Derridean mode of presentation, he gives graphic expression to the postmodern suspicion of stable values, determinate meaning, and progress (16). Similarly, "all eight essays and our response essay stand in parallel columns, alongside and near to one another, yet never converging into a single meaning or final conclusion" (16). If any commonalities emerge from these discrete universes, it is only by happenstance.

This postmodern motif, above all as it finds expression in the metaphor of parallel lines, harbors a potential difficulty—a difficulty that deserves scrutiny precisely because it sharpens the challenge of self-reckoning. Lines that never meet lack any shared point of contact. If we use this metaphor to interpret the more specific claim that we lack a shared, readily understandable expression of the "Jesuit way of acting and thinking"—a historical memory, set of images, or formulation by which we could present ourselves at the level of higher education—then Jesuit scholarship is in serious trouble. If we cannot agree on any shared self-understanding of the aims or characteristics of specifically Jesuit scholarship, if we lack any definable mode of solidarity or cohesion as Jesuit scholars, then a disconnect develops between official pabulum and the self-understanding of Jesuit scholars themselves; consequently, scholarly work loses its quality as a corporate apostolate, something Jesuits work at together. The danger then looms that the diversity of Jesuit scholarship is a sign, not of an open-ended search for the more universal good but of self-indulgence or a "lone wolf" mentality. The passionate search for truth masks a "passionate uncertainty" about religious identity and corporate mission, a deficit of substantive vision at the institutional level.[8]

By choosing this postmodern metaphor, Clooney slides from the healthy caution of the evidence-minded inductivist to the debilitating doubts of the linguistic skeptic. Postmodernist thought stems in large measure from Friedrich Nietzsche, who notably influenced, *inter alia,* poststructuralist thought in France (for example, Derrida) and Richard Rorty's pragmatist brand of postmodernism in the United States.[9] Although postmodernist motifs and methodologies encompass a range of forms, many of them involve skepticism about linguistic meaning and discourse. Nietzsche, for example, targeted essential definitions of moral ideas such as justice and conscience.[10] Other postmodernists doubt that authors can successfully intend to write texts that do not undermine themselves.[11] Still others conceive of discourses as so heterogeneous that ideals of consensus, unifying meta-narratives, and the like must harbor violence and oppression.[12] Although Clooney's metaphor recalls this last strand of postmodern skepticism, I do not claim that any particular postmodernist thinker would fully endorse the metaphor itself. I read Clooney's image, rather, as extending a particularly skeptical trend of postmodernist thought to the problem of Jesuit scholarly identity.

To be sure, postmodern skeptical methods can be useful for social-political critique insofar as they help unmask hypocrisy and ideology.[13] But insofar as it rejects common norms of discourse, postmodern skepticism represents a "logic of disintegration."[14] Before Jesuit scholars accept metaphors of discursive fragmentation as an adequate language of self-reckoning, they must ask what sort of commonality, or shared meaning, their common texts and history afford them at the level of actual practices of Jesuit scholars. That is, we must attend to how Jesuit scholars actually appropriate the themes briefly sketched in section I.

The best place to start is the essays of this collection. As Clooney notices, the authors do not share a single theory of postmodernity.

III. Stances toward Postmodernity

A "postmodern" Jesuit might mean a number of different things. In his introduction, Clooney opposes postmodern to classical and modern styles of twentieth-century Jesuit higher education. In what follows, however, I use a philosophical frame of reference suggested by the skeptical literature described in the previous section. If we examine representative essays in the collection from that perspective, we find a range of stances regarding the postmodern. In ascribing these stances, I characterize not the attitudes of the living authors but their texts, as I fallibly read them. I situate these stances along a kind of spectrum: at one end are views and projects that fail to qualify as postmodern in any real sense, at the other end, thoroughly postmodern views, in a substantive theoretical sense. The collection exhibits at least four distinct positions on this spectrum.

1) At the one end of the spectrum we find Arthur Madigan's essay, which contains little or nothing that qualifies its stance as postmodern. His chief philosophical interlocutors are Aristotle and contemporary neo-Aristotelians, and among his theological lights he numbers neo-Thomists like Bernard Lonergan and John Courtney Murray. To my knowledge, none of Madigan's chief interlocutors are generally considered postmodern thinkers.[15] The choice of intellectual heroes reflects the general thrust of his essay, namely that he draws energy from the attempt to bring modern and contemporary trends into a

fruitful critical dialogue with Aristotle. On the one side, then, Madigan seeks to expand Aristotle by confronting him with modern ideas and movements (for example, Kant's idea of human dignity, sensitivity to the equality of women); on the other side, he relies on Aristotle both to challenge contemporary assumptions and to provide nuanced methods of dialectical inquiry for clarifying current issues. In light of Madigan's description of his driving interests, I see him as a socio-historically informed Aristotelian responding above all to modernity and its influences on contemporary culture and politics.

2) Roger Haight's essay stakes out a position a step closer to the postmodern end of the spectrum, namely a position that characterizes (and responds to) the context for Jesuit scholarship as specifically postmodern. According to Haight, "postmoderns by definition try to characterize and respond to a period with qualities that distinguish it from the modern" (89). As he specifies those qualities (n. 1), they include increased awareness of cultural diversity, the historical and social conditioning of thought, local bias, and perspectival pluralism. On this view, to be a postmodern Jesuit is to notice and respond to a certain set of cultural circumstances that make it difficult to speak from a universally valid position of intellectual authority. In response to this postmodern situation, Haight recommends an autobiographical method, for it allows one to make potentially general, but not preemptory universal, statements on the basis of personal evidence. That is, the biography provides a text that invites (rather than commands) others to find commonalities with their own personal experiences.

However, in responding to the postmodern condition Haight remains decidedly non-postmodernist in key respects. To begin with, the appeal to personal experience provides evidence that is subject to standards of truth. This suggests that Haight believes biography involves a kind of self-reckoning whose validity depends on norms and values not entirely at the author's disposal; biography is not merely self-creation in the Nietzschean mode, which was highly skeptical of truth as a value. Moreover, Haight frames his autobiographical account in terms of theories of personal development (for example, Piaget, Kohlberg, Erikson). Developmental theories, which hearken back to Kant and Hegel, presuppose objective—usually cross-cultural—standards that give development a definite direction and logic.[16] Such theories easily fit with "grand narratives" of one sort or another—a favorite target of postmodern critics of the Enlightenment.[17] Haight himself, to be sure, measures development not by narrow Western standards but by the cross-culturally informed expansion of horizons. But this expansion remains subject to non-relativistic criteria of truth (103).

As I read it, then, Haight's essay expresses a socio-historically minded modernist stance that is keenly attuned to postmodernist cultural conditions. To be sure, he remains postmodern on his above definition: he attends and responds to postmodern features of today's world. But he does this from a non-postmodern position that accepts central Enlightenment commitments. If there is an exception to this characterization, it lies in his strongly apophatic Christology, but even here he remains a realist about the transcendent (103).[18]

3) James Bernauer represents yet a further style of "Jesuit postmodern": the use of postmodern methods, not for skeptical purposes, but in the service of critical-social aims. Specifically, he draws on Michel Foucault's critical methods in the service of speaking truth to the power that masquerades as truth. Driven by the haunting collective memory of the Holocaust, Bernauer uses Foucault's methods to excavate the history and language that implicate Catholics and Jesuits in promoting anti-Jewish sentiment over the ages. This critical-historical recollection, however, aims at a positive rather than skeptical outcome, championed by Pope John Paul II himself: the Church's confession of its sins against the Jews and its request for their forgiveness.[19]

Although Bernauer uses a postmodern methodology, he also finds inspiration in two figures one would hardly call postmodernists: Pope John Paul II and Alfred Delp, the Jesuit priest executed by the Nazis for alleged complicity in a plot to kill Hitler. Moreover, his goal of reconciliation based on confessing the truth about one's past hardly qualifies as distinctively postmodern, as though such a goal depended on a postmodern theory. Indeed, the depth of Foucault's postmodern skepticism was ambiguous, and it receded in later years.[20] In my view, it is primarily the apophatic character of Foucault's critical approach that distinguishes it from more rationalist approaches found in thinkers like Habermas. Whereas the latter is willing to articulate positive ideals and norms of reason, Foucault seems to have preferred negative critique, on the assumption that any positive statements of ideals must harbor seeds of social oppression.[21] Similarly, Bernauer situates Foucault not in the skeptical tradition but in Greek and Christian traditions of parrhesia, the practice of speaking the truth, for the sake of others, even at the risk of one's life. On this reading, Foucault sounds more like Socrates than Nietzsche.

4) Whereas Bernauer's stance is *methodologically* postmodern, Ronald Anderson heads toward a *substantively* postmodern position, one that not only employs poststructuralist methods of analysis but also affirms postmodern theses. Precisely Anderson's very modern quest for foundations—a quest reflecting his immigrant wanderings—leads him to poststructuralism as an "unsettled foundationalism" (152). Beginning with the conventionality of the constant speed of light, Anderson marshals the theoretical arguments from

modern physics, mathematics, and logic that ground postmodern conclusions regarding the unavailability of determinate interpretations, certain foundations, and absolute truths—precisely in those disciplines that laypersons most expect to yield undeniable "hard facts."

One can, to be sure, reach many of Anderson's conclusions by other routes.[22] But Anderson draws on poststructuralist theory to formulate these insights. Moreover, his postmodernism inclines him to accept a very postmodern view of the self—even if he comes by the idea from Buddhism—as impermanent, an absence of enduring stability (151).

I thus read Anderson as adopting substantive theses associated with postmodernism. Notice, however, that he does not reach skeptical conclusions; he also rejects relativist interpretations of poststructuralism (150). This rejection suggests that claims of linguistic incommensurability—a major source of postmodern skepticism—is not decisive for Anderson's postmodern stance. Although aware of his inability "fully to translate" between cultural worlds (147), Anderson takes his immigrant's sense of never-fully-belonging as occasion for an ongoing quest toward a "distant . . . foundational home on the horizon" (153)—a horizon whose very objectivity and "independence from me" (152) gives direction and meaning to the ongoing quest. If this reading is on target, then Anderson deboards the postmodern express just one stop short of its terminal destination at the other end of our spectrum, where we find the debilitating skepticism suggested by the parallel-lines metaphor.

Notice that William Stempsey also employs some substantive postmodern favorites, in particular the theses that scientific knowledge is socially constructed and subject to communicative incommensurabilities. But like Anderson, he too stops short of anti-realist or relativistic conclusions: incommensurability is only partial, it is not the final word—"some accounts of medical reality are objectively better than others" (61). Thomas J. Brennan, although skeptical of essentialist views of personal identity, does not commit himself to the logic of disintegration suggested by the skeptical metaphor.

Indeed, as we shall see below (section IV), Clooney's own project is not well served by his skeptical metaphor. After all, he clearly draws energy from a commitment to dialogue, as do a number of the other contributors—which seems to mark a point of convergence. This suggests we take a closer look at this motif as a unifying strand in the collection.

IV. Dialogue and Jesuit Scholarship

The term "dialogue" admits of various uses. Although its primary sense refers to a conversation between equals, we also speak of a reader's dialogue with a text, of the "dialogue" between tradition and contemporary culture, and so on. The Documents of GC 34, which provide the most complete articulation of the Society's commitment to dialogue, further specify the idea of dialogue connected with the Jesuit charism. Two kinds of dialogue have pride of place: the dialogue with contemporary culture and interreligious dialogue, both of which are understood as inextricable from a concern for justice.[23] In each case, the Jesuit enters into a "spiritual conversation" between equals (n. 101) in which he strives both to learn from, and share his faith with, his dialogue partners. According to GC 34, then, the dialogical interchange is not arbitrarily structured, but has a specific directionality or focus, at least for the Jesuit, given by his Christian faith and the concern for justice.

I claim that each contributor's scholarly project accords with this vision. Clooney and Bernauer, and to some extent Haight, focus on interreligious dialogue. All of the authors in the collection attempt to engage in dialogue with contemporary culture. How they carry out the dialogue and how they articulate the dialogical aspects of their work differ in interesting ways. But in each case we can understand the project as plausibly linked to the dialogical goals set by GC 34. Moreover, two metaphors for dialogue give apt expression to most of the specific endeavors: the Jesuit intellectual as crossing boundaries, and as missionary. I start with the first metaphor as it applies to authors engaged in interreligious dialogue.

1) Haight introduces the first metaphor when he suggests that Jesuits straddle boundaries (99). Although he emphasizes boundaries between ideologies and between Church and world, the essays suggest we understand the metaphor broadly: Jesuit scholars cross boundaries between religions, cultures, intellectual traditions—and more. Haight himself is known for theoretical concerns that lead him across the boundary between Christian sources of tradition and a postmodern hermeneutics sensitive to the challenges of cultural pluralism and interreligious dialogue.

Of all the essays, however, those by Bernauer and Clooney provide the fullest examples of interreligious boundary crossing. In striving to rectify past injustices and reconcile Christians and Jews, Bernauer links a particular dialogue with overcoming barriers of mistrust and contempt that Christians (and Jesuits) erected against the Jews. By linking interreligious dialogue with a concern for justice, Bernauer's project deeply responds to the call of GC 34.

Clooney explicitly links the dialogical agenda of GC 34 with interreligious boundary crossing (176), applying this metaphor to his work at fostering dialogue between Christianity and Hinduism. In negotiating this boundary, Clooney also probes the historical divide between the early Jesuit missionary style and a more contemporary one. In Clooney's struggles with interreligious dialogue and Jesuit history one senses the source of his postmodern metaphor: unlike earlier missionaries such as Robert de Nobili, Clooney arrives at a somewhat ambiguous, uncertain position about the requirements of interreligious dialogue, specifically about the relation between understanding and critique. Although passionate about witnessing to the Gospel of Christ as universally relevant, the long years of cross-cultural study have softened the critical moment, the willingness to challenge other cultures with the Christian message as cross-culturally valid. He seems, at the end of his essay, to have shifted from the pluralist but ultimately unitary model of Dupuis to Barnes's postmodern approach. This shift need not negate Christian witness to other religions, but it does require the Christian to allow members of the other religious culture to remain forever somewhat strange, not fully assimilated into (Western) Christian categories. Clooney then goes on to extend this model to relations among Jesuits themselves, a point I take up in section V.

2) The boundary-crossing metaphor can also describe the work of authors whose efforts involve a dialogue with contemporary culture. Consider Arthur Madigan's work with Aristotle. An effort to retrieve Aristotelian thought could simply aim to reaffirm the classical roots of our tradition. In fact, Madigan makes it a kind of cultural challenge. Specifically, he wants us to sense the strangeness of Aristotle, an outsider whom he brings into current discussion to challenge us with an ancient, thus foreign, cultural perspective. Madigan, in other words, strives to bring Aristotle across a historical-cultural boundary.

Although Madigan is modest about his work as directly religious or justice-oriented, we can see his scholarship as serving an important propaedeutic role. This is the case with Jesuit philosophers in general: their dialogue with culture aims to prepare the way for more explicitly religious witnessing by showing how Christians can cross the conceptual divides separating contemporary postmodern culture and traditional Catholic modes of thought. As philosophers, both Anderson and Stempsey engage in such work. Stempsey, in fact, casts such work in terms of reconciliation, specifically as "reconciling what seems to be irreconcilable," namely the natural and supernatural realms (62). To carry out his project, he also must negotiate boundaries between disciplines, even vocations: medicine and philosophy, physician and Jesuit priest.

3) The boundary-crossing metaphor does not describe every aspect of Jesuit scholarly endeavor. I thus turn to the second metaphor: the Jesuit scholar as missionary, which overlaps with ideas of boundary-crossing and reconciliation, but which also links Jesuit scholarship to the Society's history. The missionary metaphor, that is, has the advantage of fitting with, and expanding, a well-known feature of Jesuit history, exemplified by such heroes as Francis Xavier, Robert de Nobili, and Matteo Ricci. Although most Jesuits in the history of the order have probably not been missionaries in the traditional sense, the Society has certainly been known for this kind of work.

This missionary spirit, I suggest, characterizes much of the scholarly dialogue between Jesuits and contemporary culture. If we conceive missionary work as a two-way exchange, then missionaries not only bring to others insights and consolation from their own religious faith and culture, they also *bring back* to the Church insights from the religions, cultures, and disciplines to which they are sent. They can teach only because they have learned from those they want to teach. Such mutual exchange between the Gospel and culture (both contemporary postmodern Western culture and other cultures) constitutes the process of "inculturation."[24]

Notice that some authors find themselves more on one side of this activity than on the other: some Jesuits, that is, engage more in bringing back from the other culture, some more in bringing to the other culture. But each approach contributes to missionary work in some sense, and each might be understood as contributing to the inculturation of Christian faith: rendering the Gospel both meaningful and challenging for contemporary contexts. The propaedeutic efforts of Stempsey, Anderson, and Madigan contribute to inculturation insofar as they prepare the ground for rethinking Christian categories in contemporary terms, so that the Gospel message can be recast in a language that makes it rhetorically cogent for contemporary audiences. Like traditional missionary work, scholarship aimed at inculturating the Gospel is inherently risky and experimental—in adapting Christian language and practice for other cultures, one runs the risk of betraying the Gospel.

Although Bruce Morrill's essay, focused on issues of liturgical reform within the Church, involves a kind of boundary-crossing within Catholicism, namely that between the individualism of contemplation in the *Spiritual Exercises* and the corporate character of liturgical worship, I think his work is primarily missionary in spirit: he wants to foster a liturgical practice that works for contemporary postmodern contexts. He is, in other words, committed to inculturating the faith, specifically the liturgical tradition of the Church, rendering it symbolically accessible for contemporary sensibilities.

4) Brennan's elusive essay sets an interesting puzzle for the dialogical analysis I propose: it contains hints of the above metaphors, but it also introduces something new. We see a kind of inculturation in his work: he grapples with contemporary culture, as it concerns the status of gays and lesbians in the Church; his reflections draw on literature informed, I assume, by postmodern theory as well as critical social theory. In his case, however, a *particular* act of boundary crossing serves a missionary aim. By publicly coming out as gay, he "transgresses" a boundary—in some respects a boundary between Church and culture, but more a boundary between the private and the public—thereby risking a very personal self-integration in a public forum, where it could become an object of discussion. Brennan hopes to address others by his coming out: specifically, to challenge the opposed, one-sidedly essentialist

discourses of gay liberation and homophobia. The missionary work here, I suggest, consists in a two-way exchange: insisting to the Church on the gift of being gay or lesbian, and to gays and lesbians that "salvation is not simply a matter of an individual's 'coming out' with the allegedly essential 'truth' of one's identity" (193).[25]

Notice that Brennan's missionary transgression, his challenge to contemporary culture (both secular and Catholic) depends on a formative contrast experience: his experience of being accepted as he is by other Jesuits, from formation onward. This experience—which I read as a lesson in genuine freedom—gives him the background against which the public act of coming out can emerge in all its cultural complexity, ambivalence, and illusion of freedom. Brennan thus brings to his work not so much a set of categories, but something gained from Jesuit life itself. In the end, this commonality of living, Jesuit life as a set of shared social practices, unites the Jesuits in the collection far more than any adherence to a set of official declarations.

Might this be the key to the coherence of Jesuit scholarship? That is, might the shared basis and rule of Jesuit scholarship lie less at the level of explicit pronouncements and more at the level of our (more or less) common Jesuit background—thus in the largely tacit dispositions, intuitions, and know-how acquired over years in formation and community life?

V. The Solidarity and Coherence of Jesuit Scholarly Endeavor

I opened this reflection with the question of how a Jesuit scholar connects the Jesuit charism with being a scholar. This question calls for more than a merely descriptive answer. That is, the question requires a *collective self-reckoning*, in which together we search for the images, motifs, formulations and the like that can form the basis for a scholarly Jesuit solidarity. The Jesuits who contributed to the current collection have supplied the autobiographical material relevant to collective self-reckoning, but they have also embedded their contributions in a postmodern rhetoric that emphasizes the obstacles to articulating a shared solidarity. To sharpen the challenge still further, I have focused on Clooney's postmodern image of Jesuit scholars working along parallel lines that never meet, whose labors never cohere. This metaphor, I claim, harbors the more radical, skeptical aspects of postmodern thought. In particular, it suggests that we cannot share a common discourse that does not do violence to our differences.

Does the metaphor do justice to the contributions? I have adduced two sorts of evidence from the essays themselves to argue that the metaphor fails. First, the essays do not support, indeed many explicitly reject, the skeptical aspects of postmodernism. Even Clooney assumes nonviolent points of discursive contact between Hindus and Christians. Second, as I read them, each of the contributions exhibits some version of the commitment to dialogue that GC 34 placed at the heart of the Jesuit mission. Not only do most of the authors articulate their self-understanding in dialogical terms, the work of each author, I contend, can be understood in terms of some dimension of inculturation: bringing the Gospel experience into contact with contemporary culture and other religions in a way that affects both sides of the exchange. Dialogical inculturation requires participants to find or forge common ground, shared terms of discourse. Thus the two sorts of evidence hang together: if the authors are committed to dialogue across boundaries, between the Church and culture, then they must reject the skeptical metaphor.

That said, my overview of the authors' contributions does not fully dispel the skeptical postmodern challenge. The skeptic can object that the common terms my authors invoke—"justice," "dialogue," "Christian faith," "Gospel," and the like—are so abstract that they leave open the crucial question of whether Jesuit scholars are pulling in the same direction when they invoke such terms. Terms such as "justice" and "Gospel" have, historically, been open to wildly divergent interpretations. In this final section, I respond to this objection by clarifying the degree of coherence and solidarity we may reasonably expect of Jesuit scholars. I begin by picking up the point at the end of section IV, concerning the priority of lived practice over general statements.

1) We can express this priority with the following broad thesis: *General statements of the Jesuit charism have their full sense only as they are grounded in lived practice.* To understand this claim, recall the idea of the Jesuit charism as a gift for whose uptake Jesuits, both individually and collectively, bear responsibility. Sociologically, the Jesuit charism is lived out in the various social practices that make up the "Jesuit life." General statements merely attempt to articulate the charismatic reality of such practices as a coherent form of life. Although these statements have a literal meaning connected with the dictionary meaning of the words themselves, their full sense resides in how Jesuits actually strive to live out their charism.[26]

I deliberately say "actually *strive* to live out" rather than simply "actually live out." The reason is that social practices, together with the general statements that articulate them, are normative realities: ways of living and acting together that are structured by (linguistically expressible) rules, ideals, and values and that group members (that is, participants in the practice) expect one another to accept and follow. Normative standards state the exigencies of the practice for its participants, and a coherent social practice is identifiable as such insofar as members share more or less similar expectations about how they and others ought to behave. (To be sure, expectations can and often do diverge, but if they diverge too much then the practice either disintegrates into subcultural variants or else develops into a new form.)

Thus the normatively demanding character of practices means that participants understand themselves as subject to standards to which they hold one another accountable and which their actual behavior often fails to satisfy. General statements of normative standards provide the linguistic means for such accountability—for criticizing, praising, defending, excusing, and explaining behavior. However, participants' statements of their norms and values—their "accounts" of what they do—typically gloss the situational complexities of realizing values and following rules. Exactly what counts as meeting a standard is highly context-sensitive. Consequently, an adequate descriptive analysis of a practice requires the sociological observer to adopt the perspective of the participants. This poses a two-fold challenge. On the one hand, understanding what participants say about their values and norms draws on a background of experience and know-how about the various situations and contextual variations in which such normative standards are relevant. On the other hand, one cannot get at the reality of a social practice simply by observing external behavior, but only if one can distinguish appropriate exceptions from failures in the participants' efforts to realize the values, rules, and goods that structure their practices.

Consider, for example, the value of daily Eucharist (the Mass) as part of Jesuit life. One might state the value in a general formula, for example, "all of our members should consider daily celebration of the Eucharist as the center of their religious and apostolic life."[27] As grounded in practice, such a statement merely reflects or articulates an exigency that primarily resides *within* the shared practice. Its exigency reveals itself in very concrete ways, at the level of interpersonal interactions. For example, if I decline a lunch invitation from another Jesuit with the excuse, "That's my only chance for Mass today," it would probably strike me as quite inappropriate, even puzzling, if he replied by calling my excuse lame, or by saying, "Why is Mass so important?"[28] Jesuits normally expect one another to place a high value on the Eucharist, and my presumption that we share such a value structures my expectations of how our interaction should proceed. A rejoinder such as the one above jars this presumption, and it might well provoke me to question or criticize my interlocutor's attitude.

Still, the social fact that the value of daily Eucharist has an interpersonal exigency for Jesuits does not allow one to realize the value simply by reading off its demands from its formulaic expression (as given above) and acting accordingly. What exactly does it mean, for example, to "consider daily Eucharist the center" of our Jesuit life? Does that mean Eucharist specifically in community, and if so, how often per week? Are there circumstances when one may legitimately forgo Eucharist on a given day? If so, what are those circumstances?

The literal meaning of stated formulas usually remain somewhat vague and open-textured in relation to their full practical sense, their exigency in practice.[29] Rather, determinate sense emerges only at the level of actual practice, when members bring formulations to bear in their daily interaction to explain, criticize, excuse, praise, or justify their behavior and choices, to exhort and encourage, praise or forgive one another. Only in actual practice do we see whether the rule is taken strictly or loosely, which circumstances permit exceptions and which do not, and so on. Often the various maneuvers seem to have an ad hoc character, driven by particularities of circumstance, temperament, the actors' relational history, and the like. That is, at the level of locally situated practice, living up to shared values and norms commonly involves some degree of interpersonal "negotiation" about what behavior is mutually acceptable. Authentic modes of negotiation, we might say, are those that hit the mean between the extremes of mindless rigorism and self-serving laxity. To hit this mean, the actors cannot simply follow official rules blindly, but must bring their skills as agents intelligently to bear on the concrete situation with its particular, perhaps unique, demands. This Wittgensteinian approach to social practices thus leads us back to Aristotle's familiar point that one cannot escape the need for practical judgment informed by *phronesis*, a perceptual insight into the concrete situation.[30]

2) What does this conception of Jesuit life have for articulating a shared ideal of Jesuit scholarship? Statements of the scholarly Jesuit charism—in the official documents of the Society, or the ideas of dialogue presented in the essays—are general formulations (or the touchstone for possible general formulations) that articulate ways in which scholarly practices might be imbued with the charisms constituting the Jesuit form of life. If Jesuit scholarship indeed represents a genuine charism, then there are ways of engaging in scholarship that imbue research and teaching with features of the Jesuit charism, and other ways that work against the charism. On the one hand, then, the general statements are not empty formulas but express interpersonal exigencies of actual practice—exigencies that constitute standards for the Jesuit scholar's self-reckoning. On the other hand, the practical exigency of such formulations necessarily remains more or less indeterminate, or vague, until we understand how mature Jesuits strive to contextualize them in their everyday practice of scholarship at the local level. Given the foregoing analysis of practices, we should expect neither a deductively tight fit between the formulas and actual practice, nor a laissez faire, anything-goes attitude toward scholarly projects. Jesuits must contextualize ideals of Jesuit scholarship in ways that are not fully predictable in advance, but that other participants can nonetheless recognize

as appropriate both to the Jesuit charism and to the demands of intellectual honesty.

Appropriate contextualization presupposes intelligent exercise of agency in the company of other scholars, Jesuit and non-Jesuit. We should not underestimate the challenges such exercise involves. If scholarship is a social practice structured by shared values and norms, and if Jesuit scholars are to appropriate those values and norms in a specifically Jesuit manner, then the scholar who is first of all a Jesuit aims at a dauntingly complex achievement. Specifically, he must master the various shared expectations of diverse groups (some secular, some Jesuit, some mixed) across the range of social situations in which scholars do their work (classrooms, conferences, departmental meetings, publishing situations, research projects, etc.) in such a way that he presents himself, on the one hand, as a competent participant whose behavior and speech make sense in the situation and, on the other, as a dedicated Jesuit whose Jesuit vocation makes a publicly evident difference. One can hardly overemphasize the high level of agency—active, intelligent engagement—this process requires of the individual Jesuit.

This agency must be exercised socially, in concert with other participants in the relevant situations. But as an exercise of agency, more than mechanical conformity to general statements is required. Thus the shared normative expectations at issue are always to some extent open to contestation and adaptation at the local level, in light of circumstantial demands and the identities of the particular actors involved in the situation—their personal histories, needs, interests, and so on. Thus the process of contextualization often requires actors to engage in a certain amount of ad hoc negotiation, as already mentioned above. Superiors dealing with unruly Jesuits are well aware of this, I suspect: the ideal of obedience as conformity to the superior's "will" meets its reality check in the living, unique personality of the Jesuit subject. Even the official statements on obedience recognize the importance of active agency on the part of the obedient Jesuit.[31]

3) We can now address the postmodern objection explicitly. The foregoing observations suggest that any shared rationale that Jesuit scholars adopt for their work will remain an empty generality if we ourselves do not master the kind of social contextualizing achievement just described. Given how deeply this mastery must engage our multi-layered identities—as Jesuits, as scholars, as members of a given culture, as embodied persons with a sexuality, and so on—any general articulation that a Jesuit perceived as "erasing" some aspect of his identity would probably fall short as a guide for his actual practice. To this extent, the postmodern objection names a real risk: that general accounts always leave out significant differences and particularities. But this risk does not negate the necessity of general accounts as shared touchstones for Jesuit

scholars who take self-reckoning as a serious responsibility. We ameliorate the risk if we recognize the important role of agency and local negotiation in the situated appropriation of generalized values and norms. This recognition opens up the possibility of contestation, adaptation, and development at the grass-roots level, but without foreclosing the possibility of shared rationales and statements that, though vague in themselves, make a difference at the level of practice insofar as Jesuits can contextualize them in their own lives.

The observations so far show that a shared vocabulary and discourse need not erase differences among Jesuit scholars. But that point still leaves open the further question of whether Jesuit scholarly endeavor actually coheres. Might not the indeterminacy of general rationales conveniently conceal embarrassing contradictions at the level of practice?

To answer this further aspect of the postmodern objection, we must notice something about the Jesuit intellectual apostolate in particular, namely its *experimental* character. Not all scholarship is experimental: one might, for example, simply strive to understand a medieval author. But scholarship driven by the demands of dialogue with culture—the inculturation of the Gospel in contemporary cultural contexts or in foreign cultures—demands a kind of experimentation that is fraught with risks. I do not mean the empirical experiments of the scientist. Rather, the Jesuit engages in a kind of conceptual experimentation in which he seeks new ways to express the Christian faith. The risks arise from the fact that this faith, the Gospel, imposes demands of its own—one can get the faith wrong, betray its message, water it down so that it no longer challenges people to conversion.

Consequently, if we scrutinize the substantive projects of Jesuit scholars who engage in such experimentation, we should *expect* some measure of contradiction beneath the shared commitment to dialogical inculturation—just as we should not be surprised to find scientists in a given domain, particularly areas at the growing edge of research, to pursue conflicting lines of research. The presence of such contradictions in science does not lead most theorists of science to skeptical conclusions, however. Rather, the pursuit of conflicting hypotheses serves cooperative aims: by testing alternative lines of inquiry, scientists weed out dead ends and false hypotheses, and thereby contribute to the growth of public knowledge.[32]

Because all the contributors to the present collection practice scholarship in this experimental vein, we should not expect a fully substantive coherence in their respective projects. But if the comparison with science is apt, then the tensions and even contradictions at the level of details do not preclude coherence and growth at a collective level of endeavor. If this observation is on target, then the real problem with the postmodern metaphor of parallel lines lies in its overly simplistic two-dimensionality. Coherence and solidarity among

Jesuit intellectuals does not consist in the convergence of their projects into a "single black line," but in their contribution to the growing body of attempts to probe the possibilities of encounter between faith and culture. The coherence, in other words, is organic not linear. Thus Stempsey's metaphor of the body provides the better description of Jesuit scholarly solidarity. I only want to add this further complication: because this body of scholarly endeavor grows by experimentation, we cannot conclusively determine in advance which efforts will survive the test of criticism and find an enduring place in the Church's pantheon of successful theoretical developments in its self-understanding.

4) In conclusion, I want to suggest a way of thinking about the articulation of Jesuit scholarly identity as a way of realizing the vow of obedience, specifically obedience to the directives of GC 34. At one level, the vow of obedience finds expression in a rather specific norm, namely to carry out the commands of one's superior when the latter explicitly makes the command "under holy obedience." But this bottom-line employment of the norm is rare, and it scarcely suffices as an expression of the vow's practical exigencies. Like other norms and values of Jesuit life, the determinate meaning of obedience is grounded in practice, and its appropriate realization depends on the individual Jesuit's exercise of agency.

This practice-based understanding of obedience leads us back to the postmodern problem, however. As grounded in practice, the practical sense of obedience can shift over time: the concrete behaviors and expectations connected with obedience can evolve in ways that belie the official statements. In fact, McDonough and Bianchi maintain that just such a shift has occurred in the concrete practice of obedience in the Society, specifically a shift from a more group-centered, collectivist pre-Vatican style to a "therapeutic model," which accords considerably more emphasis on the individual Jesuit's personal satisfaction and fulfillment.[33] Precisely this re-orientation toward individual satisfaction, they say, has made it difficult for the Society to develop a coherent corporate direction. In my opinion, McDonough and Bianchi's analysis describes a transitional period in the Society; they do not adequately account for shifts in practice since GC 34. Nonetheless, their description of the therapeutic model of obedience conjures up the specter of fragmentation yet again. Does the practice-based account of solidarity, with its emphasis on individual agency, imply a therapeutic model of obedience that would undermine corporate self-reckoning and solidarity?

It does not. To say that obedience is grounded in practice, such that Jesuit scholars answer the call of GC 34 only by appropriately exercising their agency as individuals, is not to say they simply follow their own individual preferences to the detriment of corporate goals. The active contextualization of Jesuit values and norms presupposes that Jesuit subjects strongly identify with the Society and its aims, and that they are willing to make sacrifices for one another and for the whole Society—a crucial component of solidarity. But this model of obedience, understood in terms of social practice, links this solidaristic side of the equation with a closer attention to the necessity of individually appropriating and appropriately contextualizing general aims and values at the local level. Insofar as both sides of this dialectic remain in tension, the model of obedience goes beyond an individualistic therapeutic approach.

If the obedience of Jesuit scholars has this dialectical character, then obedience requires us to engage in a common effort to articulate a shared rationale that specifies our solidarity as Jesuit scholars. To work, such an articulation must be genuinely connected with the Jesuit charism and, at the same time, genuinely common to the efforts of Jesuit scholars. Moreover, the effort of articulation must itself be dialogical, carried out in common. The reason is that the exigency of shared rationales and norms depends on the capacity of individual Jesuits to contextualize the relevant values and norms in their daily practice—specifically, in how they organize and balance their various activities and duties, in what choices they make regarding research projects and collaborations, in how they present themselves in a department, and so on. This high level of responsibility incumbent on the individual Jesuit can easily slide into rationalization and self-serving choices if not balanced by self-critical discussions with other Jesuit scholars. Consequently, both the stated articulation and our daily efforts to live up to it demand ongoing, collective scrutiny. Jesuits sent to the intellectual apostolate negotiate their obedience, in other words, precisely by engaging in an ongoing collective self-reckoning. The contributors to this volume have attempted to do just that.

Notes

1. Liddell and Scott's Abridged Greek-English Lexicon (Oxford: Clarendon, 1982).
2. See, for example, the index entries for "charism" in *Documents of the 31st and 32nd General Congregations of the Society of Jesus* (St. Louis: Institute of Jesuit Sources, 1977).
3. Formula of the Institute of the Society of Jesus, n. 3, in St. Ignatius of Loyola, *The Constitutions of the Society of Jesus*, trans. G. E. Ganss, S.J. (St. Louis: Institute of Jesuit Sources, 1970), 66. (As customary in citing Jesuit documents, "n. 3" indicates paragraph number or margin number.)
4. "To proceed more successfully in this sending of subjects to one place or another, [the superior] should keep the greater service of God and the more universal good before his eyes as the norm to hold oneself on the right course." *Constitutions*, n. 622a.

5. Ignatius's desire to "help souls" live upright, religious lives is evident, for example, in his autobiography. See *A Pilgrim's Journey: The Autobiography of Ignatius of Loyola*, trans. J. N. Tylenda, S.J. (Wilmington, Del.: Glazier, 1985).

6. *Constitutions*, nn. 440–52.

7. See John Paul II, *Ex corde ecclesiae*, in *Origins* 20, no. 17 (October 4, 1990): 265–76; and *Documents of the Thirty-Fourth General Congregation of the Society of Jesus* (St. Louis: Institute of Jesuit Sources, 1995). The papal document emphasizes forms of dialogue as an important component of intellectual work; GC 34 links the Jesuit vocation in particular with dialogue—more on which in section IV below. More recently, the Jesuit Superior General Peter Hans Kolvenbach has designated the intellectual apostolate as one of the four top priorities of the Society. Christmas letter on "Our Apostolic Preferences," January 1, 2003; French version available in *Acta Romana Societatis Jesu* 23 (2003): 31–36.

8. See Peter McDonough and Eugene C. Bianchi, *Passionate Uncertainty: Inside the American Jesuits* (Berkeley: University of California Press, 2002). However, I do not entirely accept their analysis, which has not adequately assimilated developments beginning with GC 34.

9. See, for example, Rorty's *Objectivity, Relativism, and Truth* (Cambridge: Cambridge University Press, 1991). On poststructuralism, see Peter Dews, *Logics of Disintegration* (London: Verso, 1987).

10. See his *On the Genealogy of Morality*, trans. M. Clark and A. Swensen (Indianapolis: Hackett, 1998).

11. For example, see Paul de Man, *Allegories of Reading* (New Haven, Conn.: Yale University Press, 1979).

12. Jean-François Lyotard, *The Differend*, trans. G. van den Abbeele (Minneapolis: University of Minnesota Press, 1988); also his *Postmodern Condition*, trans. G. Bennington and B. Massumi (Minneapolis: University of Minnesota Press, 1984).

13. This is especially true of Michel Foucault's approach. For a sensitive treatment, see Beatrice Hanssen, *Critique of Violence* (London: Routledge, 2000). For an overview of postmodernism in relation to political theory, see Stephen K. White, *Political Theory and Postmodernism* (Cambridge: Cambridge University Press, 1991).

14. The term comes from Adorno. See Dews, *Logics*, 224–26.

15. At one point (33) he alludes favorably to some postmodern critics of modernity (Nietzsche, Foucault, Heidegger), but only in passing, and only as contributing to a general departmental environment critical of modernity.

16. See Jürgen Habermas, *Communication and the Evolution of Society*, trans. T. McCarthy (Boston: Beacon, 1979), especially chs. 2–4.

17. For example, Nietzsche's genealogical analysis of morality directly targets the idea of linear cultural development in the area of morals and law. On the idea of a grand narrative, see Lyotard, *The Postmodern Condition*.

18. The apophatic character of Haight's Christology does not stop him from insisting on a universal normative claim, namely that Christians must take Christ as cross-culturally normative. See his *Jesus: Symbol of God* (Maryknoll, N.Y.: Orbis, 1999).

19. See also James Bernauer, S.J., "The Holocaust and the Search for Forgiveness: An Invitation to the Society of Jesus?" *Studies in the Spirituality of Jesuits* 36, no. 2 (Summer 2004).

20. See Thomas McCarthy, "The Critique of Impure Reason: Foucault and the Frankfurt School," in *Critique and Power*, ed. M. Kelly (Cambridge, Mass.: MIT Press, 1994), 243–82; Dew, *Logics*, chs. 5–7.

21. See Foucault's "What is Enlightenment?" in *The Foucault Reader*, ed. P. Rabinow (New York: Pantheon, 1984), 32–50; "What Is Critique?" trans. K. P. Geiman, in *What Is Enlightenment? Eighteenth-Century Answers and Twentieth-Century Questions*, ed. J. Schmidt (Berkeley: University of California Press, 1996), 382–98. My understanding of Foucault is indebted to Kendall Phillips, "Divided by Enlightenment," a paper delivered at the Ontario Society for the Study of Argumentation, Windsor, Ontario, May 17–19, 2001.

22. Compare Jürgen Habermas, *Postmetaphysical Thinking*, trans. W. M. Hohengarten (Cambridge, Mass.: MIT Press, 1992); Thomas E. Uebel, "Logical Empiricism and the Sociology of Knowledge: The Case of Neurath and Frank," *Philosophy of Science*, supplement to vol. 67, no. 3 (2000): S138–S150.

23. GC 34, decrees 3–5. For the interconnection between dialogue and the concern for justice, see decree 2. Intralinear references to this document refer to margin numbers of the 1995 St. Louis edition (see n. 7 above).

24. See GC 34, decree 4.

25. As I understand it, to say that sexual identity (gay or straight) is a gift in the vowed celibate life means that such identity does not reduce simply to a specific mode of sexual attraction (or "orientation") but rather encompasses a whole range of affective energies and modes of attentiveness that can foster caring celibate relationships and community life.

26. On the relationship between literal meaning and fully determinate sense, see Jean Widmer, "Wörtliche Bedeutung und reflexiver Sinn," *Zeitschrift für Semiotik* 8 (1986): 63–69. More generally, my analysis of social practices draws on ethnographic sociology and the later Wittgenstein. See, for example, John Heritage, *Garfinkel and Ethnomethodology* (Cambridge: Polity, 1984); Erving Goffman, *The Presentation of Self in Everyday Life* (Garden City, N.Y.: Doubleday-Anchor, 1959); Ludwig Wittgenstein, *Philosophical Investigations*, 3rd ed., trans. G. E. M. Anscombe (New York: Macmillan, 1968). I also draw on Alasdair MacIntyre's influential description of practices. See his *After Virtue*, 2nd ed. (Notre Dame, Ind.: University of Notre Dame Press, 1984).

27. GC 32, n. 235.

28. Even this general claim glosses over possible complexities that could affect my reaction: perhaps this particular Jesuit has a way of teasing me that I've come to expect; perhaps his challenge is an understandable move in a running debate over the Mass; perhaps he is a teacher challenging me to think, etc.

29. Even very strict formulas and rules often have tacit ceteris paribus conditions and vagueness, which competent practitioners fail to notice because they have become so familiar with the accepted interpretive moves that determine their practical sense.

Ethnographers of cultural practices thus make it their aim to notice and describe all
the subtle presumptions, maneuvers, gestures, and the like that mature members witness but have learned to ignore—until the other person fails to enact them.

30. See his *Nicomachean Ethics* 1109b21–24, where Aristotle discusses the difficulty
of hitting the mean of virtue in the concrete situation: "it is not easy to determine by
reasoning, any more than anything else that is perceived by the senses; such things rest
on particular facts, and the decision rests with perception."

31. See Complementary Norms, nn. 150–51, 153, in *The Constitutions of the Society of Jesus and Their Complementary Norms* (St. Louis: Institute of Jesuit Sources,
1996).

32. One need not assume the old linear model of knowledge growth as straightforward accumulation to hold this non-skeptical view of science; the old model has been
discredited by critics like Thomas Kuhn, but since then a number of more sophisticated non-skeptical accounts have been proposed. See, for example, Helen Longino,
The Fate of Knowledge (Princeton, N.J.: Princeton University Press, 2002); Miriam
Solomon, *Social Empiricism* (Cambridge, Mass.: MIT Press, 2001).

33. McDonough and Bianchi, 160ff, 192–96.

About the Editor and Contributors

Ronald Anderson, S.J., is Associate Professor of Philosophy at Boston College. He received a doctorate in elementary particle physics from the University of Melbourne in 1979 and a doctorate in philosophy of physics from Boston University in 1990. His recent research and area of publications have been in the philosophy of space and time and the history of nineteenth-century British electromagnetism.

James Bernauer, S.J., is Professor of Philosophy at Boston College. He received his doctorate from the State University of New York at Stony Brook in 1981. A student of Foucault for two years, he is the author of *Michel Foucault's Force of Flight: Toward an Ethics for Thought* (Humanity Books, 1990). His most recent publication is a collection of essays that he coedited with Jeremy Carrette: *Michel Foucault and Theology: The Politics of Religious Experience* (Ashgate, 2004).

Thomas J. Brennan, S.J., is Assistant Professor of English at St. Joseph's University in Philadelphia. A specialist in nineteenth-century British literature, he has published on William Wordsworth's poetry and is currently working on an essay on Algernon Charles Swinburne's poem "Ave atque Vale."

Francis X. Clooney, S.J., received his doctorate from the University of Chicago's Department of South Asian Languages and Civilizations in 1984. His books include *Preaching Wisdom to the Wise: Three Treatises by Roberto de Nobili, Missionary and Scholar in 17th-Century India* (Institute of Jesuit Sources, 2000), *Hindu God, Christian God: How Reason Helps Break Down the*

Boundaries Among Religions (Oxford University Press, 2001), and *Divine Mother, Blessed Mother: Hindu Goddesses and the Virgin Mary* (Oxford University Press, 2005). He taught at Boston College for twenty-one years and was Professor of Comparative Theology there until July 2005, when he became the Parkman Professor of Divinity at the Harvard Divinity School.

Roger Haight, S.J., received his doctorate from the University of Chicago in 1973 and taught successively in Jesuit schools of theology in Manila, Chicago, and Toronto before coming to Cambridge, Massachusetts, in 1990. He is currently working in the field of ecclesiology after writing an extensive systematic work in christology entitled *Jesus: Symbol of God* (Orbis Books, 1999). He is a past president of the Catholic Theological Society of America. He was for many years Professor of Historical and Systematic Theology at Weston Jesuit School of Theology. He is currently teaching at Union Theological Seminary in New York.

Arthur Madigan, S.J., is Professor of Philosophy in Boston College. He received his Ph.D. from the University of Toronto in 1979. He has translated and annotated Alexander of Aphrodisias's commentaries on books III and IV of Aristotle's *Metaphysics* (Duckworth & Cornell, 1992, 1993), and his own commentary on *Metaphysics* III (Clarendon, 1999). He also teaches and writes about ethics in the Aristotelian tradition. He was rector of the Jesuit community at Le Moyne College in Syracuse, New York, from 2002 to 2005.

Bruce T. Morrill, S.J. (Ph.D., Emory University, 1996), is Associate Professor of Theology at Boston College. He is the author of *Anamnesis as Dangerous Memory: Political and Liturgical Theology in Dialogue*, The Liturgical Press, 2000, as well as numerous journal articles and book chapters. His current project is a book entitled *Divine Worship and Human Healing*.

William Rehg, S.J. (Ph.D., Northwestern, 1991), is Associate Professor of Philosophy at Saint Louis University. His chief areas of interest include science and technology studies, argumentation theory, and ethical-political theory. He is the author of *Insight and Solidarity: The Discourse Ethics of Jürgen Habermas* (University of California Press, 1994), the translator of Habermas's *Between Facts and Norms* (MIT Press, 1996), and coeditor (with J. Bohman) of *Deliberative Democracy* (MIT Press, 1997) and *Pluralism and the Pragmatic Turn: The Transformation of Critical Theory* (MIT Press, 2001).

William E. Stempsey, S.J. (M.D., State University of New York, 1978; Ph.D., Georgetown University, 1996), is Associate Professor of Philosophy at the College of the Holy Cross in Worcester, Massachusetts. He is the author of *Disease and Diagnosis: Value-Dependent Realism* (Kluwer Academic Publishers, 1999).